PRACTICAL HANDBOOK

THE COOK'S GUIDE TO
CHOCOLATE

PRACTICAL HANDBOOK

THE COOK'S GUIDE TO
CHOCOLATE

CHRISTINE McFADDEN
CHRISTINE FRANCE

HERMES
HOUSE

This Paperback edition published by Hermes House
an imprint of Anness Publishing Limited
Hermes House88-89 Blackfriars Road
London SE1 8HA

A CIP catalogue record for this book is available from the British Library

ISBN 1 84038 841 2

Publisher: Joanna Lorenz
Text by: Christine McFadden
Recipes by: Christine France
Project Editor: Joanne Rippin
Designer: Nigel Partridge
Special Photography: Don Last
Production Controller: Don Campaniello
Picture Researcher: Vanessa Miles
Handcrafted dishes on pp: 58, 206, 231, 237 by Sue Shaw 01252 726684

Previously published as *The Ultimate Encyclopedia of Chocolate*

Printed and bound in Hong Kong

The authors and publishers would like to thank the following people for supplying additional recipes in the book: Catherine Atkinson, Alex Barker, Carla Capalbo, Maxine Clark, Frances Cleary, Carole Clements, Roz Denny, Nicola Diggins, Joanne Farrow, Silvana Franco, Sarah Gates, Shirley Gill, Patricia Lousada, Norma MacMillan, Sue Maggs, Sarah Maxwell, Janice Murfitt, Annie Nichols, Angela Nilsen, Louise Pickford, Katherine Richmond, Hilaire Walden, Laura Washburn, Steven Wheeler, Judy Williams, Elizabeth Wolf-Cohen.

Additional recipe photographs supplied by: Karl Adamson, Edward Allwright, David Armstrong, Steve Baxter, James Duncan, Michelle Garrett, Amanda Heywood, Tim Hill, David Jordan.

CONTENTS

INTRODUCTION

O ne of the greatest treasures ever discovered was the bean from the tree *Theobroma cacao,* the original source of chocolate. Smooth in texture, intense in taste, subtly perfumed and elegant to behold, chocolate is a rich source of sensory pleasure, adored by almost everyone.

The Ultimate Encyclopedia of Chocolate is a celebration of this divine food, and divine it really is – translated from the Greek, *theobroma* literally means "food of the gods". In the first chapter chocolate's journey is traced from the land of the Maya in Central America to Spain and the rest of Europe, and then back across the Atlantic to the United States. Through doing so, it is evident that since the earliest days of its discovery chocolate has woven intricate links among people on every imaginable level – national, cultural, social, economic and spiritual. Chocolate has never failed to make an impact, initiating comment from the church, the medical profession, scientists, social reformers and royalty. Over the centuries it has been eagerly consumed in one form or another by all levels of society.

The chapter on Cultivation and Processing outlines where and how cacao is grown and harvested, and describes the different types of bean. The book follows the American, and less confusing, convention of using the term "cacao" for the plant and all

its products before processing; and the term "chocolate" for the processed beans, regardless of whether they are ground, liquid or in solid form. The word "cocoa" refers only to the concentrated cocoa powder invented by the Dutch.

The chapter goes on to trace the transformation from bean to beverage and from beverage to confectionery, and describes how this was made possible on a commercial scale. The industry's founding fathers, from the Quaker families in Britain – the Frys, the Terrys, the Cadburys and the Rowntrees – to the colourful Domingo Ghirardelli in San Francisco, and the persistent Dutch chemist Coenraad Van Houten, were all acutely aware of chocolate's popular appeal and commercial potential and went on to establish businesses that in most cases are still providing the world with chocolate today.

The taste and quality of chocolate is examined as we look at the specialist world of quality chocolate, demystifying terms such as couverture and cacao solids, praline and ganache. There is also a guide on how to taste chocolate properly – in the same way that wine-tasters evaluate a fine wine – for it is only by doing so that we learn to appreciate the alchemy that takes place during manufacture.

The international world of chocolate, including the characteristics of each country's chocolate, is also investigated. Flavourings and sweetness may vary, but what unites them is that smooth, sensuous, melt-in-the-mouth quality that is so hard and so pointless to resist. The book then delves into the physiology and psychology of chocolate, covering nutritional aspects, craving and addiction, passion and pleasure.

With this wealth of background knowledge, chocolate is then taken into the kitchen. The book's recipe section covers essential techniques to help you make the most of the two hundred tempting recipes that follow. You will find mouthwatering ideas for every kind of chocolate cake imaginable, from homely Chocolate Chip Walnut Loaf to the decadent White Chocolate Cappuccino Gâteau. A chapter on hot desserts will devastate you with Hot Chocolate Zabaglione, Hot Mocha Rum Soufflés and Chocolate Pecan Pie. Recipes for chocolate tarts and chilled desserts include classics such as luscious Mississippi Mud Pie and Tiramisu; and there are plenty of recipes for biscuits and little cakes. You will also see how to make your own chocolates and truffles, and the most deeply indulgent chocolate drinks. The recipes finish with a section on sauces, frostings and icings.

The *Ultimate Encyclopedia of Chocolate* is not only a celebration of a wonderful food, it will also fascinate, inform and instruct you in the history and production of this unique gastronomic treasure. Indulge yourself in a visual chocolate feast and accept the fact that if chocolate is not already an intrinsic part of your life, this book will make sure that it becomes so.

THE HISTORY OF CHOCOLATE

DRINK OF THE GODS

The origins of the solid, sensuous and, to some, addictive substance we know as chocolate are rooted in New World prehistory in the mysterious realm of the Olmec and the Maya. It was these ancient Mesoamerican civilizations living in the heart of equatorial Central America who were responsible for cultivating the tree from which chocolate is derived.

THE OLMEC

Three thousand years ago the Olmec people, one of the earliest Mesoamerican civilizations, occupied an area of tropical forests south of Veracruz on the Gulf of Mexico. Modern linguists have managed to reconstruct the ancient Olmec vocabulary and have found that it includes the word "cacao". Given the cacao tree's requirement for hot, humid and shady conditions, such as the land of the Olmecs, many historians are certain that the first civilization to cultivate the tree was the Olmec, and not the Aztecs, as is commonly believed.

THE MAYA

Around the fourth century AD, several centuries after the demise of the Olmec, the Maya had established themselves in a large region just south of present-day Mexico, stretching from the Yucatán peninsula in Central America across to the Chiapas and the Pacific coast of Guatemala. The humid climate there was perfect for the cacao tree, and it flourished happily in the shade of the tropical forest.

The Maya called the tree *cacahuaquchtl* – "tree" – as far as they were concerned, there was no other tree worth naming. They believed that the tree belonged to the gods and that the pods growing from its trunk were an offering from the gods to man.

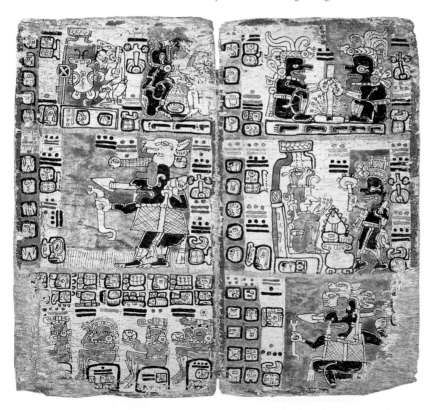

LEFT: The Maya wrote their books on folding screens of bark paper. These two pages show a black-faced merchant god with cacao growers.

BELOW: Fifteenth-century Aztec stone figure holding a cacao pod.

ABOVE: This pre-Columbian codex shows Theobroma cacao, *with its pods, growing in a soil-filled sink-hole.*

The period around AD 300, known as the Classic Mayan civilization, was a time of great artistic, intellectual and spiritual development. The Maya built magnificent stone palaces and temples, carving into the sacred walls images of cacao pods – for them the symbol of life and fertility.

Known as "the people of the book", the Maya also devised a system of hieroglyphics, which were written down on fragile sheets of bark paper. Today only four of the Maya's books

---

— *THEOBROMA CACAO* —

The eighteenth-century Swedish botanist Linnaeus, who invented the binomial system of classification for all living things, later named the tree *Theobroma cacao,* meaning "drink of the gods", from the Greek *theos* (god) and *broma* (beverage). He felt it deserved a name that reflected the Mayan belief that the tree belonged to the gods, rather than the New World name of cacao or chocolate tree.

---

survive, and these are all from the post-Classic period. The books are full of drawings of gods who are depicted performing various religious rituals in which cacao pods frequently appear, and the text often refers to cacao as the god's food.

The Maya were the originators of a bitter brew made from cacao beans. This was a luxury drink enjoyed by kings and noblemen, and also used to solemnize sacred rituals. In their books the Maya describe several ways of making and flavouring the brew. It could be anything from porridge thickened with ground maize meal, to a thinner concoction for drinking. An early picture shows the dark brown liquid being poured from one vessel to another to produce an all-important froth. Various spices were used as flavourings, the favourite being hot chilli.

More evidence of Maya use of cacao survives on the many painted vessels that have been unearthed from their burial grounds. A tomb excavated in Guatemala in 1984 contained several vessels obviously used for chocolate drinking. One exotic and beautiful specimen bears the Mayan symbol for chocolate on its lid and was found still to contain residues of the drink.

THE TOLTECS AND AZTECS

After the mysterious fall of the Mayan empire around AD 900, the gifted and supremely civilized Toltecs, later followed by the Aztecs from Mexico, settled in former Mayan territory. Quetzalcoatl, the Toltec king, was also believed to be the god of air, whose mission was to bring the seeds of the cacao tree from Eden to man and to teach mortals how to cultivate various crops.

Because of political uprisings, Quetzalcoatl and his followers left the capital and fled south to the Yucatan. During a period of ill-health he was persuaded to drink a mysterious cure, which, in fact, drove him insane. Convinced he must leave his kingdom, Quetzalcoatl sailed away on a small raft, promising to return in a preordained year to reclaim his kingdom. The legend of his exile became part of Aztec mythology, and astrologers predicted that in 1519 a white-faced king would return to release his people. This belief was to influence the whole future of the New World.

RIGHT: Aztecs greeting the white-skinned explorers landing on the coast of Tabasco. The Aztecs believed they were gods returning to recover their kingdom.

THE SPANISH ADVENTURERS

Although the Spanish explorer Hernán Cortés is generally considered to be the first European to recognize the potential of Aztec chocolate, the initial discovery must be attributed to Christopher Columbus. In 1502, on his fourth and final voyage to the Caribbean, Columbus reached the island of Guanaja off the Honduran coast. The story goes that he was greeted by Aztecs who offered him a sackful of what looked like large almonds in exchange for some of his own merchandise. Noticing his puzzlement, the Aztecs explained that a very special drink, *tchocolatl* (or *xocolatl),* could be made with these beans. Their chief demonstrated by having his servants prepare some on the spot. Columbus and his crew found the resulting dark and bitter concoction repellent but nevertheless took some cacao beans back to Spain for curiosity value, little realizing their future economic worth.

ABOVE: Hernán Cortés, the Conquistador.

CACAO AS CURRENCY

When Hernán Cortés arrived in the New World seventeen years later, Montezuma II, the then Aztec Emperor, believed Cortés to be a reincarnation of Quetzalcoatl, the exiled Toltec god-king whose return had been predicted to take place in the same year. The confusion made it easy for Cortés to gain access to Tenochtitlán, the Aztec capital, where Montezuma received him and his men with a royal welcome. The emperor offered them numerous gifts, including a cacao plantation, and an extravagant banquet was prepared in their honour.

Despite the overwhelming welcome, Montezuma eventually realized that he had made a mistake and had wrongly identified the Spaniard. Immediately recognizing the insecurity of his position, Cortés enlisted the help of sympathetic natives and managed to take Montezuma prisoner. Within the space of two or three years he brought about the downfall of the Aztec kingdom. Unlike Columbus, Cortés quickly realized the enormous economic value of the cacao bean, both as food and a form of currency. A contemporary of Cortés reported that a slave could be bought for one hundred cacao beans, the services of a prostitute for ten, and a rabbit for four. The Jesuit, Pedro Martyre de Angleria, called the beans "pecuniary almonds" and described them as "blessed money, which exempts its

ABOVE: A painting showing Montezuma giving a royal welcome to Cortés.

RIGHT: Aztecs greeting Columbus and his fleet with welcoming gifts as he lands on Guanaja.

possessors from avarice, since it cannot be hoarded or hidden underground". It is presumed that he was referring to the fact that the beans could not be stored for long without rotting.

The writings of Thomas Gage, a seventeenth-century English Dominican friar, are a rich source of information on chocolate. Visiting the City of Mexico, Gage describes how the cacao bean is used as "both meat and current money". Basing the exchange rate on the Spanish real, which at that time (1625) was worth sixpence (2½p), he explained that two hundred small cacao beans were worth one Spanish real, and "with these the Indians buy what they list, for five, nay for two cacaos, which is a very small part of a real, they do buy fruits and the like".

THE CACAO PLANTATIONS

When Cortés set out on his voyage to the New World, his primary goal was to find El Dorado – Aztec gold. When he failed to unearth the dreamed-of riches, his attention turned to cacao beans. Having seen them used as currency, and noticing the importance attached to them, Cortés soon realized that money could literally be made to grow on trees. He devoted the next few years to exploiting the commercial potential of this "liquid gold" by setting up cacao plantations around the Caribbean.

Cacao was cheap to cultivate and reasonably profitable, and the prospect of easy riches attracted plenty of Spanish colonists. Before long, the Spanish had established plantations in Mexico, Ecuador, Venezuela, Peru, and the islands of Jamaica and Hispaniola (now called Haiti and the Dominican Republic). Cacao production has since spread all over the world, but the plantations in these original regions still produce the most highly prized varieties of bean.

THE SPANISH SECRET

The Spanish colonists had tried to keep the secret of cultivating and preparing cacao to themselves, and with good reason – they were making fat profits out of processing the beans in Latin America before shipping them to Europe. However, the colonists did not remain in sole possession of their secret forever. In 1580, the first ever chocolate-processing plant was set up in Spain. From then on the popularity of chocolate gradually spread to other European countries.

LEFT: An early illustration showing cacao pods drying and a cacao tree growing under a shade-creating "mother" tree.

ABOVE: This lithograph, produced by the Empire Marketing Board, shows cacao pods being gathered.

These, in turn, established their own plantations, trade routes and processing facilities.

The Dutch transplanted the tree to their East Indian states of Java and Sumatra in the early seventeenth century, and from there it spread to the Philippines, New Guinea, Samoa and Indonesia with a degree of financial success made possible by the exploitation of hundreds of thousands of African slaves. The French settled in Martinique in 1660, and in Brazil in 1677, along with the Portuguese. Trinidad was fought over by the Dutch, the French and the British for years; it eventually went to the British in 1802. In the early nineteenth century, the Portuguese successfully transplanted Brazilian cacao saplings to the island of São Tomé off the African coast, and later to the island of Fernando Póo (now called Bioko) and West Africa. By the end of the nineteenth century, the Germans had settled in the Cameroons and the British in Sri Lanka. Plantations have since spread to South-East Asia, and Malaysia is now one of the world's leading producers.

CACAO FEVER

It was no easy job for the early planters to clear the jungle, but their fierce determination spurred them on. A Brazilian writer, Jorge Amado, described the vision of those early planters gripped by "cacao fever": "He does not see the forest ... choked with dense creepers and century-old trees, inhabited by wild animals and apparitions. He sees fields planted with cacao trees, straight rows of trees bearing golden fruit, ripe and yellow. He sees plantations pushing the forest back and stretching as far as the horizon."

THE POWER OF CHOCOLATE

To the Aztecs, chocolate was a source of spiritual wisdom, tremendous energy and enhanced sexual powers. The drink was highly prized as a nuptial aid, and, predictably, was the favourite beverage at wedding ceremonies. The Emperor Montezuma was reputed to get through fifty flagons of chocolate a day, always fortifying himself with a cup before entering his harem.

Although drunk on a daily basis, chocolate was still considered an exotic luxury and consumed primarily by kings, noblemen and the upper ranks of the priesthood. (Some historians say that priests would not have drunk chocolate, arguing that it would have been the equivalent of a priest quaffing champagne every day.)

Because of its renowned energy-boosting properties, chocolate was also given to Aztec warriors to fortify them on military campaigns. The chocolate was compressed into conveniently travel-sized tablets and wafers. Perhaps as a kind of incentive scheme a special law was instated declaring that unless a warrior went to war, he was forbidden to drink chocolate or eat luxury meats, or wear cotton, flowers or feathers – even if he was a royal prince or nobleman.

The Spanish colonists, too, became infatuated by the chocolate mystique. Once they had become accustomed to the strangeness of the drink, they took to it with enthusiasm. The Jesuit, José de Acosta, wrote "The Spaniards, both men and women, that are accustomed to the country, are very greedy of this chocolaté. They say they make diverse sortes of it, some hote, some colde, and put therein much of that chili."

Increasingly aware of its restorative values, Cortés convinced Carlos I of Spain of the enormous potential of this New World health food: "… the divine drink which builds up resistance and

> ## — THE MIDAS TOUCH —
> Chocolate has always been associated with gold, possibly originating from Montezuma's ritual of drinking chocolate from a golden goblet, which, immediately after use, was thrown into the lake beside his palace. The lake turned out to be quite literally a gold mine for the Spanish after the conquest. Evidence of the association with gold can still be seen today with chocolate manufacturers, especially the Swiss, selling fake gold bars and chocolate coins encased in gold wrapping.

fights fatigue. A cup of this precious drink enables a man to walk for a whole day without food".

Thomas Gage was heavily reliant on it too. He wrote: "Two or three hours after a good meal of three or four dishes of mutton, veal or beef, kid, turkeys or other fowles, our stomackes would bee ready to faint, and so wee were fain to support them with a cup of chocolatte".

RIGHTS, RITUALS AND CEREMONIES

The writings of New World travellers give us fascinating insights into the strange and sometimes barbaric rites, rituals and ceremonies attached to the cacao bean and the drinking of chocolate.

Religious rituals took place at different stages during cultivation. The Maya always held a planting festival in honour of the gods during which they sacrificed a dog with a cacao-coloured spot in its hair. Another practice, calling for a certain amount of commitment, required the planters to remain celibate for thirteen nights. They were allowed to return to their wives on the fourteenth night, and then the beans were sown. Another somewhat gory planting ceremony involved placing the seeds in small

LEFT: Chocolate was drunk by Aztec warriors in military campaigns, but it didn't win them victory over the Spanish.

RIGHT: An Aztec with his chocolate pot and molinillo. The molinillo has shaped paddles for making the drink frothy.

— CHOCOLATE AND CUISINE —

Contrary to what some cookery writers would have us believe, the Aztecs did not use chocolate as an ingredient in cooking. To do so would have been considered sacrilegious – rather like devout Christians using communion wine to make gravy. What possibly causes confusion is a classic Mexican recipe called *Mole Poblano,* turkey or chicken in a chilli sauce flavoured with chocolate. The recipe is often assumed to have Aztec origins, but the ingredients include several items – onions, tomatoes and garlic, for instance – that would not have been available then. This is a recipe for Mole Poblano:

8 dried mulato chillies; 4 dried ancho chillies; 4 dried pasilla chillies; 2 dried chipotle chillies; 1 small turkey; 50g / 2oz / 4 tbsp lard (or vegetable oil); 60ml / 4 tbsp sesame seeds; 115g / 4oz / 1 cup blanched almonds; 1 corn tortilla; 2 crushed garlic cloves; 1 chopped onion; ¼ tsp each of ground cloves; cinnamon and anise; 6 black peppercorns; 50g / 2oz / ⅓ cup raisins; 3 peeled tomatoes; 5ml / 1 tsp salt; 50g / 2oz / 2 squares unsweetened chocolate; chicken or turkey stock

Arrange the dried chillies in a single layer in a roasting tin and soften in a hot oven for 2–3 minutes, taking care not to let them burn. Discard the stems and seeds and put the chillies in a bowl. Cover with barely boiling water. Leave to soak for 20–30 minutes.

Divide the turkey into portions. Heat the lard or oil in a heavy-based flameproof casserole and fry the turkey until golden brown. Using a slotted spoon, remove the turkey portions from the casserole and set aside.

Roast the sesame seeds and almonds in a dry frying pan over a medium heat until golden. Remove from the pan. Cut the tortilla into strips and heat in the pan until brittle.

Put the almonds, tortilla and all but 5ml / 1 tsp sesame seeds into a food processor. Add the garlic, onion, spices, raisins, tomatoes and salt. Drain the chillies, reserving the soaking water, add them to the processor and purée until smooth, adding some of the chilli soaking water if necessary. Add this purée to the fat remaining in the casserole. Fry gently for about 5 minutes, stirring constantly.

Return the turkey to the casserole, with the chocolate and enough stock to just cover. Bring to the boil, then lower the heat, cover and simmer gently for 45–60 minutes until the turkey is tender and cooked through and the sauce has thickened. Garnish with the reserved sesame seeds and serve with rice and tortillas.

NOTE: If you have difficulty in finding Mexican dried chillies, use 115g / 4oz fresh green chillies and 2 small dried red chillies, and do not preheat them in the oven. Simply remove the seeds, tear the chillies into shreds and soak as above.

LEFT: A Mexican metate *was used for grinding cacao beans to a paste.*

LEFT: A mosaic of Quetzalcoatl, the Toltec king and god who, according to legend, brought the cacao bean as a gift to human kind.

bowls before performing secret rites in the presence of an idol. Blood was then drawn from different parts of the human body and used to anoint the idol. Other practices include sprinkling "the blood of slain fowls" over the land to be sown. There were also tales of frenzied dancing, orgiastic rituals and bloody sacrifices. The sixteenth-century Italian historian and traveller, Girolamo Benzoni, recorded that during festivals "they used to spend all the day and half the night in dancing with only cacao for nourishment". Another legend tells of how, as a prize, the winner of a type of ball game would be offered as a sacrifice. The unfortunate man was first fed vast quantities of chocolate in order "to colour his blood" before his heart was cut out and presented to the gods, who, it was believed, would be honoured by the chocolate-rich blood.

Another use of chocolate was as a face paint with which the Aztecs adorned themselves in religious ceremonies. Even the early Spanish planters believed that secret rites were necessary for a successful crop and performed planting ceremonies. From its earliest days, then, chocolate was regarded as a substance of power, a gift from the gods, a source of vitality and life.

BELOW: Cacao beans laid out to dry on plantain leaves.

FROM BEAN TO BEVERAGE

ABOVE: A seventeenth-century lithograph showing an imaginary scene on a plantation, with Aztecs harvesting, preparing and cooking chocolate.

The Aztec drink bore little resemblance to the deliciously smooth, rich and creamy beverage we know today; it was bitter, greasy and served cold. Early travellers give differing accounts of how it was made. Giramolo Benzoni, a sixteenth-century Italian botanist, described the method used in rural areas: "They take as many fruits as they need and put them in an earthenware pot and dry them over the fire. Then they break them between two stones and reduce them to flour just as they do when they make bread. They then transfer this flour into vessels made of gourd halves …, moisten the flour gradually with water, often adding their 'long pepper' [chilli]."

Still on the subject of ingredients, Thomas Gage described additions other than chilli: "But the meaner set of people, as Blackamoors and Indians, commonly put nothing in it, but Cacao, Achiotte, Maize, and a few Chillies with a little Aniseed". Maize was used to blot up the cacao butter which floated to the top, and also to bind and thicken the drink.

It seems that the grinding stone, or *metate,* was an important part of the production process. One writer describes the process in some detail: "For this purpose they have a broad, smooth stone, well polished and glazed very hard, and being made fit in all respects for their use, they grind the cacaos thereon very small, and when they have so done, they have another broad stone ready, under which they keep a gentle fire". Because of the crude manual processing, all sorts of undesirable bits and pieces – shells, husks and pith – were allowed to remain in the resulting

RIGHT: Aztec chocolate-making equipment: chocolate pot, drinking goblet, whisk and rolling pin.

liquor. In Benzoni's opinion: "This mixture looks more fit for the pigs than like a beverage for human beings".

A FROTHY BREW

The Jesuit José de Acosta wrote: "The chief use of this cacao is in a drincke which they call chocolaté, whereof they make great account, foolishly and without reason: for it is loathsome to such as are not acquainted with it, having a skumme or frothe that is very unpleasant to taste, if they be not well conceited thereof."

For the Maya and Aztecs the froth was an all-important and most delicious part of the drink. One historian pointed out the importance "of opening the mouth wide, in order to facilitate deglutition, that the foam may dissolve gradually and descend imperceptibly, as it were, into the stomach". The Maya made the drink frothy by pouring it from one bowl to another from a height. Later, the Aztecs invented a device that the Spanish called a *molinillo* – a wooden swizzle stick with specially shaped paddles at one end, which fitted into the hole in the lid of the chocolate pot.

The eighteenth-century missionary, Father Jean-Baptiste Labat, described this indispensable item in one of his books: "A stick is about ten inches longer than the chocolate pot, thus enabling it to be freely twirled between the palms of the hand." The *molinillo* is still in use today and can be found in Latin American shops and markets. The design of the basic wooden stick remains unchanged, but there are also beautiful antique pots and swizzle sticks in silver and other decorative materials, which have become collectors' items.

There is evidence of yet more ingredients than those

— CHAMPURRADO (CHOCOLATE ATOLE) —

The addition of maize would have turned the Aztec drink into a thin gruel or porridge known as *atole.* This is a type of fortified drink, not necessarily flavoured with chocolate, still served at meals or used as a pick-me-up by workers in the fields in Latin America today. The chocolate-flavoured version is always referred to as *champurrado,* from *champurrar,* meaning to mix one drink with another:

Put 65g/2½oz/½ cup masa harina (treated maize flour) or finely ground tortillas in a large pan with 750ml/ 1¼ pints/3 cups water. Stir over low heat until thickened. Remove from the heat and stir in 175g/6oz/1 cup soft light brown sugar (or to taste), and 750ml/1¼ pints/ 3 cups milk. Grate three 25g/1oz squares unsweetened chocolate and add to the pan. Beat well with a molinillo *and serve steaming hot.*

A MEXICAN RECIPE FOR HAND-MADE CHOCOLATE

Take 6 pounds [2.75kg] of good quality cacao beans, at least three different types, in equal quantities. Roast in a metal pan studded with holes just until they begin to give off their oil. Take care not to remove the beans from the heat too soon, or the resulting chocolate will be discoloured and indigestible. If the beans are allowed to burn, the chocolate will be bitter and acrid.

Rub the roasted beans through a fine hair sieve to remove the husks. Next, place your metate (grinding stone) on a flat pan containing hot coals. Once the stone is warm begin to grind the chocolate. Grind the chocolate with 4 to 6 pounds [1.75–2.75kg] of sugar, depending on desired sweetness, pounding it with a large mallet.

Shape the resulting paste into tablets as preferred — round, hexagonal or oblong — and place on a rack to air. If you wish, make dividing lines on the surface of the chocolate with the tip of a sharp knife.

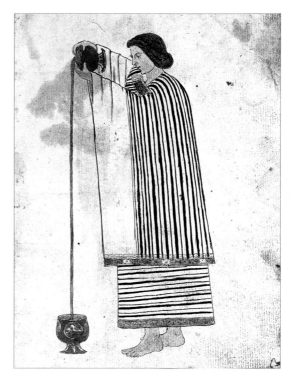

ABOVE: Aztecs poured chocolate from a height to make it frothy.

mentioned by Thomas Gage. The Spanish historian, Sahagún, describing a menu of chocolate drinks to be served to lords, tells us that there were "ruddy cacao; brilliant red cacao; orange cacao; black cacao; and white cacao". Many of the very early recipes for chocolate share common ingredients, and from these we can tell that the likely flavourings for the lords' impressive choice of cacao were chilli, allspice, cloves, vanilla, a type of black pepper, various flower petals, nuts and annatto.

BELOW: A modern chocolate pot, whisk and chocolate from Colombia. The design of the whisk has not changed since the days of the Aztecs.

Sugar was not added until much later. There is a story that the nuns of Oaxaca, an Aztec town occupied by the Spanish until 1522, developed new recipes in deference to the Spanish sweet tooth. They added sugar and sweet spices such as cinnamon and aniseed, and so the bitter beverage of the Aztecs began its transformation to the delicious drink that we know today.

THE SPANISH VERSION

In 1701 an Englishman travelling in Spain gave a detailed and lengthy account of the manufacturing process developed by the Spanish. After the preliminary roasting, dehusking and grinding, the cacao mass was ground again to a fine paste with plenty of sugar, cinnamon, vanilla, musk and annatto. The chocolate was formed into blocks, along the lines of modern block chocolate, but even so, these were still used only for making the beverage, rather than as confectionery.

As far as we know, this is the recipe that was used throughout Spain and the rest of Europe until the process was revolutionized in the nineteenth century by the technological achievements of the Dutchman Van Houten.

FROM BEVERAGE TO CONFECTIONERY

ABOVE: A 1893 poster with a background of cacao pods and leaves.

VAN HOUTEN'S PRESS

In its early days chocolate was an extremely rich beverage. It contained a fatty substance known as cacao butter, which tended to rise to the top, where it would float in unappetizing greasy pools. Manufacturers overcame this to some extent by adding starchy substances to absorb the fat – a process similar to the Aztec tradition of adding ground maize.

Manufacturers had also tried unsuccessfully for years to devise a way of separating out the greasy cacao butter. Breakthrough came in 1828 when, after years of trial and error, a Dutch chemist named Coenraad Van Houten patented a new and extremely efficient hydraulic press. His machine was able to extract about fifty per cent of the cacao butter present in the "liquor" (the paste produced after grinding the beans), leaving behind a refined, brittle, cake-like residue that could then be pulverized to a fine powder.

Not satisfied, Van Houten went one step further. He treated the powder with alkaline salts in order to improve the ease with which it could be mixed with water. The process, which came to be known as "Dutching", also darkened the colour of the chocolate and lightened the flavour – a curious anomaly since plain chocolate is usually assumed to have a stronger flavour. Today many people believe they prefer Dutch chocolate because of its strong flavour, but it may simply be the colour that attracts them.

Van Houten's inexhaustible patience revolutionized the chocolate industry. It led to the manufacture of what we now know as cocoa powder, which in Van Houten's time was called "cocoa essence". It also led to an all-round improvement within the industry. Van Houten sold his rights ten years after he took out the patent, and the machine came into general use. Among the first customers were the Frys and the Cadburys, ever eager to outdo

RIGHT: Modern packaging based on the art nouveau style.

ABOVE: An early advertisement for Van Houten's cocoa powder – "the best liquid drinking chocolate".

each other. Both firms were quick to enter the cocoa essence market, actively promoting the product's purity and ease of preparation. The old-style starch-based products were classified as adulterated, resulting in several fierce legal battles between rival firms. Van Houten's press also initiated the industry's next step in gearing up – the large-scale production of chocolate as confectionery.

EATING CHOCOLATE

Having separated out the butter from the bean, the industry was left with the question of what to do with it – it was certainly too good to waste. What happened was that somehow one of the cocoa manufacturers – and there are conflicting claims as to who was the first – hit upon the idea of melting the cacao butter and combining it with a blend of ground cacao beans and sugar. The resulting mixture was a smooth and malleable paste

ABOVE: A charming poster for Bovril's nourishing new chocolate bars, or cakes. The lettering on the box refers to them as "the perfect food".

that tolerated the added sugar without becoming gritty; the fat helped to dissolve it. The paste was also thin enough to be poured into a mould and cast, and it is from this concept that "eating chocolate" was developed.

The Fry family claim to have been the first to market the new product. Reflecting the current popularity of French-style products, they named the bars "Chocolat Délicieux à Manger" and exhibited them at a trade fair in Birmingham in 1849. The bars were an immediate success, and eating chocolate

RIGHT: Hershey's famous little Kisses were introduced in 1907.

caught on in a big way. Not to be outdone Cadburys introduced the first box of small individual chocolates, followed by a Valentine's Day presentation box. Other companies, such as Bovril, began producing eating chocolate, and the new confectionery was firmly established.

As a result of the new craze the price of cacao butter rocketed and, predictably, eating chocolate became an expensive sought-after product popular with society's élite. Meanwhile, cocoa was relegated to the masses.

The United States developed their version of chocolate bars a little later on. After experimenting with cream and chocolate – time and time again, the mixture scorched or failed to set – Milton Hershey's milk chocolate bars finally appeared on the market in 1900. His world-famous Kisses followed in 1907. Over on the west coast, Ghirardelli was making use of new chocolate-moulding technology, and soon added chocolate bars to their

ABOVE: Modern packaging with old-fashioned appeal.

lines too. Specialist chocolate shops began to spring up all over the country and most towns had at least one well-respected establishment producing hand-made chocolates. The early chocolatiers were too small to import cacao beans or invest in expensive processing machinery. Instead, they bought industrial-sized blocks of coating chocolate from large companies such as Guittard and melted them down to use as "couverture" for their own hand-dipped fillings. Alice Bradley's 1917 *Candy Cook Book*, published in America, devoted a whole chapter to "Assorted Chocolates" with over sixty recipes for fillings. Bradley stated: "More than one

ABOVE: Ghirardelli's first chocolate bars were "full of toasted almonds".

hundred different chocolates may be found in the price lists of some manufacturers." The American chocolate industry got its biggest boost during the Second World War, when millions of chocolate bars were issued to the American armed forces in Europe. By this time both Ghirardelli and Hershey were well-equipped for the challenge of supplying them.

CHOCOLATE TRAVELS THE WORLD

During the sixteenth century chocolate began its journey into the countries of Europe as colonialists exploited their new world discoveries. Reaching Spain first, then following trade routes to Northern Europe and Great Britain, chocolate eventually made its way back across the Atlantic to North America.

SPAIN

It was probably through merchants and also through contact between New World convents and monasteries and their Spanish counterparts, that chocolate found its way to Spain.

Once the first commercial cargo of beans from Veracruz had been unloaded in 1585 and the official trade routes established, chocolate quickly became part of the Spanish way of life, especially among society's élite. However, a French noblewoman visiting Spain was unimpressed. She says of the drink: "They take it with so much pepper and so many spices, that it is impossible they don't burn themselves up." Nor was she impressed by their dental care and personal habits: "Their teeth are good, and would be white if they took care of them, but they neglect them. Besides the sugar and the chocolate which spoil them, they have the bad habit, men and women alike, of cleaning them with a toothpick, in whatever company they are."

Chocolaterías, chocolate houses, sprang up in cities all over the country, and it became the fashion to visit them in the afternoons to drink a cup of the foaming fragrant brew, accompanied by *picatoste,* fried bread, to dip in it. Today, the chocolate drinking habit remains strong in Spain, and there are still many *chocolaterías.* A traditional time to take the beverage is in the

RIGHT: The chambermaid model for "The Beautiful Chocolate Girl" married a wealthy aristocrat and so got to drink chocolate herself.

BELOW: This early eighteenth-century Spanish tiled panel shows gentlemen serving chocolate to their ladies.

The Spanish like their chocolate thick — so thick that a spoon will stand up in it, and it can almost be classified as a food rather than a drink. Cornflour is used as a thickener, or sometimes eggs, which practically turn the drink into chocolate mousse.

— *SPANISH EGG CHOCOLATE* —

In a double boiler, melt 50g/2oz/2 squares unsweetened chocolate in 475ml/16fl oz/2 cups milk until thick and smooth. Keep stirring and add 115g/4oz/½ cup sugar, pinch of salt, 10ml/2 tsp ground cinnamon and 5ml/1 tsp vanilla essence. Beat 1 egg in the bottom of a jug with a molinillo, pour over the hot chocolate mixture, whisk until frothy and serve immediately.

ABOVE: The pleasures of taking chocolate are captured in this seventeenth-century still life by Philippe Rousseau.

morning with freshly cooked *churros* (piped strips of deep-fried choux pastry), which replaced the *picatoste*.

In Spain, as in the rest of Europe, chocolate was always associated with stimulating foods such as spices, coffee and tea; it was a long while before chocolate was used as an ingredient for confectionery and desserts. Although its first use was as a beverage, chocolate was also a flavouring ingredient in savoury dishes. Both the Spanish and the Mexicans traditionally add chocolate to sauces for meat and game, and even fish.

THE NETHERLANDS

The Netherlands became part of the Spanish territories in the fourteenth century. Because of this, the Dutch were familiar with chocolate from an early stage.

The Dutch West India Company eventually defied the Spanish ban on foreign traders and started shipping cacao beans in bulk to Amsterdam during the seventeenth century. They then re-exported the beans in small lots to foreign buyers, as well as setting up their own processing plants in the Netherlands. Until the end of the eighteenth century, production was limited and chocolate was only seen in the homes of a few wealthy merchants and financiers.

ITALY

There are conflicting theories as to how and when chocolate reached Italy. Some historians believe it was around the middle of the sixteenth century when the exiled duke Emmanuel-Philibert returned to power, having experienced the delights of chocolate in Spain. The popular theory is that chocolate was imported by a Florentine merchant, Antonio Carletti, who discovered it while travelling the world in search of new products to sell. The most likely theory is that chocolate was brought in as a medicine through the convents and monasteries.

By the seventeenth century a growing number of chocolate companies had become established in northern Italy, particularly around the towns of Perugia and Turin. These companies in turn began to export their newly developed products to other European countries.

A collection of recipes by an eighteenth-century Italian priest shows the imagination of the Italians in their use of chocolate compared with other countries. Recipes included such dishes as: Liver dipped in chocolate and fried, Chocolate soup, Chocolate pudding with veal, marrow and candied fruit, and Chocolate polenta.

FRANCE

France was also quick to fall under chocolate's spell. As with Spain and Italy, there are conflicting theories about the circumstances surrounding its first appearance. Some say it was a result of networking between Spanish and French monasteries. Another theory states that chocolate entered France as a medicine. There is certainly some evidence from the French historian Bonaventure d'Argonne that the Cardinal of Lyons drank chocolate "to calm his spleen and appease his rage and foul temper", and that he may have "had the secret from some Spanish monks who brought it to France". However, there is also no doubt that the trend was largely set by nobility and the royal court as it was in other European countries.

ABOVE: Cardinal Mazarin travelled with a chocolate-maker.

The most popular theory is that the drink made its first appearance in 1615 when Louis XIII married Anne of Austria, the young daughter of Philip II of Spain. The new queen loved her chocolate with a passion and introduced it to members of the court. There were plenty of devotees: the king's personal adviser, the formidable Cardinal Mazarin, absolutely refused to travel anywhere without his personal chocolate-maker; and later

BELOW: A tapestry depicting the marriage of María Teresa, the Spanish princess, to Louis XIV. Chocolate and the king were her only passions.

Marie Antoinette, also very fond of chocolate, created the prestigious "Charge of chocolate-maker of the Queen". Chocolate parties held by royalty, *chocolat du roi,* became a fashionable social ritual to which it was the ultimate in chic to be invited.

The many anecdotes include the story of the Spanish princess María Theresa, who married Louis XIV in 1660. She is said to have declared: "Chocolate and the King are my only passions." (Note the order.) The princess brought with her a Spanish maid, who prepared chocolate each morning for her queen. The ladies of the French court were intrigued by this new drink, especially as word had got round that it was an aphrodisiac. Chocolate sales in France apparently sky-rocketed around that time. Another often-repeated story about the princess is that her passion for chocolate was so excessive that she developed a horrendous complexion, and that her teeth were black and riddled with cavities.

Throughout France, chocolate never failed to evoke strong feelings. In 1664 learned academics praised its food value, presumably because of the fat content, but at the same time it was violently attacked by other writers, who accused those who drank it of moral depravity. Even Madame de Sévigné, a French courtesan and a great devotee of chocolate, turned against it for a while. In one of her letters to her daughter she wrote: "Chocolate is no longer for me what it was, fashion has led me astray, as it always does … it is the source of vapors and palpitations; it flatters you for a while, and then suddenly lights a continuous fever in you that leads to death … In the name of God, don't keep it up …" In another letter she told a horrendous tale of the Marquise de

ABOVE: Chocolate consumption was often depicted as being risqué.

Coëtlogon who "took so much chocolate during her pregnancy last year that she produced a small boy as black as the devil, who died". Eventually Madame de Sévigné regained her enthusiasm, and in a wonderful letter she neatly got round the issue of fasting and chocolate: "I took some chocolate night before last to digest my dinner, in order to have a good supper. I had some yesterday for sustenance so that I could fast until the evening. What I find most pleasant about chocolate is that it acts according to one's wishes."

SWITZERLAND

After the mid-seventeenth century, chocolate was making an appearance in all the principal cities of Europe. Although

ABOVE: The elegant refreshment room where chocolate was served at Confiserie Sprüngli in Zurich.

Switzerland was later to become a major producer of chocolate as confectionery, chocolate as a beverage was relatively late in arriving. It was first noticed in Zurich in 1697 after the Mayor had enjoyed drinking chocolate on a trip to Brussels. By the mid-eighteenth century, chocolate was more widely available and was often brought into the country by travelling Italian merchants, known as *cioccolatieri*, who sold it at fairs and markets.

GERMANY AND AUSTRIA

Like Switzerland, Germany was also relatively late to take up chocolate. For years the Germans regarded it as medicine, and it was sold only by apothecaries. But by the middle of the seventeenth century, chocolate had become accepted among fashionable society, although enthusiasm varied from city to city. Berliners still looked on it as an unpleasant tonic, but the drink was a hit in Dresden and in Leipzig, where the city's *glitterati*

The popularity of chocolate spawned a whole new industry for the famous china factories in both Austria and Germany, and in France too. At the beginning of the eighteenth century, European factories from Vienna to Berlin to Sèvres started producing the most exquisite chocolate services in porcelain; before that earthenware or metal, including gold and silver, were the materials used. As well as the traditionally shaped serving pots, the new range included elegant cups known as *trembleuse*. These new porcelain wares were specially designed to protect the aristocracy from the embarrassment of accidental spills. They featured double-handled cups which fitted into a holder or a very deep saucer.

took to drinking it at the fashionable Felsche café, one of the earliest German *schokoladestuben* (chocolate houses).

Among Germany's confirmed chocoholics were the famous poets Goethe (1749–1832) and Schiller (1759–1805). Goethe was reputed to have found the beverage a deep source of inspiration and drank it well into ripe old age. During his travels he often wrote to his wife asking her to send supplies from his favourite chocolate-maker, Riquet, in Leipzig.

Germany started producing its own chocolate on a large scale in 1756 when Prince Wilhelm von der Lippe erected a factory at Steinhude and brought over Portuguese workers especially skilled in the art of chocolate-making.

In Austria, Viennese aristocracy were quick to take up the new drink, especially after the Emperor Charles VI had moved his court and his chocolate from Madrid to Vienna in 1711. Since Austria did not impose such punishing taxes on chocolate as Germany, it was drunk not just by the aristocracy but also by lesser mortals who could afford it. There is a story of a German traveller in Vienna who was horrified to see someone as common as a tailor drinking a cup of best quality chocolate.

Both the Germans and the Austrians were accomplished pastry-cooks. Indeed, in the Austrian imperial court it seemed that the head pâtisserie chef was on a par with the most senior general. Like the Italians, the German and Austrian pastry-cooks took a while to start using chocolate as an ingredient in their baking rather than just as a beverage. It was worth the wait — their most wickedly delicious creations, the rich Black Forest Cake from Germany and the Viennese Sachertorte, are now celebrated forms of indulgence the world over.

BELOW: "Goethe in the Campagna" (1787) by German painter Johann Tischbein. Goethe was a lifelong drinker of chocolate.

ABOVE: The interior of a typical seventeenth-century London chocolate house – hotbeds of gossip, frequented by politicians and the literary set.

GREAT BRITAIN

In the sixteenth century, when the Spanish were shifting cacao as if there were no tomorrow, the British couldn't have cared less about it. Even the pirates who plagued the Spanish ports and shipping routes seemed unaware of its economic and cultural importance, for they showed no interest in the valuable cargo. Like their Dutch counterparts, they are reputed to have thrown boatloads of it overboard in disgust.

When chocolate finally arrived in Britain, it did so more or less simultaneously with two other stimulants, tea from Asia and coffee from Africa. Coffee was the first to catch on in British society – it was relatively cheaper – but chocolate soon followed.

Documentary evidence of the first chocolate house in London appeared in *The Public Advertiser* in 1657, followed two years later by a paragraph in *Needham's Mercurius Politicus* that drew attention to "an excellent West India drink, sold in Queen's-Head alley, in Bishopsgate-street, by a Frenchman".

The most famous establishment was White's Chocolate House, near St James's Palace, opened by an Italian immigrant. A rival establishment was The Cocoa Tree in St James's Street.

LEFT: Sacks of cacao beans from the tropics arriving at an English warehouse.

RIGHT: "A Cup of Chocolate" by Sir John Lavery. Drinking chocolate in the new chocolate houses was a fashionable pastime for ladies of society.

By chance rather than design the two establishments catered to different political loyalties – The Cocoa Tree was the favourite haunt of members of the Tory party, while the Whig aristocrats and the literary set frequented White's. White's was the inspiration for some of the scenes from William Hogarth's famous series of paintings *The Rake's Progress*.

For the wealthy upper classes, both the coffee and chocolate houses were *the* place to be seen. They were hotbeds of vicious gossip and political intrigue, as well as popular gambling venues where vast fortunes were won and lost. In 1675, Charles II tried in vain to have both types of establishment closed down on the grounds that politicians and businessmen were frequenting them too often and were in danger of neglecting their families. It is also possible that he was trying to suppress the kind of talk that could potentially lead to a rebellion similar to the one that caused his father's execution in 1649.

The diarist Samuel Pepys (1633–1703) was an ardent fan of chocolate, or "jocolatte", and a regular frequenter of the chocolate houses. One entry in his diary records a horrendous hangover the morning after the king's coronation: "Waked in the morning with my head in a sad taking through last night's drink, which I am very sorry for; so rose, and went with Mr Creed to drink our morning draught, which he did give me in Chocolate to settle my stomach."

In England, as in other countries, the government seized on chocolate as a potential source of revenue. Importers were

LEFT: Examples of early packaging for Domingo Ghirardelli's revolutionary instant cocoa powder.

obliged to pay a hefty duty on every sack of cacao beans brought into the country, and in 1660 a tax of 8d (about 3p) a gallon was imposed on all chocolate made and sold in England.

These penalties led to an inevitable increase in smuggling cacao beans, as well as adulteration of the chocolate, for which anything from brick dust to red lead was used. Brandon Head in *The Food of the Gods* refers to "the reprehensible practice (strongly condemned)" of padding out chocolate with husks and shells. He goes on: "To prevent this practice it was enacted in 1770 that the shells or husks should be seized or destroyed." Some of these husks did not go to waste, however. Head tells us: "From these a light, but not unpalatable, table decoction is still prepared in Ireland and elsewhere, under the designation of 'miserables'."

By the mid-1800s, the high levels of taxation had come down, thanks to the vast volume of imports, as well as the influence of respected Quaker industrialists who had convinced the government of chocolate's nourishing virtues. Chocolate was now affordable by all and had become big business.

UNITED STATES OF AMERICA

The first chocolate found its way back across the Atlantic to North America around 1765, probably in the pockets of high-ranking English officials going to their posts in the east coast colonies. We also know that Domingo Ghirardelli, an Italian confectioner then trading in Lima in Peru, exported cacao beans and other essential commodities from South America to San Francisco to supply the needs of the gold rush hordes. Another possible route for cacao beans was directly from Jamaica after the Spanish had given up control there.

Thomas Jefferson (1743–1826), third president of the United States, is quoted as saying: "The superiority of chocolate, both for health and nourishment, will soon give it the preference over tea and coffee in America which it has in Spain." Because of the pioneering nature of North American society, chocolate was given a somewhat different reception to the one it had received in Europe. Although the wealthy east coast society enjoyed chocolate, they drank it at home — chocolate houses did not exist. Another difference was that chocolate was generally marketed to the masses rather than the elite (as in Europe), with the emphasis on wholesomeness rather than sophistication, so it consequently reached a far broader segment of society than it had in Spain, France and England.

The first chocolate factory was set up in 1765 in Massachusetts by Dr James Baker and John Hannon. The Walter Baker Company was established in 1780 by Baker's grandson and is still synonymous with quality chocolate. By 1884, Milton Hershey, of the Hershey Chocolate Company, was producing baking chocolate, cocoa and sweet chocolate coatings for his famous caramels; and by 1885, Domingo Ghirardelli had set up his California Chocolate Manufactory in San Francisco. Right from the start, chocolate was big business in North America.

BELOW: Nineteenth-century advertising poster for curious chocolate products from the Walter Baker Company.

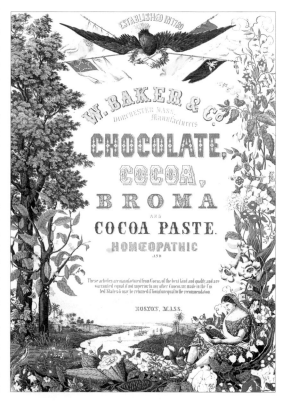

CHOCOLATE AND THE CHURCH

The Church played an important role, directly and indirectly, in the early history of chocolate. The bitter and bloody religious wars raging between Catholics and Protestants in the sixteenth and seventeenth centuries, were, in a way, the cause of chocolate's appearance and gradual dispersal through Europe. The Jesuits, actively involved in the religious wars and fiercely committed to empowering the Catholic Church, were a driving political force both in Europe and Latin America. It was almost certainly the Jesuit missionaries, rather than New World explorers, who were responsible for bringing the first chocolate into Spain, Italy and France; it would have passed through an international network of monasteries and convents. It was also thanks to the pressure of Jesuit missionaries that raw, rather than processed, cacao beans were eventually shipped to Europe. Before this, the Spanish colonists had had a monopoly on processing the beans in Latin America, making fat profits by doing so.

In Italy, the religious wars resulted in a great many high-level marriages between aristocratic families and the ruling powers.

ABOVE: Friar Drinking Chocolate *by Jose M. Oropeza.*

Until its unification in 1879, Italy was a collection of self governing states, and it was felt that marriages of this kind were the best way of cementing diplomatic relationships and consolidating the states' collective power. The aristocratic brides liked to take their maids, cooks and favourite foods with them when they moved from one Italian state or foreign country to another, and so through them chocolate began to appear in all sorts of places.

Until the eighteenth century, chocolate was made by monks and nuns, both in Europe and Latin America, using the methods handed down from the Aztecs. Thomas Gage, in his book *The English-American, His Travail by Sea and Land, or a New Survey of the West Indies* (published 1648), wrote of "cloister churches" run by nuns and friars. He said these were "talked off far and near, not for their religious practices, but for their skill in making drinkes which are used in those parts, the one called

BELOW: Part of Columbus's mission was to conquer new lands in the name of the Catholic Church. This picture illustrates that religious fervour.

ABOVE: This seventeenth-century Spanish still-life shows tablets of chocolate, which were often made by monks and nuns.

chocolatte, another atolle. Chocolatte is (also) made up in boxes, and sent not only to Mexico, but much of it yearly transported into Spain".

In the New World, the Church generally took a pragmatic view of chocolate. It was popular with nuns and monks because it sustained them through the lengthy fasts they had to endure, and they were convinced of its health-promoting properties. There was an occasional difference of opinion in the Old World, however. A Spanish monk was said to have declared the drink diabolical, claiming its invigorating properties were the work of evil spirits, but his views went unheard. In 1650 the Society of Jesus (the Jesuit school) issued an act outlawing the drink to Jesuits, but this was impossible to enforce, especially when students started to abandon the school because of it.

THE CHOCOLATE OF CHIAPA

One major objection to chocolate appears to have been raised by the Bishop of Chiapa whose Mass was continually disturbed

by its use. A famous and rather lengthy story told by Thomas Gage is worth repeating. The upper-class white ladies of Chiapa Real claimed "much weakness and squeamishness of stomacke, which they say is so great that they are not able to continue in church … unless they drinke a cup of hot chocolatte …. For this purpose it was much used by them to make their maids bring them to church … a cup of chocolatte, which could not be done to all without a great confusion and interrupting both mass and sermon".

Driven to distraction by the endless disturbances, the Bishop posted a notice stating that anyone who ate or drank in church would be excommunicated. The scornful women carried on their chocolate drinking regardless, and eventually the situation exploded into an uproar in which swords were drawn against the priests as they tried to remove the cups of chocolate from the women's maids.

The women retaliated by refusing to attend the Bishop's services, and attending Mass at the convents instead. The local priest warned the Bishop that if the women "cannot have their wills, they will surely work revenge either by chocolate or conserves, or some fair present, which shall surely carry death along with it!" Lo and behold, the Bishop fell ill and died a most unpleasant death eight days later. Gage wrote: "His head and face, did so swell that the least touch upon any part of him caused the skin to break and cast out white matter, which had corrupted and overflown all his body." Rumour had it that a gentlewoman "noted to be somewhat too familiar with one of the Bishop's pages" had persuaded the innocent young man to administer a cup of poisoned chocolate to "him who so rigorously had forbidden chocolate to be drunk in Church". A popular proverb in the region thereafter was "Beware of the chocolate of Chiapa".

DANGEROUS STIMULANTS

At the time that chocolate was becoming all the rage in Europe, there was a similar rise in the consumption of other tropical commodities such as coffee, tea, tobacco, rum and sugar; it seems that the Europeans were developing a taste for stimulants. The Church took a strong position and, with the exception of sugar, denounced the new foods as potentially dangerous. Even so, there was a certain amount of rule-bending when it came to chocolate.

RIGHT: Detail from a diorama based on a seventeenth-century engraving of monks drinking chocolate.

CHOCOLATE AS MEDICINE

Chocolate was used therapeutically as long ago as the fourth century, when the Maya first started cultivating the cacao tree. Sorcerers, the predecessors of priests and doctors, prescribed cacao both as a stimulant and as a soothing balm. Warriors took it as an energy-boosting drink, and cacao butter was used as a dressing for wounds.

ABOVE: Utensils needed "to make cocoa to perfection".

Later on, the Aztecs prescribed a potion of cacao mixed with the ground exhumed bones of their ancestors as a cure for diarrhoea. The Spanish colonists, too, were aware of cacao's healing properties. A traveller reported of his countrymen: "They make paste thereof, the which they say is good for the stomacke, and against the catarre."

However, chocolate was given a mixed reception by the scientific and medical community, who were just as vociferous as the Church when it came to debating the rights and wrongs of this mysterious new substance. In the sixteenth century, when medicine was in its infancy, many of the theories were based on the principle of "hot" and "cold" humours, or body energies, which, if not kept in balance, would cause illness. The Spanish classified chocolate as "cold" and tried to neutralize its effect by drinking it hot, flavoured with "hot" spices. They found it hard to understand why the Aztecs drank unheated chocolate when it was already a "cold" food.

By the seventeenth century, chocolate had been given the seal of approval by several botanists and medical men, who discovered that it contained all kinds of beneficial substances. Henry Stubbe (1632–72), the English court physician, visited the West Indies to investigate the physical effects of chocolate. On his return, he published *The Indian Nectar,* in which he had nothing but praise for the beverage, with the proviso that adding too much sugar or spice was unwise.

Among the many others who sang the praises of chocolate was Stephani Blancardi (1650–1702), an Italian physician. He commented: "Chocolate is not only pleasant of taste, but it is also a veritable balm of the mouth, for the maintaining of all glands and humours in a good state of health. Thus it is, that all who drink it, possess a sweet breath."

The French faculty of medicine officially approved its use in 1661. The magistrate and gastronome, Brillat-Savarin (1755–1826), summed up in *Physiologie du Gout:* "Chocolate, when carefully prepared, is a wholesome and agreeable form of food ... is very suitable for persons of great mental exertion, preachers, lawyers, and above all travellers ... it agrees with the feeblest stomachs, has proved beneficial in cases of chronic illness and remains the last resource in the diseases of the pylorus." Some of his contemporaries claimed that chocolate cured tuberculosis. A French doctor, probably sensing chocolate's ability to lift the spirits, was convinced of its merits as an antidote to a broken heart. He wrote "Those who love, and are unfortunate enough to suffer from the most universal of all gallant illnesses, will find [in chocolate] the most enlightening consolation."

Praise was by no means universal. An eighteenth-century physician to the Tuscan court threw a spanner in the works by declaring that chocolate was "hot" and that it was madness to add "hot drugs" to it. He obviously noticed the effects of caffeine for he lists as ill effects incessant chatter, insomnia, irritability and hyperactivity in children. The French, too, became disenamoured for a short period, blaming chocolate for "vapours", palpitations, wind and constipation.

In general, however, the medicinal and nutritional benefits

BELOW: French doctors believed chocolate was beneficial for chronic illnesses and broken hearts.

> — *A MEXICAN RECIPE FOR LIP SALVE* —
> *Take half a teaspoon [2.5ml] of cocoa butter from freshly roasted beans and mix to an ointment with sweet almond oil.*

RIGHT: This eighteenth-century painting shows how chocolate was adopted by well-to-do households as a nutritious breakfast drink.

BELOW: This engraving from "Physiologie du Gout ou Méditations de Gastronomie Transcendante" (1848) depicts chocolate being served to uplift the spirits.

BELOW: This nineteenth-century advertisement shows British children enjoying cocoa. Medical experts in Britain proclaimed cocoa as "the drink par excellence for children, with whom it is a universal favourite".

of chocolate were well accepted. An early English writer described it as "incomparable as a family drink for breakfast or supper, when both tea and coffee are really out of place unless the latter is nearly all milk". Brillat-Savarin commented on digestion: "When you have breakfasted well and copiously, if you swallow a generous cup of good chocolate at the end of the meal, you will have digested everything perfectly three hours later."

By the 1800s charlatans were beginning to cash in on chocolate's seal of approval by the medical profession. Various forms of "medicinal" chocolate started to appear including sinister-sounding products such as "pectoral chocolate" made with Indian tapioca, recommended for people suffering from consumption, and "analeptic" chocolate made with a mysterious "Persian tonic".

By the end of the century, the genuine article was approved of by hospitals and sanatoria, as well as by the navy, the army and various public institutions.

THE FOUNDING FATHERS

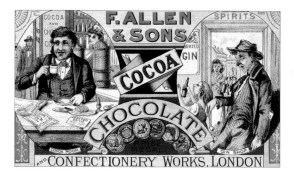

ABOVE: Nineteenth-century British cocoa manufacturers were keen to wean the poor off their favourite tipple of gin.

GREAT BRITAIN

The manufacture of drinking chocolate in Britain was transformed by the Industrial Revolution and the cultural, social and economic changes that followed in its wake. During the eighteenth century the pioneering chocolate manufacturers were still using primitive manufacturing methods, similar to those used by the Aztecs. Technology gradually entered the scene with two key developments: a hydraulic grinding press, invented in 1728 by Walter Churchman, and, in 1765, James Watt's steam engine, which changed the food industry overnight. Another crucial development in chocolate manufacture was a revolutionary type of chocolate press invented in 1828 by a Dutch chemist, Coenraad Van Houten.

In 1853 the taxes on drinking chocolate were reduced because the volume of imports had grown enormously. By then the new railways had made transport easier, and power-driven machinery had largely replaced the old slow method of making chocolate by hand. These changes radically brought down the price, meaning that drinking chocolate could potentially be enjoyed by all.

It was during this era that several

RIGHT: Cadburys printed endorsements from the medical press on their packaging.

eminent Quaker families – the Frys, the Cadburys, the Rowntrees and the Terrys – became involved in chocolate manufacturing. These families established themselves as the main producers in Britain and succeeded in transforming chocolate from the drink of the aristocracy to the drink of the people.

It was undoubtedly the Quakers' evangelical outlook which was behind their decision to choose chocolate as a commercial venture. Because the beverage was so wholesome, the Quakers hoped it would provide a means of weaning the poor off beer and gin, their favourite tipples, and improving the quality of their lives in general. The Quakers were also concerned for their employees' welfare. They created exemplary working conditions and built model villages where education, healthcare and community services were provided for the workers, both active and retired, without charge. Cadbury's Bournville village near Birmingham and Rowntree in York are famous examples.

The Frys were the sole suppliers of chocolate to the navy, making them the largest chocolate manufacturer in the world. Not to be outdone, the rival Cadbury family gained the privileged title of purveyors of chocolate to Queen Victoria.

ITALY

The Italians have always been accomplished sweet-makers. They started using chocolate as an ingredient very early on and thus established themselves as leading experts in the art of making fine chocolates. In 1884, when the Russian Czar commissioned from the jeweller Fabergé his first golden egg with its surprise filling of precious stones, Italian producers introduced what may have been the first chocolate Easter eggs containing a surprise gift.

ABOVE: Military-style packaging.

The Italian chocolate industry is centred around Turin in Piedmont and Perugia in Umbria. Production on a commercial level developed in the early nineteenth century when Bozelli, an engineer from Genoa, designed a machine capable of producing over 300kg/660lb of chocolate per day. By the end of the century the industry was booming.

There are several long-established firms in northern Italy. These include Caffarel, from whom the Italians learned to make chocolate, and Baratti & Milano, from the Turin area; Perugina (now owned by Nestlé) from Perugia, makers of the famous "Baci" (kisses) chocolates with the memorable pack; and Majani in Bologna, who now produce the ultimate in designer chocolates.

SWITZERLAND

Unsurprisingly, Switzerland boasts an incredible list of founding fathers. The first, an enterprising young man named François Cailler, travelled to Turin in 1815, learned the tricks of the trade from Caffarel, then opened the first Swiss chocolate factory four years later. Next to set up was Philippe Suchard, inventor of the world's first chocolate mixing machine. In 1845 Richard Sprüngli opened his world-famous shop in Zurich, followed by a factory in 1900. Henri Nestlé, a chemist, invented a type of evaporated milk powder, which was used by Daniel Peter, a chocolate-maker, to produce the first milk chocolate bars in 1879. In the same year Rodolphe Lindt invented the "conching" process, which revolutionized forever the texture and flavour of solid chocolate bars. Richard Sprüngli's grandson, David, bought out Lindt in 1899; five generations later, Lindt-Sprüngli is Switzerland's largest independent chocolate manufacturer. Finally, in 1908 Jean Tobler produced the famous "Toblerone" bar, now marketed by Suchard. Its distinctive triangular shape was designed to represent the Swiss Alps.

FRANCE

The first chocolate factories appeared in the mid-seventeenth century, and, as in England, production was a slow and primitive process. Life became easier in 1732, when a Frenchman named Dubuisson invented a grinding table. This allowed the workers to grind the beans standing up, instead of kneeling in front of a floor-level stone, which they had done until then.

France's most famous mass-producers were Auguste Poulain and Jean-Antoine Menier. Poulain set up shop in Blois in 1848, making chocolate in a back room. By 1878 he was producing chocolate by the ton from five different factories. In 1884 his son Albert developed a chocolate breakfast drink, now known as Grand Arôme and still loved by French children. Meanwhile, Menier, a pharmacist famous for his "medicinal powders", bought a small chocolate factory near the River Marne, intending simply to produce chocolate to coat his pills. When he died in 1853, his son Émile-Justin stepped in, concentrating on full-scale chocolate manufacture. A man of capitalist vision, Émile built a new factory in France, opened a factory in

LEFT: Menier cooking chocolate is widely used today.

RIGHT: As this 1893 poster shows, Menier chocolate has always been popular with French children.

LEFT: Established for over a hundred years, Weiss still produces quality drinking chocolate.

London, a warehouse in New York, bought cacao plantations in Nicaragua, and built a Bournville-like model village for his workers. When he died Émile's son, Henri, continued in the same expansionary spirit. In 1889 he arranged for electricity lines and telephones to be installed in the workers' homes, and, many years before the rest of the French working population, gave them the right to retire at sixty.

France's chocolatiers also include a strong contingent of smaller specialist firms that played an important role in forming the character of France's present-day chocolate industry. Debauve & Gallais was established in Paris in 1800 and are the oldest producers of hand-made chocolates in the city today. Another prestigious company is Weiss, based in Saint-Étienne for over a hundred years, and famous for its delicious drinking chocolate and hefty foil-wrapped chocolate drops.

ABOVE: The electronic automobile bought by Hershey in 1900.

UNITED STATES OF AMERICA
Chocolate arrived relatively late in North America, around the middle of the eighteenth century. The first industrial producers were Dr James Baker and his partner John Hannon, who built a chocolate factory in 1765 on the banks of the River Neponset in Massachusetts. In 1780 the company was renamed the Walter Baker Company, after John Hannon's grandson, and is still a household name today, producing baker's (a confusing generic term) chocolate as well as better quality varieties under their own name of Baker's.

Over a century later Milton Hershey, a successful caramel manufacturer from Pennsylvania, visited the 1893 Chicago World's Fair and was overwhelmingly impressed by German chocolate production machinery on display. With a shrewd sense of timing, he decided that chocolate was going to be a runaway success; and his company has never looked back. Milton sold his first milk chocolate bar in 1895, and since then Hershey Bars and Hershey Kisses have become part of the American way of life – just as he predicted.

Like his Quaker counterparts in Britain, Milton had a social conscience. He enlisted nutritionists to vouch for the sanctity of his product, set up a squeaky-clean working environment, and built the factory town of Hershey in Pennsylvania. The main thoroughfares are East Chocolate Avenue and Cocoa Avenue, while the tree-lined side streets are named after places where cacao is grown, or by types of bean – Java, Caracas, Arriba and so on. Milton went one better than the Quaker factory villages in England and provided very generous out-of-town facilities for his employees such as an amusement park, a zoo, sporting facilities and a theatre. Milton also made it clear that no "taverns, piggeries, glue, soap, candle, lamp-black factories" were allowed, making sure that his model working communities stayed as wholesome as possible.

It is interesting that the early North American and British manufacturers of a product that was, and still is, associated with sensory enjoyment and indulgence, should have had quite a puritanical outlook. A cynical view might be that their social philanthropy was a clever marketing ploy, but these businessmen did have a genuine social conscience, and it is perhaps another illustration that chocolate is all things to all people – both a luxurious treat and a wholesome daily food.

Milton Hershey was not the only American producer

pushing the wholesomeness of chocolate. Like-minded but rather more extreme companies included the Taylor brothers, who entered the market with their Natural Hygienist Practitioners, and Dr William Hay, of the still-popular Hay System of food-combining. Taylor's selling point was the curative, home-opathic nature of chocolate. This shows a continuity with the earliest European marketeers, who sold their chocolate

ABOVE: Street signs to the main thoroughfares in Hershey.

through the apothecaries, monasteries and convents of the sixteenth and seventeenth centuries, and had much to say on the beneficial properties of the cacao bean and its products.

A much more colourful American chocolate producer was

BELOW: Early publicity for Taylor Brothers demonstrating their social conscience, while promoting the nourishing powers of chocolate.

ABOVE: A picture of the original Guittard building surrounded by scenes showing early chocolate manufacture.

Domingo Ghirardelli, an Italian confectioner with South American links who was originally in business in Lima, Peru. Ghirardelli befriended an American cabinetmaker named James Lick, who, in 1847 just before the discovery of gold at Sutter's Mill, moved from Lima to San Francisco, taking with him a large quantity of Ghirardelli's chocolate. Lured by reports of a lucrative market, Ghirardelli followed Lick to California. As astute and entrepreneurial as his fellow chocolate producers, both in

BELOW: The Ghirardelli company was the first in America to make easily dissolvable powdered cocoa.

the United States and worldwide, Ghirardelli foresaw the potential in satisfying the day-to-day needs of the goldrush pioneers, who by then were arriving in hordes. He set up a business in San Francisco importing and selling commodities such as sugar, coffee and, of course, chocolate.

There were various disasters over the years, including devastating bankruptcy and a serious fire, but business continued despite the inevitable setbacks in a volatile period of American history. By 1856 the company was known as Ghirardelli's California Chocolate Manufactory. The company was to make its mark on the chocolate industry in the 1860s when, by sheer accident, a way of making a low-fat powdered cocoa was discovered. The new product was known as Sweet Ground Chocolate and Cocoa and is still sold today.

The original factory buildings have become a well-known San Francisco landmark in Ghirardelli Square, and the company continues to flourish. It was bought by the Golden Grain Macaroni Company in 1963, which in turn was acquired as a subsidiary of the Quaker Oats Company in 1983.

Another chocolate maker, Etienne Guittard from France, set off for the gold fields of San Francisco in 1860. After three years, he hadn't found any gold, but the supply of fine chocolate he had brought with him to barter for prospecting gear had been enthusiastically received. The shopkeepers he traded with assured him that there was a future for him and his wonderful chocolate in San Francisco. Guittard went back to France, where he worked and saved to buy the equipment he would need. In 1868 he returned to San Francisco and opened the business that developed into one of the important American manufacturers of top-grade chocolate for wholesale customers. Some of the country's best confectioners, bakers and ice-cream makers (Baskin-Robbins, for one) use Guittard.

— GHIRARDELLI'S ACCIDENT —

Cacao beans have a high fat content and because of this do not combine easily with liquids when ground to a powder. Ghirardelli's most important contribution to the chocolate industry was the accidental discovery of a way of making a virtually fat-free powder.

A worker left some ground cacao beans hanging from a hook in a cloth bag overnight. By the morning, the floor was covered in cacao butter that had dripped from the bag. The ground chocolate left behind was almost fat-free and was found to combine with liquids much more smoothly. Ghirardelli's ever-popular Sweet Ground Chocolate and Cocoa was developed from this.

CULTIVATION AND PROCESSING

GROWING AND HARVESTING

ABOVE: Cacao tree and seedling.

There are many stages in the processing of chocolate, and there has been a corresponding amount of development in its history as it has grown from a cold drink to the complex and adaptable substance it is today. This chapter traces the most important steps in the production of chocolate.

GROWING

The cacao bean grows in large pods on the cacao tree, *Theobroma cacao,* an evergreen which thrives in tropical areas lying between 20° north and 20° south of the equator. The tree is an exacting specimen, for it refuses to grow where it is too high, too cold or too dry, and it demands shelter from wind and sun. It also needs protection from wild animals which delight in picking its pods, and it easily succumbs to various rots, wilts and fungal diseases.

It is traditional for the cacao tree to be grown under the protection of taller shade-creating trees, the conditions resembling its natural jungle habitat. In areas such as Grenada and parts of Jamaica, cacao trees grow successfully without additional shade, as long as there are sufficient moisture and nutrients in the soil. The cacao tree grows to about the size of an apple tree and starts

BELOW: A shady cacao plantation in the garden island of Grenada, where cacao production is a staple industry.

CACAO is essentially the botanical name and refers to the tree, the pods and, at one time, the unfermented beans from the pods. The term is now also used for beans that have been fermented.

COCOA refers to the manufactured powder sold for drinking or food manufacturing purposes.

bearing fruit in its third year. With luck, it will continue to do so until at least its twentieth year, and it is not unknown for a tree to live to be a hundred years old. The glossy dark green leaves, similar to those of the laurel, grow to nearly 30 cm/ 12 in long. The small pale pink flowers grow in dense clusters straight out of the trunk and main branches on little raised cushions, a feature technically known as "cauliflory".

After pollination, the flowers take about five months to develop into cacao pods. It's a colourful crop – the pods range from bright red, green, purple or yellow, changing hue as they ripen. Ripe pods are about 20 cm/8 in long, oval and pointed, each containing 20 to 40 beans, embedded in a soft white pulp.

HARVESTING

It is by assessing the colour of the pod and the sound it makes when tapped that the picker can be sure it is ready for picking. To be absolutely certain that the pod is ripe requires years of practice, and experienced pickers are highly valued.

The pods are removed from the tree by cutting through their stalks, those within reach with a cutlass, and those on higher branches with a curved knife fixed to a long pole. Cutting must be done with extreme care so as not to damage the "cauliflory", as this continually produces the flowers and therefore the fruit.

In some countries, harvesting takes place all year round, although most heavily from May to December. In other parts of the world, West Africa for instance, the main crop is harvested from September to February.

FERMENTING

The next stage is to split the pods with a cutlass, taking care not to damage the precious beans. These are scooped out, together with their surrounding pulp, and formed into a conical heap on a carefully arranged mat of banana leaves. When the heap is complete the leaves are folded over, and yet more of these giant

ABOVE: Early lithograph issued by the Empire Marketing Board in Britain showing cacao beans being scooped from the pods.

TYPES OF CACAO BEAN

There are two distinct species of cacao bean used in the manufacture of chocolate: the criollo (meaning "native") and the forastero (meaning "foreign").

The criollo, the Rolls Royce of beans and the most delicate, is in a way a "limited edition", representing only 10 to 15 per cent of the world's production. It is cultivated mainly in the countries where cacao originated, namely Nicaragua, Guatemala, Mexico, Venezuela and Colombia, as well as Trinidad, Jamaica and Grenada. The criollo's exceptional flavour and aroma are prized by chocolate manufacturers the world over. Not surprisingly, the bean is always used in combination with other varieties.

The much hardier and higher-yielding forastero bean is grown mainly in Brazil and Africa, and it accounts for about 80 per cent of the world's production. It has a stronger, more bitter flavour than the criollo and is mainly used for blending.

The one exception is the amenolado variety, known as the "Arriba" bean, grown in Ecuador. Its delicate flavour and fine aroma are considered equal to the world's best beans.

Finally, there are also several hybrid beans, of which the trinitario is the best known. As the name suggests, it began life in Trinidad where, following a hurricane in 1727 that all but destroyed the plantations, it was a result of cross-breeding. It has inherited the robustness of the forastero and the delicate flavour of the criollo, and it is used mainly for blending.

leaves are added to enclose the heap completely. This is the start of the fermentation process, which lasts for up to six days.

The chemical processes involved are complicated, but, basically, bacteria and yeasts present in the air multiply on the sugary pulp surrounding the beans, causing it to decompose to an acidic juice. The process raises the temperature of the heap and under these conditions magical changes take place within the bean itself. The colour changes from purple to chocolate brown and the familiar cacao smell begins to emerge – the first crucial stage in developing beans of superior quality. That said, the fermentation process is sometimes omitted, with planters and manufacturers arguing both for and against.

DRYING

After fermentation, the beans are spread out on bamboo mats or wooden drying floors. During the ten to twenty days needed for drying, the beans are regularly turned to keep them well aired and to prevent moulds forming. In some places, where rainfall and humidity are high, the beans are dried in commercial drying plants. However, the best quality cacao comes from beans that have been dried naturally in the warm tropical sun.

BELOW: The large and beautiful cacao pods grow directly from the tree branches and change colour as they ripen.

Modern Manufacturing

ABOVE: *A chocolate manufacturer inspects a shipment of beans.*

Cleaning and Grading

Cacao beans arrive at a chocolate factory in the condition in which they leave the plantations in cacao-growing countries. They have been fermented and dried but are still a raw material with the edible part enclosed inside the hard skin, which is dusty with the remains of the dried pulp.

The beans are given a preliminary cleaning, during which any stones or other objects that may have arrived in the sacks are removed by sieving. The beans pass on a moving belt to storage hoppers, and from there they travel on another conveyor belt to the cleaning and grading machines. The beans are carefully inspected, and any shrivelled or double beans are discarded, as is any undesirable material still clinging to the beans. Next, the cleaned and graded beans are collected either in containers or passed on another continuous conveyor belt to the roasting machines.

Roasting for Flavour

Roasting is a crucial part of the process and serves several functions. First, it develops the flavour and aroma, and it enriches the colour. Roasting also dries the husk surrounding the "nib", or edible inner part of the bean, making its removal easier, and dries the nib itself so that it is ready for grinding.

The degree of roasting is extremely important. Overdoing

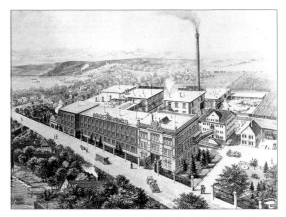

ABOVE: *A contemporaneous picture of Richard Sprüngli's famous factory, which opened in Switzerland in 1900.*

it destroys the natural flavour of the bean and produces a bitter product, while under-roasting makes the removal of the husk more difficult and also fails to eradicate the natural bitterness of the raw bean. Some manufacturers who want their chocolate to have a strong flavour, but who are not prepared to increase the cacao content, attempt to achieve the required intensity by roasting the beans longer.

Different types of bean need different roasting temperatures, depending on their texture and flavour; the mild varieties are usually roasted at lower temperatures than the stronger types.

After roasting, the beans are cooled as quickly as possible to prevent further internal roasting.

BELOW: *The beans are cleaned and sifted through a mesh to get rid of small or shrivelled beans and foreign bodies.*

BELOW: *The beans are gently roasted to develop the aroma, enrich the colour and to dehydrate them prior to grinding.*

WINNOWING

During the next stage the beans are passed through the husking and winnowing machine, which cracks open the roasted beans, and blows the lighter husks away from the heavier pieces of nib.

Manufacturers send the husks off for recycling as garden mulch, or use them to make low-quality soft "shell" butter.

THE CRUCIAL BLEND

During the blending process, specified quantities of different varieties of cacao nibs are weighed and transferred to a cylindrical blender before they are fed into the grinding machines.

The blending of beans for cocoa powder is generally less exacting than for eating chocolate. The latter requires the utmost skill from the chocolatier since knowledge of the characteristic flavours imparted by different beans is only acquired by years of experience. There are subtle differences of flavour in each type of bean, and the final flavour is obtained by blending two, three or more types of bean after roasting. In the same way that the winemaker blends his grapes, the chocolatier needs to determine the proportion of strong and mild cacao beans necessary

ABOVE: A picture of the grinding hall in the Sprüngli factory. The rollers can be seen on the left.

to produce a blend that will result in a satisfying chocolate, and the formulae are jealously guarded secrets.

GRINDING

Once in the grinding mill, the nibs pass through a series of rollers, resulting in coarse particles that eventually turn into a warm paste because of the frictional heat of the grinding action. Then follows a second grinding to bring the particles down to the required size, usually between 25 and 50 microns (about 0.001in). Large particles result in coarse grainy chocolate, while very finely ground particles will produce a pasty and slightly sticky chocolate. After grinding, the cacao mass or "liquor" flows out of the machine into shallow metal containers.

THE PARTING OF THE WAYS

At this stage, further treatment of the liquor depends on whether it is to be made into cocoa powder or eating chocolate. For cocoa powder the next step is the extraction of a large proportion of the cacao butter. This is pressed out of the liquor, and the residue is formed into cakes, which go through one more grinding. Some cocoa is "dutched", which helps to make cocoa powder easier to mix with water. It also improves the colour and lightens the flavour. Sometimes a wetting agent is added, especially to the "instant" varieties of cocoa intended for use as a cold drink; it makes the powder easier to mix with cold water or milk. The wetting agent is usually lecithin, a vegetable fat found in egg yolks and soy beans. Chocolate destined for eating is treated very differently from cocoa powder.

RIGHT: Two types of instant drinking chocolate.

— *BEAN BLENDS* —

The final flavour of chocolate depends largely on the chocolatier's skill and experience in selecting and blending various types of beans. Availability of supplies and cost also have to be taken into account.

Types of cacao beans may be divided into strong and mild varieties:

STRONG VARIETIES	MILD VARIETIES
Accra	Caracas
St Lucia	Mauritius
Para	Sri Lanka
Trinidad	Arriba
Grenada	Java
Surinam	Madras
Cuba	Jamaica
Dominica	Seychelles

If made only with Accra beans, for example, chocolate will have a very strong, harsh flavour, whereas Caracas beans make mild but excellently flavoured chocolate. Superb chocolate can be made with a blend of 42 per cent Trinidad beans (strong), 21 per cent Accra beans (strong) and 37 per cent Caracas (mild).

THE MANUFACTURE OF EATING CHOCOLATE

ABOVE: Rolls of ground chocolate paste (foreground) are moulded into bars and various shapes in the moulding hall.

ABOVE: Prolonged conching transforms the chocolate paste into velvety smoothness.

MIXING

Cacao beans used for manufacturing eating chocolate are processed in a different way from beans used in cocoa manufacture. First, a carefully selected blend of roasted and ground nibs, the edible centre of the bean, is mixed with pulverized sugar and enriched with cacao butter, not necessarily extracted from the same batch of nibs. The mass producers in the chocolate industry are very keen on adding lecithin, a vegetable fat, to replace some or all of the cacao butter. This means they can sell the valuable butter at a profit.

The mixture then goes to the *mélangeur,* a round machine with a horizontal rotating base on which run heavy rollers. After mixing, the chocolate paste that is discharged from the *mélangeur* resembles well-kneaded dough.

When manufacturing milk chocolate, powdered milk or evaporated sweetened milk is added to the rest of the ingredients in the mixer.

REFINING

Next, the chocolate paste is ground between a series of five rollers, each succeeding roller rotating faster than the previous one. The paste enters the first pair of rollers as a thin film, which is then taken up by the next pair, through a carefully adjusted gap – rather like making pasta with a machine. By the time the paste emerges from the fifth roller it is wafer-thin.

As far as some mass-producers are concerned this is the end of the process, but the finest quality chocolate needs further treatment known as "conching".

CONCHING

The conching machine was invented in 1880 by the Swiss chocolatier, Rodolfe Lindt. The name comes from the French (*conche,* meaning "shell") and is derived from the shape of the machine, a large shell-shaped container.

The function of the machine is to agitate the liquid chocolate gently over a period that may be as long as seven days. It is a vital process in which the flavour of the chocolate is developed and mellowed, any residual bitterness is removed, and the texture reaches that essential stage of velvety smoothness.

Manufacturers of cheaper chocolate give as little as twelve hours to the process. Quality producers will continue conching for up to a week, sometimes adding extra cacao butter to make the chocolate smoother still.

During conching, various flavours are added, such as vanilla, cloves or cinnamon.

LEFT: Luscious slices of crystallized fruit are enrobed with smooth, dark chocolate.

Vanilla is almost always used and dates back to the days of the Aztecs. Our palates have become so accustomed to its flavour in chocolate that leaving it out would be like making bread without salt. Pure vanilla extract is used for the best quality chocolate, but cheaper varieties are likely to contain vanillin, a synthetic substitute.

TEMPERING

Once the conching stage is complete, the chocolate is fed into tempering kettles, where it is stirred and carefully cooled but still remains liquid. This is a tricky process since cacao butter contains various types of fat, all with different melting and setting points. If the chocolate mass is cooled too slowly, some fats will remain liquid and separate from the mass, creating a bloom on the surface when the chocolate finally solidifies. Tempering causes rapid cooling resulting in a more even distribution of the various fats.

After tempering, chocolate to be made into bars is pumped into moulding machines, while chocolate to be used as coating is pumped into enrobing machines.

BELOW: Hollow Easter eggs, filled with small chocolates, are a classic example of chocolate moulding.

Mr R. Whymper in *Cocoa and Chocolate* (1921) told an interesting story of how, in the early 1900s, the popularity of milk chocolate "raised hopes in the breasts of manufacturers that a similar demand might be created among the masses for such articles as Date Chocolate, Egg Chocolate, Malt Chocolate". A number of patents were taken out, one of which was for mixing cacao beans and dates to a pulp, and covered the use of apples, pears and apricots for the same purpose. There was apparently a shortage of cane sugar at the time, and the fruit pulp was intended to be a sweetener.

Another patent was for "dietetic and laxative" chocolate. As Mr Whymper pointed out: "Such preparations must have only a very limited sale, so long as the chocolate-consuming public does not seek to find cures in its confections."

MOULDING

Liquid chocolate is also moulded into hollowed-out shapes which are sometimes filled with small chocolates. These products are often marketed as gifts for children, and specialist chocolate-makers give full rein to their creativity here, producing not simply exquisite Easter eggs, bunnies and hearts, but also pigs, fish, lions, hippos, crocodiles and

ABOVE: 1930's metal moulds for producing novelty chocolates.

cars. Because of the contact with the smooth tinned surfaces of the mould, good quality hollow chocolate has a high degree of gloss, which adds to its attraction.

ENROBING

Enrobing is the tricky process of coating confectionery centres. Liquid chocolate of a slightly "thin" consistency is pumped into the enrobing machine, where it is agitated once more and maintained at a temperature just high enough to keep it liquid. The centres themselves have to be warm when they enter the coating chamber, but not so warm that they lose their shape. The danger of a cold centre is that it is likely to expand when it comes in contact with the warm coating, resulting in burst chocolates. Enrobing is the process used not only for top quality chocolates in their luxury packaging, but also for the mass-produced candy bars that are bought as snacks around the world.

TASTE, QUALITY AND PRESENTATION

TYPES OF EATING CHOCOLATE

There is a wealth of wonderful chocolate products available, with an often confusing array of types, qualities, fillings and flavourings. Here is a brief guide on what you should look for and how to enjoy chocolate at its best.

PLAIN CHOCOLATE (ALSO KNOWN AS BITTERSWEET)

Plain or bittersweet chocolate must contain a minimum of 34 per cent cacao solids, but generally speaking, the higher the proportion the better the chocolate. Not so long ago, plain chocolate containing just 30 per cent cacao solids was considered high quality. Nowadays, as our taste and awareness of chocolate grows, 60 per cent is the preferred minimum, while for chocoholics 70-80 per cent is even more desirable. High quality dark chocolate contains a correspondingly small proportion of sugar. Adding sugar to chocolate has been compared with adding salt to food. You need just enough to enhance the flavour but not so much that the flavour is destroyed. Quality chocolate contains pure vanilla, an expensive flavouring sometimes called Bourbon Vanilla, extracted from a type of orchid grown in Madagascar. It also contains the minutest amount of lecithin, a harmless vegetable stabilizer. In unsweetened chocolate, which is found only in specialist shops, cacao solids are as high as 98 per cent.

ABOVE: Quality white, milk and dark chocolate.

COUVERTURE

This is high-quality chocolate in the professional league, used mainly for coating and in baking. Couverture usually has a minimum of 32 per cent cacao butter, which enables it to form a much thinner shell than ordinary chocolate.

LEFT: Couverture chocolate, which has a very high proportion of cacao solids.

RIGHT: Best quality couverture with a good sheen. Blocks of this size are supplied to chocolatiers.

> **— FORMULA FOR QUALITY CHOCOLATE —**
> 56-70% cacao solids, to include 31% cacao butter
> 29-43% finely ground sugar
> 1% lecithin and pure vanilla extract
>
> **— FORMULA FOR MASS-PRODUCED MILK CHOCOLATE —**
> 11% cacao solids
> 3% vegetable fat
> 20% milk solids
> 65% sugar
> 1% lecithin and synthetic vanillin

MILK CHOCOLATE

To some *aficionados,* milk chocolate is not really chocolate, but, increasingly, there are good brands around even though they may be difficult to find. A good brand will have a cacao solid content of around 40 per cent, but most mass-produced milk chocolate contains only 20 per cent. Mass-produced milk chocolate has a high sugar content, often up to 50 per cent. It can also contain up to 5 per cent vegetable fat, used as a substitute for expensive cacao butter, and artificial flavouring.

WHITE CHOCOLATE

This is basically cacao butter without any cacao solids, with some added sugar, flavouring and milk. White chocolate does not have the same depth of flavour as plain chocolate. It is mainly sold for its novelty value or to provide an attractive colour contrast

LEFT: A layered bar of plain, white and milk chocolate.

in chocolates and chocolate desserts. The best quality brands tend to be French and Swiss. British brands usually contain vegetable oil instead of cacao butter, as well as synthetic flavourings.

ASSESSING QUALITY

All our senses – sight, smell, sound, touch and taste – come into play when assessing the quality of plain chocolate. There are several points to watch out for:

APPEARANCE: The chocolate should be smooth, brilliantly shiny and pure mahogany-black in colour.

SMELL: The chocolate should not smell excessively sweet.

SOUND: The chocolate should be crisp and make a distinct "snap" when broken in two. If the chocolate splinters, it is too dry; if it resists breaking, it is too waxy.

TOUCH: Chocolate with a high cacao butter content should quickly start to melt when held in the hand – this is a good sign. In the mouth, it should feel ultra-smooth with no hint of graininess, and it should melt instantly.

TASTE: Chocolate contains a kaleidoscope of flavours and aromas which continue to develop in the mouth. The basic flavours are bitterness with a hint of acidity, sweetness with a suggestion of sourness, and just a touch of saltiness which helps release the aromas of cocoa, pineapple, banana, vanilla and cinnamon.

STORAGE

Humidity and heat are chocolate's greatest enemies; both can cause a "bloom" to appear on the surface. Heat-induced bloom

---

— WHAT TO DRINK WITH CHOCOLATE —

Generally speaking, chocolate and wine do not mix. The lingering intensity of the chocolate competes with the aroma of the wine, and chocolate's bitterness can mask the tannins essential to the wine's flavour. White wine or champagne drunk with chocolate is a particularly uneasy combination. At the end of a meal, coffee, perhaps accompanied by a fine cognac, whisky or bourbon, is the best choice. Professional chocolate tasters swear by a glass of cold, fresh water; as it not only quenches the thirst but also cleanses the palate.

— TASTING TECHNIQUES —

It is best to taste chocolate on an empty stomach. If your chocolate is correctly stored, you will need to allow an hour or so for it to reach the recommended temperature of 19–25°C/66–77°F.

PLAIN CHOCOLATE: Allow the chocolate to sit in your mouth for a few moments to release its primary flavours and aromas. Then chew it five to ten times to release the secondary aromas. Let it rest lightly against the roof of your mouth so that you experience the full range of flavours. Finally, enjoy the lingering tastes in your mouth.

FILLED CHOCOLATE: Allow the chocolate to sit in your mouth for a few moments to release its primary flavours and aromas. Then chew it three to five times to mix the chocolate and the filling. Let the mixture melt slowly in your mouth so that you experience a new range of flavours. Enjoy the lingering tastes.

LEFT: The perfect bar of chocolate has a glossy sheen and a rich dark colour.

is the result of cacao butter crystals rising to the surface and recrystallizing. The flavour is unaffected but the appearance is spoiled.

Humidity-induced bloom is more damaging. It is a result of sugar crystals being drawn to the surface, where they dissolve in the moist atmosphere and eventually recrystallize to form an unpleasant grey coating. As the texture and taste of the chocolate deteriorate, too, the dustbin is the best place for chocolate that has suffered in this way. The ideal temperature for storage is 10–15°C (50–60°F), slightly warmer than the refrigerator, and the humidity should be 60–70 per cent. Chocolate also absorbs surrounding odours easily and should be kept in an airtight container.

BELOW: A bloom has formed on the surface of the chocolate on the right. An unaffected piece on the left shows the difference in appearance.

Flavourings and Fillings

Every chocolate manufacturer has a secret condiment or blend of flavourings that he or she claims gives their product a unique character. Fillings and flavourings from the same tropical latitude as the cacao bean itself – vanilla, cinnamon, cardamom, coffee, rum, ginger, even pepper and chilli – are the ones most commonly used. Even in this age of "culinary fusion", when we happily mix and match cuisines in our never-ending quest for novelty, flavouring chocolate with spices from a more northerly latitude simply seems wrong – it is hard to imagine fennel or caraway-flavoured chocolate, for instance – but perhaps it is merely a matter of time before it happens.

Secret flavours

Every chocolate-consuming country has its favourite flavourings. Italy prefers its chocolate mixed with hazelnuts, almonds or chestnuts. France likes a nutty flavour too, but strongly flavoured dark bitter chocolate is also popular there. Spain likes spiced chocolate, and fillings such as almonds and dried fruits, America consumes mostly milk chocolate, often with whole peanuts or almonds embedded in it, while Britain

Above: Handmade "tartufini" from southern Italy – whole almonds coated in praline and dusted with dark cocoa and powdered sugar.

Left: Spanish chocolate packed with plump almonds.

— Fillings —

Boiled: based on sugar and glucose and including caramels, butterscotch and fudge.

Creams and fondants: a mixture of sugar crystals in a sugar syrup, with fruit or other flavourings, coated with tempered chocolate.

Croquet (or brittle): molten sugar with crushed nuts.

Ganache: a mixture of chocolate, cream and butter, either rolled in cocoa powder to make a truffle or enrobed in tempered chocolate.

Gianduja: finely ground nuts and sugar mixed with plain or milk chocolate.

Marzipan: molten sugar mixed with ground almonds, coated with plain or milk chocolate.

Nougat: a mixture of beaten egg white, boiled sugar, nuts and/or candied fruit. Known as *Montélimar* in France (after the town where it is made), *torrone* in Italy, and *turrón* in Spain.

Praline: similar to *gianduja* but with a coarser texture and usually coated with plain or milk chocolate.

likes vanilla. Not only that, every country uses different blends of beans, and, as already mentioned, the subtle variations in the flavour of different bean varieties play their part in determining the final flavour of the chocolate. If we also take into account different processing methods used by individual factories, the number of flavour combinations is almost endless.

Within the scientific community, the complexity of chocolate's flavour is a source of enormous fascination to the flavour scientists who are regularly producing learned papers on the subject. Daniel Querici, speaking at the 1992 Oxford Symposium on Food & Cookery, summed up the subject of chocolate's flavour in a delightful way: "Its complex flavour profile looks like a royal peacock tail, although not fully deployed, as food scientists keep discovering new components."

Below: Plump and glistening, these unusual, luscious chocolate-covered figs come from Italy.

ABOVE: Italian chocolates with succulent fillings of walnuts, dried fruit and pistachio marzipan.

FANTASTIC FILLINGS

Chocolate has been used as a coating for anything from almonds and dried fruit to bizarre ingredients such as ants, and a look at the contents of a global box of chocolates will reveal many more.

In the United States, chillies and chocolate come together once more in the whacky confectionery range created by two chocolatiers from Oregon. Their products, which won an award at the Fiery Foods Show at Albuquerque, New Mexico, include Mexican Zingers, a creamy, green jalapeño salsa encased in a white chocolate shell, and Southwest Coyote Kickers, a red jalapeño salsa cream covered in light milk chocolate.

Although chilli-filled chocolates are legal in the United States, alcoholic fillings are not universally acceptable. As recently as 1986, only one American state permitted the manufacture of alcoholic chocolates, only eleven states permitted their sale, and

BELOW: Handmade British chocolates with melt-in-the-mouth fondant fillings, delicately flavoured with violet and rose.

— A FILLING STORY —

In 1987, Ethel M Chocolates owned by 82-year-old Forrest Mars and named after his mother, attempted to introduce liqueur-filled chocolates to Las Vegas, Nevada. The chocolates were spiked with crème de menthe, brandy, Scotch and bourbon.

Mr Mars found that the sale and/or manufacture of alcoholic chocolates was illegal in most American states. Things were not looking good, especially as an appeal to legalize alcoholic chocolates had recently been rejected in Pennsylvania, home of Hersheyville. As was to be expected, the squeaky-clean Hershey Company added their support to the rejection on the grounds that "liquor-laced chocolates are inconsistent with values emphasized by religious and medical communities".

Not one to give up easily, the determined Mr Mars successfully petitioned the sale and manufacture of alcoholic chocolates in his home state of Nevada. This meant he could sell his chocolates there but not across the border, and so he had to content himself with selling to the twenty million tourists who visit Las Vegas each year. Ethel M Chocolates are still to be found at Las Vegas airport and in many of the city's luxury hotels.

even then the permitted alcohol levels were severely restricted.

Move on to Europe, however, and it is a different story. In Italy smooth dark chocolates are filled with decadent liqueur-soaked fruits – cherries, kumquats, slices of dried peach, pear, apricots and oranges. There are also plump prunes, dates and walnuts filled with marzipan and covered with dark chocolate.

In Britain, chocolate lovers can enjoy delicate fondant fillings such as violet and rose creams or marzipan; truffle fillings laced with champagne, Cointreau or Drambuie; or chunks of stem ginger, and whole Brazil nuts. France is the birthplace of the dusky chocolate truffle created in the late nineteenth century by the Duc de Praslin, one of Louis XIV's ministers. At that time it was considered amusing to create a food resembling something totally unrelated. *Truffes au chocolat* were deeply rich, buttery chocolate balls that were then rolled in dark cocoa powder to resemble the savoury black fungi from Périgord.

The dragée is a French confectionery classic that in its original form, almonds coated with sugar and honey, dates back to the thirteenth century. The dragée adapted well to the introduction of chocolate and now consists of praline or nuts covered in chocolate and a hard sugar coating.

Chocolate Wrappers and Boxes

Wrapping and packaging tell a great deal about what kind of chocolate is inside. Much can be learnt from the nutritional information on a bar, while the style of its presentation says much about who is expected to buy it.

Wording on Wrappers

As with the label on a bottle of fine wine or virgin olive oil, the wording on a chocolate wrapper can provide significant clues as to the quality of the product, so for a chocolate lover it is worth becoming familiar with the terminology.

LEFT: As well as listing the ingredients, some wrappers are packed with other interesting information.

An area of confusion arises over the terms "cacao liquor" and "cacao solids". Liquor is the term used in the United States, while Europe favours solids, but both refer to the same thing – the entire cacao content including the butter. This is usually expressed as a percentage of the net weight of the end product. Cacao content ranges from 15 per cent, which hardly comes into the category of chocolate, to an incredible 99 per cent, which is an almost inedible but interesting experience.

ABOVE: A wrapper that makes a feature of the high cacao content.

Since the setting up of the European Union, legislation on the labelling of food has become much more regulated, and the classification of chocolate has become an issue. Some chocolate-producing countries feel that Britain's product should be classified as "vegolate" because of its use of vegetable fat and low cacao content. Happily for British chocolate producers this has as yet remained a discussion point only.

What to Look For

The key indicator of quality is the cacao content – the combined total of cacao solids (liquor) and cacao butter. In some cases, couverture for instance, the cacao butter content is itemized separately. In the case of plain chocolate, a minimum of 50 per cent total cacao is an indicator of quality. Quality milk chocolate should have a minimum of 30 per cent. Since sugar makes up the balance of the ingredients, a high sugar content is a warning of a correspondingly low cacao content.

Unlike wine labels, which mention the grape variety, chocolate wrappers rarely divulge the type of cacao bean used and are not obliged to do so. An exception is in France, where the words *fine cocoa* mean that the superior varieties of bean, such as the criollo, have been used.

Vegetable or animal fats are used as a cheap substitute for some or all of the cacao butter, so if either is listed as an ingredient, the chocolate is not going to come up to scratch. The fact that they are not listed, however, does not always necessarily mean they are not present. In Britain, for example, up to 5 per cent cacao butter substitutes can be included without mentioning them on the wrapper.

Lecithin, an emulsifier derived from egg yolk and soya beans, is used in all types of chocolate, and at 1 per cent or less is not an indicator of inferior quality. Its function is to stabilize the chocolate and to absorb any moisture.

As far as flavourings are concerned, look for the words "pure vanilla extract". If "vanillin", a synthetic substitute, or simply the word "flavouring" is listed, the chocolate is likely to be of inferior quality.

The Americans outdo any other nation in the world when it comes to providing information on the ingredients that go into their chocolate; the wrappers and packaging often read like a book. There are very precise

LEFT AND BELOW: Early chocolate boxes often featured inlaid metal decorations and intricate decorative painting.

LEFT: The ultimate in kitsch packaging, this opulent white plastic "grand piano" chocolate box comes from Germany.

— NATIONAL PREFERENCES —
According to the American writer, Nika Standen Hazelton, "Chocolate in a blue wrapper won't sell in Shanghai or Hong Kong because the Chinese associate blue with death. Neither Swiss nor Germans like girl pictures on their chocolate packages, but want a realistic reproduction of the contents."

specifications for the quantity of cacao solids in different types of chocolate; all flavouring ingredients must be fully declared; there are additional lists of sugars, such as dextrose and glucose, which all have maximum permitted levels; and there is always a detailed panel of nutritional information.

CHOCOLATE BOXES

Chocolate-makers have been strongly aware of the value of shelf-appeal since the industry's early days. In France the most exquisitely designed chocolate boxes came into vogue as early as 1780, featuring beautiful paintings, intricately embossed plaques and inlaid semi-precious stones. Britain's chocolate boxes were not so ostentatious; they featured sentimental images that were very much the fashion when boxed chocolates came on the market. The first was produced in 1868 by Cadbury and featured a painting of a young girl cuddling a kitten; the model was Richard Cadbury's daughter Jessica.

Also part of the appeal are the beautiful papers used to line boxes and separate layers of chocolate. Although grease-resistant, the types of paper used have always had a special quality. They may be elaborately padded or embossed with gold or silver, or mysteriously translucent, like crisp tracing paper, with a swirly hammered finish. Another type of paper is known as glasine. It has a waxy feel and comes in wonderfully glossy, dark colours, almost smelling of chocolate in its own right.

Nowadays, packaging design veers from one extreme of style to another. Reminiscent of the glamourous thirties, there are amazingly lavish fabric-covered boxes trimmed with satiny ribbons and roses. In the kitsch category there is a large, white grand-piano-shaped box from Germany with chocolates hidden beneath the lid, and at the other end of the spectrum there is the ultimate in modern minimalist designer chocolates and packaging with slim chocolates wrapped in gold leaf.

BELOW: The packaging room at Cadbury's factory in 1932. Cadbury were the first manufacturer in Britain to produce boxed chocolates.

BELOW: Espresso-infused dark chocolate truffle fingers from the United States, end-wrapped with delicate gold foil.

A WORLD OF CHOCOLATE

In the next few pages of the book we survey some of the world's highest quality chocolate products. This is not a comprehensive selection, and it includes some of the most familiar quality brands as well as the more exclusive. Some products, such as the famous Toblerone bars, are internationally popular and universally available, and others, such as the exquisite chocolates made by the small specialist companies in America, are known to a much smaller market, but their first-class products are available by mail order and their market will increase as our appreciation of chocolate becomes more discerning.

BELGIUM

Belgium is renowned for its *ballotins,* chocolate-covered pralines, invented by Jean Neuhaus who, in 1912, developed coating chocolate capable of containing liquid fillings. Today NEUHAUS is well known for its flavoured Côte d'Or bars.

Of all Belgian chocolate companies, GODIVA must be the most recognized internationally. Established in 1929 by the Drap family, the company has 14-year old Joseph Drap to thank for its success. Realising people needed a little luxury in the austere post-war years Joseph created the chocolate truffle. They were marketed under the name of Godiva and were an instant success. Belgium also boasts many smaller specialists producing their own excellent chocolates.

ABOVE: A selection of Kim's Cachet chocolates, exported worldwide.

CHARLEMAGNE produces superior quality thin squares of plain and white chocolate with exotic flavours such as spiced ginger, cardamom and coffee, and spiced Earl Grey tea.

KIM'S, established in 1987 and manufacturer of the widely available luxury Cachet brand, specializes in handmade fillings. Kim's range includes white, milk and plain chocolate bars with luscious cream fillings such as hazelnut, coconut truffle, mocha and vanilla.

PIERRE COLAS specializes in unusual bars of plain and milk chocolate that are set in antique moulds and flavoured with esoteric combinations of cardamom, juniper, pink peppercorns and lavender. The company supplies specialist retailers in Belgium, Spain, France and the London chocolate shop Rococo.

WITTAMER probably ranks highest with connoisseurs. The range includes unusual seasonal specialities and Wittamer's famous Samba cake made with two contrasting chocolate mousses.

THE NETHERLANDS

The Netherlands is the birthplace of Coenraad·Van Houten who revolutionized the chocolate industry with his cocoa press. With this background, it is not surprising that the Dutch chocolate industry today concentrates largely on cocoa rather than eating chocolate. The four biggest companies, VAN HOUTEN, BENSDORP, DE ZAAN and GERKENS, were all set up in the nineteenth century and continue to supply the world with fine-quality unsweetened cocoa powder. Van Houten is now based in Germany, having undergone several takeovers

and mergers, and trades in Europe, the United States, Hong Kong and Singapore.

The Netherlands do produce a certain amount of eating chocolate, however, and enthusiasts enjoy Dutch chocolate for its dark colour and distinctive flavour. DROSTE, of the distinctive "Droste man" logotype, makes delicious chocolate discs, or pastilles, from which the logotype is derived. Bensdorp and Van Houten also make quality chocolate.

LEFT: Droste are famous for their chocolate pastilles.

GERMANY

The Germans are one of the largest consumers of chocolate in Europe. Faced with this demanding clientele, German chocolate manufacturers pride themselves on producing fresh, quality chocolates made with the very best ingredients.

CONFISERIE HEINEMANN, based in München-Gladbach and run by master chocolatier Heinz Heinemann, makes over sixty varieties of freshly made chocolates every day, including exceptional champagne truffles. Heinemann also offers an interesting range of moulded chocolate-filled seasonal specialities.

DREIMEISTER is a long-established family enterprise set up by the father of Hans Wilhelm Schröder, the present owner, and originally known as Café Schröder. Although the company has a large turnover and supplies to hotels, restaurants and airlines, Dreimeister produces the freshest of chocolates and truffles, made only with top-quality ingredients.

FEODORA is probably Germany's best-known brand

RIGHT: Leysieffer's freshly made seasonal chocolate.

internationally. Their chocolate is wonderfully smooth due to lengthy conching. The elegantly packaged quality chocolates include champagne truffles, bitter milk chocolate wafers, espresso Brazil chocolates and luxury pralines.

HACHEZ, based in Bremen since 1890, makes chocolates exclusively with rare cacao beans from Venezuela and Ecuador. Loved by generations of chocolate connoisseurs, the range includes melt-in-the-mouth cat's tongues, gold-covered nut sticks, ginger sticks, chocolate leaves and fruit cream-filled chocolate pastilles.

LEYSIEFFER has produced handmade chocolates in its Osnabrück bakery since 1909. In order to guarantee absolute freshness, the company starts manufacture only on receipt of an order. Its products include good quality white and milk chocolate, flavoured with a tempting range of ingredients — cinnamon, ginger, orange, pistachio and a mouthwatering combination of mocca and Jamaica rum.

STOLLWERCK in Cologne began as a bakery in 1839 and is now an international group with impressive headquarters on the banks of the River Elbe. The Imhoff-Stollwerck Museum boasts a fascinating collection of chocolate-related exhibits, including a collection of vending machines resembling grandfather clocks, porcelain chocolate services and printed ephemera, as well as a tropical greenhouse planted with young cacao trees. The company produces a wide range of chocolates for all levels of the market.

BELOW: Feodora's elegant range produced for the international market.

AUSTRIA

Austria's chocolate delicacies include both pâtisserie and confectionery. World-famous pâtisserie establishments are the palatial HOTEL IMPERIAL, Vienna's grandest, and home of Imperial Torte, an unbelievably rich layered square chocolate cake; and the HOTEL SACHER, famous for its delectable Sachertorte, a moist apricot-glazed rich chocolate cake; and DEMEL, the celebrated Viennese pâtisserie, which produces a rival version of Sachertorte based on a recipe said to have been given to Anna Demel by Franz Sacher's son. Demel also

produces whole roasted cacao beans coated with fine chocolate.

ALTMANN & KÜHNE, established in Vienna for more than eighty years, produce exquisite hand-dipped miniature chocolates, appropriately called Liliputconfekte, in the most unusual shapes. The chocolates are beautifully packaged in miniature chests of drawers and treasure chests.

MIRABELL in Salzburg produces traditional Mozartkugeln, an Austrian speciality consisting of creamy marzipan and hazelnut-nougat balls with a delicate chocolate coating.

ITALY

ABOVE: Gianduja *are Italy's favorite chocolate.*
RIGHT: Italians prefer chocolate in bite-size pieces.

Hazelnuts, chestnuts, almonds and honey have always been an integral part of Italian cuisine. It comes as no surprise therefore, that Italians like their chocolate nutty and sweet. They also like their chocolate small, so bars are often sold in single serving sizes – handy for a quick fix, should the need arise. Neapolitans, which look exactly like miniature chocolate bars, complete with individual wrappers, are well known throughout Europe.

The Italians are creative chocolate makers, and they excel at presentation too; Italian packaging is stunning, whether the design is traditionally ornate or 1990s minimalist.

CAFFAREL in Turin is one of Italy's oldest chocolate makers. Established in 1826, the company purchased a chocolate-making machine designed by Bozelli, a Genoese engineer, and so became the pioneers in setting out on the route to industrialization. In 1865 Caffarel developed Italy's favorite confection, *gianduja,* a rectangle of luscious chocolate and hazelnut paste, instantly recognizable by its triangular profile and rounded ends. Nowadays most Italian chocolate makers produce their own special version of *gianduja* using jealously guarded recipes. There is a glorious giant-sized version, *grangianduja,* as well as miniature *gianduiotti.*

An ancient culture of confectionery lives on in Italy's far south, and it was here in Salantino, in Italy's heel, that MAGLIO opened their factory in 1875. The business has passed from father to son and is now run by brothers Massimo and Maurizio. The Maglio range is based on plump, dark chocolates with inspirational fillings, including liqueur-infused dried kumquats, peaches, pears and oranges, marzipan-stuffed dates and prunes, and lemon-zest-coated figs stuffed with a whole almond.

Founded in 1796, MAJANI in Bologna is one of Italy's most creative chocolate makers. Their specialties are *scorze,* deliciously bittersweet chocolate sticks still made from the same ancient recipe, and *"Fiat" Cremino,* launched in 1911 as a publicity stunt to celebrate the Fiat Tipo 4 car. The car has since gone out of production but *"Fiat" Cremino* live on. These stunning miniature squares are made with four types of layered chocolate, something like a brown striped licorice allsort.

PERUGINA, based in the medieval city of Perugia, Umbria, was set up in 1907 by Francesco Buitoni, a descendant of the well known pasta-making family. From its humble beginnings making sugared almonds, Perugina is now one of Italy's largest chocolate manufacturers. The most popular brand in their extensive range is *Baci* (kisses), introduced in 1922 and still going strong. Lovers still like to discover the romantic messages hidden under the wrapper.

PEYRANO, an exclusive chocolatier in Turin, is almost unique in grinding their own cacao beans – very, very few chocolatiers do so. The chocolates are superb, especially their *gianduja.* Peyrano also sell *bicerin,* a very rare paste of bitter chocolate, cocoa, hazelnuts and honey used for sweetening coffee.

BELOW: Romantically packaged Baci conceal a lover's message.

SWITZERLAND

ABOVE: The Confiserie Sprüngli in Zurich, around 1895.

Three key developments undoubtedly contribute to Switzerland's national preference for its very delicate, melt-in-the-mouth milk chocolate. Switzerland is the birthplace of Rodolphe Lindt, inventor of the conching machine which transforms chocolate from a rough gritty paste to a state of silky-smooth perfection. Lindt also created soft, creamy fondant chocolate by adding cacao butter to the paste before conching. We have the Swiss to thank, too, for the invention of milk chocolate.

SPRÜNGLI in Zurich is one of the most famous chocolate establishments in the world. The shop in Bahnhofstrasse is renowned for its freshest of fresh *Truffes du Jour,* a heart-stopping mixture of finest chocolate, cream and butter, made to the highest possible standards. The company operates a worldwide delivery service which guarantees that the longed-for parcel will arrive within 24 hours of despatch.

Set up by master confectioner Rudolf Sprüngli in 1845, the company has been handed down through six generations of Sprünglis. When Rudolf retired, he divided his empire between his two sons. The younger, David, received the confectionery shops. The elder brother, Johann, became the owner of the

ABOVE: A 1935 street poster.

chocolate factory. In the same year he retired, Rudolf Sprüngli also decided to purchase Rodolphe Lindt's chocolate factory in Berne. Overnight, the company acquired all Lindt's manufacturing secrets, and it was this transaction that was the foundation for the success of the now world-famous Lindt & Sprüngli company.

LINDT & SPRÜNGLI operates entirely independently from Sprüngli. The company produces an enormous range of excellent quality chocolates sold in supermarkets and specialist shops world-wide. One of their best products is the tastefully thin Excellence bar, a sublime blend of finest cacao beans with a hint of pure

vanilla, and a cacao solid content of 70 per cent. This is closely followed in quality by Excellence Milk, possibly one of the best milk chocolate bars available. Another Lindt bar, called Swiss Bittersweet Chocolate, which is easily recognized by its traditional wrapper design, is also good.

SUCHARD in Berne is another long-established and respected company, now owned by the American multinational Philip Morris. Suchard was a gold medallist several times over at the 1855 Exposition Universelle in Paris, and their milk chocolate bar, Milka, produced in 1901, is well-known all over Europe. Since 1970, Suchard have been the manufacturer of the famous Toblerone bars, although these were originally produced by their inventor Jean Tobler. The bars were designed with a triangular profile representing the Swiss Alps. The name is derived from merging that of the inventor, Tobler, together with the word *torrone,* the Italian word for nougat. Toblerone is made with a blend of chocolate, nougat, almonds and egg white, and the bar is one of Switzerland's most popular products – outside the country at least. Enthusiasts can enjoy giant bars weighing more than 4kg/8.8lb, miniature bars and a whole range in between.

ABOVE: Bars of superior chocolate.

ABOVE: Lindt's mini chocolate bars.

ABOVE: The famous Toblerone bars.

FRANCE

ABOVE: *Early poster for the French Chocolate and Tea Company.*

ABOVE: *Chocolate almonds.*

A large part of the French chocolate industry is made up of small, independent firms making ever more innovative *grand cru* chocolates to jealously guarded recipes. The French, who prefer dark, intensely flavoured chocolate, have a wide choice at their disposal.

BERNACHON, a greatly respected family of artisan chocolatiers, set up in 1955 in Lyon. Sharing the caring attitude of the Quakers, the company provides daily lunch for the workers and, until recently, housed them in dormitories above the workshop. The Bernachons travel the world in search of the rarest cacao beans and the best nuts and fruit. Their chocolates are the very best. The range includes unusually flavoured chocolate bars, truffles, pralines, *giandujas* and marzipans.

BONNAT in Voiron near Grenoble is one of the few companies that roasts its own beans. A purist at heart, master chocolatier Raymond Bonnat uses a single *grand cru* bean, rather than a blend, for each of the chocolates in his range. Bonnat's choice of seven *crus,* which consist of Côte d'Ivoire, Madagascar, Ceylon, Trinité, Chuao, Maragnan and Puerto Cabellois, is selected from the world's finest cacao plantations. Bonnat chocolates are available from specialist outlets in France, and from Mortimer and Bennett's shop in London, which is the sole British importer.

CLUIZEL, in Paris, is a family-run business set up in 1947, producing excellent chocolate with rare South American and African beans ground and roasted on the premises. It is perhaps best known for a small and rather sinister chocolate bar containing 99 per cent cacao solids. Cluizel's chocolates are available throughout Europe.

CHRISTIAN CONSTANT, set up in 1970 in Paris, produces matchless ganache-filled chocolates. The flavourings read like an exotic travel brochure: Malabar cardamom, Yemeni jasmine, Chinese ginger and Tahitian vanilla.

The famous FAUCHON shop in Paris was established in 1925 by August Fauchon, whose passion was for collecting unusual merchandise. The company was taken over after his death by Joseph Pilosoff, whose granddaughter runs the business today. Fauchon specialities are the very best quality chocolate *marrons glacés,* truffles, pralines and ganaches, all exquisitely packaged.

LA MAISON DU CHOCOLAT in Paris was opened in 1977 by Robert Linxe, master chocolate-maker *extraordinaire*. Linxe's rigorous training and deep understanding of chocolate's complexities have played a major part in furthering the reputation

ABOVE: *One of Bonnat's superb* grand cru *bars.*

of France's chocolate-makers. It was Linxe's collaboration with Valrhona which set the quality of their *grand cru* couvertures, which they in turn supply to smaller chocolate-makers. Linxe's specialities are exquisitely shaped squares, pyramids and lozenges of the very best plain and milk chocolate, filled with praline, buttery caramel or the lightest and creamiest ganache. The chocolates are sold in Paris and by leading specialist outlets in New York, Houston and Dallas.

LE ROUX, founded in 1977 in Quiberon, Brittany, is renowned for *Caramel au Beurre Salé* (salted butter caramel), and for rare chocolate truffles containing fragments of Périgord truffle.

MICHEL CHAUDUN set up shop in Paris in 1986. His award-winning work includes not only the highest quality chocolates but ambitious chocolate sculptures. Only the rarest cacao beans are used together with top quality fruit and nuts. His chocolates are available in Paris and Tokyo.

RICHART DESIGN ET CHOCOLAT started life in 1925 in the laboratory of Lyon-based master chocolatier Joseph Richart. Using

ABOVE: Elegant chocolates and packaging from Richart Design et Chocolat.

only the finest cacao beans, Richart produces exquisite, smoother than smooth, miniature chocolate squares silk-screened with designs in cacao butter. Fillings and flavourings are equally inspired. The choice includes pure malt Scotch, green tea, blackcurrants, pineapple, clementines, the very best Andalucian almonds, chestnuts from the Ardèche, and pralines and ganaches flavoured with thyme, curry, bergamot, anise or nutmeg. Beautifully packaged in slim trays, Richart's chocolates are sold in boutiques in Paris, Lyon and New York.

VALRHONA, set up in 1922 and based in the Rhône valley, is the leading supplier of couverture chocolate for smaller chocolate-makers. The beans are all of superior quality and include guanaja, pur caraibe, manjari and jivara. Each shipment is tested by a panel of experts. Its products include *Carré,* small chocolate squares made from individual bean varieties, packed in beautiful tins; *BonBons de Chocolat,* individual chocolates packed in gift boxes with a guide recommending the order in which they should be eaten; and the well-known Valrhona bars in their distinctive black wrappers. The cacao content of the bars ranges from 71 per cent for *Noir Amer* (bitter) to a relatively high 40 per cent for *Le Lacté* (milk).

BELOW: A Chocolat Carpentier poster from 1895.

RIGHT: Valrhona Lacté has a high cacao content.

SPAIN

As recently as 1920, chocolate-makers in Spain were still using the curved granite metate for grinding cacao beans. The *chocolateros* would travel around with the *metate* strapped to their backs and bags of cacao beans under their arms. They would kneel on a little cushion in front of the stone and grind the beans in full public view so that the buyer could be sure he was getting unadulterated stone-ground chocolate. Nowadays chocolate-making in Spain is a fully industrialized process, but, even so, the tradition of quality craftsmanship is very much alive and well.

In some ways Spanish chocolate is indistinguishable from quality chocolate made in the rest of Europe. What sets it apart is the creativity and imagination of the chocolate-makers, and their use of the very best quality Mediterranean fruits and nuts. Spain grows some of the best nuts in the world, so there is no shortage of supply. Plump almonds, hazelnuts, pine kernels and mouth-puckeringly bitter Seville oranges are all used by the chocolate-makers with excellent results.

BLANXART, set up in 1954 in Barcelona, is one of Spain's smaller specialist firms, producing handmade high-quality chocolates from the very best cacao beans. The company prides itself on roasting and grinding the beans itself to achieve the desired perfection of flavour and aroma. The mouthwatering range includes a delicate curl of candied Seville orange dipped in bitter chocolate, clusters of chocolate-covered pine nuts, as well as liqueur-filled chocolates and several types of praline.

LUDOMAR, in Barcelona, specializes in superior, made-to-order chocolates, which they sell to pâtisserie shops in Spain, France, Germany and Britain. Specialities are plump, chocolate-smothered cherries; *postre de músico,* a chocolate-covered cluster of fresh almonds, hazelnuts and raisins; and *grageas,* almonds or hazelnuts drenched in dark chocolate, white chocolate or toffee.

RAMÓN ROCA is a large company set up in Gerona in 1928 by the Roca family. Roca chocolates are said to be a favourite of former US Secretary of State Henry Kissinger, and they certainly grace the tables of Spain's society élite, as well as finding their way on to first class intercontinental flights and the pillows of Spain's grandest hotels. Roca has always been imaginative in a showy type of way, producing masterpieces such as a 500g/1¼lb chocolate sculpture of the Statue of Liberty, and a hand-painted chocolate reproduction of the twelfth-century tapestry that hangs in Gerona cathedral. The company also

ABOVE: The Spanish love chocolate "a la taza" (in the cup).

produces a unique range of edible board games, particularly popular with the Japanese, which includes a draughts set in luxury dark and white chocolate. Their Victoria Bonbons (named after Ramón Roca's mother) – an elegant wafer of dark chocolate decorated with a perfectly positioned almond, a hazelnut, a walnut and four raisins – won first prize at the 1988 Chicago Fancy Food Fair.

RIGHT: The Valor range of chocolates.
LEFT: Chocolate croquettes from Roca.

VALOR in Villajoyosa, Alicante, was founded in 1881 by López Lloret, one of Spain's itinerant *chocolateros*. The fledgling enterprise has been handed down through three generations and is now one of Spain's largest and most technologically advanced chocolate companies with a gleaming stainless-steel fully computerized factory. Even though Valor has an enormous turnover and a vast range of products, the company prides itself on maintaining traditional quality, creativity and attention to detail.

Drinking chocolate is still widely enjoyed

RIGHT: Chunks of chocolate in tablet form, used in Spain for making thick, dark drinking chocolate.

in Spain, and Valor is the country's leading producer. It is sold both in powdered form and, more commonly, as a solid bar to be broken off as required and dissolved in foaming hot milk.

On the confectionery side, Valor's specialities are Chocolate Pearls – chocolate-covered almonds gathered from local almond groves; *doblones* – individually wrapped chocolate wafers; foil-wrapped hazelnut pralines; exquisite miniature four-piece gift boxes of chocolates; and luxury chocolate bars filled with toffee, cream caramel or *tiramisu*. Eye-catching and attractive packaging is a crucial part of the presentation, particularly as Valor's luxury chocolates are exported to speciality shops all over the world.

MEXICO

Chocolate as confectionery never really caught on in Mexico. The most important use of chocolate is still as a beverage, and as a flavouring in some of the special *moles* – rich, savoury sauces thickened with ground nuts and seeds. Chocolate is sold in rough, grainy tablets made with cacao, sugar, ground almonds and cinnamon – not so very different from the tablets made by the Spanish in the days of the conquistadors.

The most widely available brand outside Mexico is Ibarra, manufactured by CHOCOLATERA DE JALISCO in Guadalajara, and packaged in a striking red and yellow striped hexagonal box. The individually wrapped tablets are delicious whipped to a froth in hot milk and served with freshly baked *churros* (fried pastries).

RIGHT: Coarse, grainy tablets of Ibarra chocolate in traditional wrappers.
BELOW: The melted tablets make a delicious sauce for vanilla ice-cream.

They can be used in baking to give a unique spicy flavour to chocolate cake. The tablets can also be melted to make a wonderfully fudgey chocolate sauce that goes particularly well with good quality vanilla ice-cream.

GREAT BRITAIN

ABOVE: Ackermans chocolates, a favourite of the Royal family.

ACKERMANS, a small family firm founded fifty years ago by German-born Werner Ackerman and his wife, is one of the major producers of handmade chocolates in Britain. Ackermans has a shop in north London, and also supplies leading supermarkets and specialist outlets in Britain, mainland Europe and the United States. Its chocolates are a favourite with Queen Elizabeth The Queen Mother, who awarded the firm her Royal Warrant in 1969. Ackermans offers a range of fresh cream truffles, chocolate-coated whole nuts, ginger wafers, hand-dipped crystallized fruits, and rose and violet fondant creams. It also produces a wonderful chocolate menagerie of hollow moulded hippos, crocodiles, bears and bunnies.

BENDICKS OF MAYFAIR, founded in the late 1920s by Colonel Benson and Mr Dickson, was granted a Royal Warrant by Elizabeth II in 1962. Bendicks are famous for their excellent peppermint chocolates – an essentially British taste not shared by other European countries. Best-loved by connoisseurs are Bendicks Bittermints, a powerful mint fondant disc drenched with smooth, dark unsweetened chocolate – a devastating combination. As well as the mint collection, Bendicks produces delicious truffles, chocolate-coated stem ginger, and the delightfully named Sporting & Military Chocolate.

CHARBONNEL ET WALKER, founded in 1825, is one of Britain's earliest producers of chocolates. With the encouragement of

During the last few years British taste in chocolate has been undergoing a quiet revolution. Following the establishment of The Chocolate Society, a sort of sub-culture of chocolytes has emerged. Perhaps as a result of this new-found fervour, superior varieties of chocolate are increasingly finding their way into supermarkets, where they provide much-needed competition for the old-style sweet British milk chocolate.

BELOW: Bendicks are the premier supplier of superior mint chocolates.

BELOW: Exquisite chocolates from the Charbonnel et Walker range.

LEFT: Organic chocolate made with Maya beans.

Edward VII, the company began life as a partnership between Mrs Walker and Madame Charbonnel from the Maison Boissier chocolate house in Paris. Tempting items from the magnificent range include truffles flavoured with chartreuse, muscat or port and cranberry; chocolate-covered espresso beans; and cointreau-flavoured marzipan. The packaging is superb and caters for styles ranging from elegant navy-trimmed white boxes, nostalgic boxes with a faded pink floral pattern, and outrageously lavish, ruched red satin boxes.

GERARD RONAY is one of Britain's most highly respected private chocolatiers. A former psychiatric nurse, Ronay set up in 1989 having trained with the very best teachers – Linxe, Constant and Bernachon in France, Wittamer in Belgium and Charbonnel et Walker in Britain. His highly secretive recipes include geranium chocolate and superb hand-painted eggs.

GREEN AND BLACK'S, set up in the 1980s by Josephine Fairly, sells organic chocolate endorsed by The Soil Association. The company launched with its Organic Dark Chocolate, soon followed by its latest brain child, the "ethically correct" Maya Gold Organic Dark Chocolate, made with beans grown by the Kechi Maya in Belize. This product was the first in Britain to be awarded the Fairtrade mark which guarantees that small farmers are not exploited. Maya Gold contains 70 per cent cacao solids, but no cacao butter, and is described on the wrapper as having "the authentic Maya taste of rain forest spices and

BELOW: Rococo's grand cru *single bean bars with distinctive wrappers.*

ABOVE: A tempting and imaginative range from The Chocolate Society.

orange". Even though oranges were unknown to the Maya in pre-Conquest days, the chocolate still tastes pretty good.

ROCOCO, in London's King's Road, is an Aladdin's cave of a shop founded in 1983 by chocolate enthusiast Chantal Coady. Using cacao from the world's finest plantations, Rococo specialize in *grand cru* single bean bars; artisan bars with exotic flavourings such as pink pepper and juniper, lavender, petitgrain and cardamom; stunning chocolate dragées – try the dark green *Olives de Nyons;* and handmade boxed chocolates moulded into the most beautiful shapes.

SARA JAYNE, a London-based private chocolate-maker, is also public relations manager of the Académie Culinaire de France. She learnt her chocolate-making skills first hand from leading experts, including the Roux brothers. Blackberry and calvados, ginger and spice, and champagne are among the tempting flavourings used in her celebrated handmade truffles.

TERRYS OF YORK, founded in 1797, is perhaps alone among the mass-producers in manufacturing plain chocolate with a reasonable flavour. Their famous chocolate orange has been tucked in the toe of British children's Christmas stockings for generations, while their individually wrapped miniature Neapolitans have always been a welcome gift.

THE CHOCOLATE SOCIETY was formed in 1990 to promote the consumption of the finest chocolate. The society manufactures a range of products under its own label, as well as selling quality brands made by other companies. Its own range includes the most delicious chocolate-dipped candied citrus fruits; imaginative moulded items such as pigs, egg-filled nests, fish, hens and hearts; fresh handmade truffles with luscious flavourings such as raspberry, whisky or champagne; and elegant tins of drinking-chocolate flakes, cocoa powder and cooking chocolate.

THE UNITED STATES OF AMERICA

Chocolate consumers in the United States share the British liking for sweet milk chocolate, and the American chocolate industry is therefore dominated by a small number of very large mass-producers who satisfy this national need. However, in the same way that British consumers have become aware of and learned to appreciate quality handmade plain chocolate, American taste has been changing too. A number of small but sophisticated chocolate-makers have appeared on the scene and are taking advantage of the increasing popularity of European-style chocolate.

ABOVE AND RIGHT: Ghirardelli, new and old.

ABOVE: Glossy sugar-coated dragées from Dilettante.

DILETTANTE, in Seattle, was established in 1976 by Dana Davenport, a third-generation chocolatier and descendant of Hungarian master chocolatier Julius Franzen. Franzen emigrated to the USA in 1910, after studying in Paris, and won prestigious appointments in Vienna as Master Pâtissier to Emperor Franz Joseph, and later in St Petersburg as Master Chocolatier to Czar Nicholas II. Franzen passed on his skills to his brother-in-law Earl Remington Davenport, whose grandson Dana carries on the business today. Dilettante's signature product is its Aristocrat range of chocolate truffles, flavoured with ginger, raspberries, hazelnuts, pecans or coffee. Dilettante also makes intensely rich buttercream fondant, beautiful chocolate dragées with various coatings, and slim bars of good quality milk or dark chocolate.

FRAN'S, set up in Seattle by ex-accountant Fran Bigelow, is at the forefront of America's new generation of chocolatiers. She trained in cookery under

Josephine Araldo, a 1921 graduate of the Cordon Bleu school in Paris, and later enrolled at the California Culinary Academy, where desserts became her passion. Bigelow opened a tiny dessert shop in 1982, supplying local restaurants with speciality cakes. Her reputation went from strength to strength, and, soon after, she started making the European-style chocolates on which her business is now founded. An award-winning speciality are Fran's baton-shaped Fixations — individual sticks of Belgian chocolate with soft, creamy centres, flavoured with espresso, peanut butter, orange or mint. Her range also includes rich dark truffles, hand-dipped fruit and nuts covered in smooth dark Belgian chocolate, GoldBars studded with macadamia nuts, and the smaller GoldBites with almonds, as well as chocolate and caramel sauces, and various seasonal items.

GHIRARDELLI, founded in 1856 in San Francisco and one of

ABOVE: Irresistible luxury from Fran's.

RIGHT: Joseph Schmidt's stunning truffles.

America's pioneering chocolate-makers, produces quality eating chocolate, chocolate products for use in baking, and powdered drinking chocolate. Ghirardelli's Sweet Ground Chocolate with Cocoa has been a signature product for over a century. Although a mass producer, Ghirardelli uses methods based on European traditions, producing bittersweet eating chocolate as well as the popular sweet milk varieties. Ghirardelli still grinds and roasts its own cacao beans shipped from quality plantations in Central

and South America, and West Africa. Its range includes milk, white and plain chocolate squares and attractively wrapped bars with tempting flavours such as raspberry, white mocha and biscotti, and double chocolate mocha.

JOSEPH SCHMIDT CONFECTIONS was opened in San Francisco in 1983 by master chocolatier Joseph Schmidt and partner Audrey Ryan. Born in 1939 and raised in what was formerly known as Palestine, Schmidt looks to his Austrian roots for his skills. He was trained as a baker, but his supremely imaginative and sometimes outrageous creations show no evidence of this conventional background. Unusual in the chocolate world for his bold use of colour, and the large size of the individual chocolates, Schmidt's truffles gleam with perfect hand-painted spots of bright red or green, and his Slicks, thin chocolate discs, are beautifully painted in various colours. Special commissions include amazingly opulent sculpted creations for visiting dignitaries from abroad – including a giant panda for Prince Philip and a

RIGHT: Elegance from Richard Donnelly.

white dove for Nelson Mandela. Schmidt's chocolates are available from department stores in the United States and Harrods in London.

RICHARD DONNELLY, in Santa Cruz, California, is another of America's new breed of young, inspired artisan chocolate-makers.

Donnelly trained with several renowned chocolatiers both in Europe and the United States before setting up on his own in 1988. Donnelly uses French couverture chocolate to which he adds flavourings and fillings geared to the American market — coffee buttercream, and roasted salted macadamia nuts, for instance. His speciality is very slim, smooth chocolate bars which, in terms of quality, are among the very best chocolate in the world. The bars are beautifully wrapped in handmade Japanese papers.

MOONSTRUCK CHOCOLATIER in Portland, Oregon, is a young company set up by an impressive consortium of live-wire marketing experts. With more then a hundred outlets in the United States and a thriving mail order business they look set to make their name in the world of chocolate.

Moonstruck's chocolates are inspired creations from master chocolatier Robert Hammond, who served his apprenticeship in America and France, and who is now thought to be one of the leading experts in modern chocolate-making. Moonstruck's signature product is a moon-shaped, metallic blue box containing a stunning selection of beautifully designed chocolates. Flavourings include wine, brandy, coffee, *sake* and various fruits, often using award-winning local products. Favourites are wild huckleberry truffles made with white chocolate ganache and Clear Creek apple brandy truffles. There is also an impressive *gianduja* almond praline tower of crisp buttery toffee and toasted almonds.

PHYSIOLOGY AND PSYCHOLOGY

CHOCOLATE'S THERAPEUTIC POWERS

The therapeutic properties of chocolate were much written about in the seventeenth and eighteenth centuries. The Aztec beliefs in the power of chocolate travelled with it, and great claims were made by manufacturers and converts alike for its powers as an antidote to exhaustion and weakness. Soldiers, scholars and clerics used it to keep them going during prolonged periods of physical, intellectual or spiritual endurance.

We now know that it is the fat and carbohydrate in chocolate which provide fuel for the body, and the fat content means that chocolate is digested slowly, thus maintaining a feeling of fullness and satiety. Even the iron content, which helps transport oxygen to the brain, may result in greater mental alertness, although this has yet to be proven.

(PER 100G)	PLAIN CHOCOLATE	MILK CHOCOLATE	WHITE CHOCOLATE
Protein (g)	4.7	8.4	8.0
Fat (g)	29.2	30.3	30.9
Calories	525	529	529
Carbohydrate (g)	64.8	59.4	58.3
Calcium (mg)	38	220	270
Magnesium (mg)	100	55	26
Iron (mg)	2.4	1.6	0.2
Zinc (mg)	0.2	0.2	0.9
Carotene (vitamin A) (mcg)	40	40	75
Vitamin E (mg)	0.85	0.74	1.14
Thiamin (vitamin B1) (mg)	0.07	0.10	0.08
Riboflavin (vitamin B2) (mg)	0.08	0.23	0.49
Niacin (vitamin B3) (mg)	0.4	0.2	0.2
Vitamin B6 (mg)	0.07	0.07	0.07
Vitamin B12 (mcg)	—	trace	trace
Folate (mcg)	10	10	10
Vitamin C	0	0	0

Source: McCance and Widdowson's The Composition of Foods, fifth edition.

NUTRITIONAL ANALYSIS

Although the relevance of nutritional analysis is questionable if the level of cacao solids or brand of chocolate used is not known, we can see from the comparative table above that plain chocolate, considered by the chocolate fraternity as infinitely superior, does not fare as well as might be expected.

Containing no milk, plain chocolate provides roughly half the protein of white and milk chocolate, and much less calcium. Protein is vital for the growth, repair and maintenance of the body; calcium is essential for muscle contraction, including the muscles which make the heart beat, and for healthy nerve function, enzyme activity and clotting of blood.

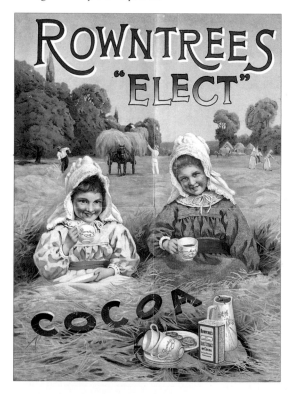

LEFT: Early publicity material depicted cocoa as wholesome.
RIGHT: Chocolate fortified the army in the First World War.

CHOCOLADE
der Sportsleute

ABOVE: Carbohydrate in chocolate provides fuel for vigorous activity.

Plain chocolate contains slightly less fat, something we are advised to cut down on, and comes out on top in terms of carbohydrate, magnesium (an essential constituent of our body cells and involved with releasing energy from the food we eat), iron (essential for the production of red blood cells, and for transporting oxygen around the body) and niacin (also involved in energy release from food). Plain chocolate also contains slightly fewer calories.

White chocolate, sometimes dismissed by chocolate experts, contains more calcium, zinc, carotene and riboflavin (vitamin B2) than plain chocolate.

A NATURAL STIMULANT

As well as the more well-known nutrients, chocolate contains certain alkaloids – organic substances found in plants – which have a potent effect on the body. The most important is theobromine, which stimulates the kidneys as a mild diuretic. Chocolate is also a stimulant of the central nervous system, with an effect similar to caffeine, which is also present in chocolate. Theobromine makes up about 2 per cent of the cacao bean and about 200 mg finds its way into an average-sized bar. The caffeine content is much smaller – about 25 mg per bar, roughly one quarter the amount found in a fresh cup of coffee.

BELOW RIGHT: Many manufacturers depicted chocolate as providing growing children with plenty of energy for healthy activity.

HOMEOPATHIC "PROVING" OF CHOCOLATE

Experimental "provings" of chocolate by homeopaths clearly indicate its stimulating effect. One experiment conducted with a decoction of roasted ground cacao beans in boiling water produced "an excitement of the nervous system similar to that caused by a strong infusion of black coffee" and "an excited state of the circulation, shown by an accelerated pulse". Interestingly, when the same decoction was made with unroasted beans neither effect was noticeable, leading the provers to conclude that the physiological changes were caused by aromatic substances released during roasting.

MYTHS AND PREJUDICES

Claims that chocolate is bad for you are almost certainly based on the excess sugar and added vegetable fat in poor grade, mass-produced chocolate. Quality chocolate contains pure cacao butter with no added fat, as well as a high percentage of cacao solids and correspondingly less sugar – in some cases hardly any. Specific claims that chocolate causes migraine, obesity, acne, tooth decay and allergies have also been refuted by several medical experts:

MIGRAINE Cheese and chocolate have been cited as the cause of migraine, which can be set off by large doses of tyramine. Chocolate, however, contains only a very small quantity of tyramine, far less than cheese.

OBESITY Good quality plain chocolate is unlikely to be the cause of obesity because it contains far less sugar than junk chocolate and, because it is more expensive, is less likely to be eaten to excess.

ACNE American surveys show no correlation between chocolate consumption and acne in teenagers. Likely culprits are hormonal imbalances and a lack of fresh fruit and vegetables in the diet.

TOOTH DECAY Chocolate melts in the mouth and is therefore in contact with the teeth for a relatively short time. While the sugar content will contribute to tooth decay, the risk is far less than that associated with sticky sweets or toffee, which remain in the mouth for longer.

ALLERGY Less than 2 per cent of the population have a genuine food allergy, and an allergy to chocolate is extremely rare. It is more likely to be the nuts and milk in chocolate that are the cause, so check the ingredients.

KOHLER'S CHOCOLATES

"Worth Struggling for"

CHOCOLATE AND THE MIND

The question of whether or not chocolate is an addictive substance always raises spirited discussion. Some social historians have even reported tales of chocolate addiction and associated crimes committed in order to satisfy an ever-increasing need. And as recently as 1991, the French dietary expert Michel Montignac advised in his book *Dine Out and Lose Weight:* "Be sure to limit yourself, since chocolate is of an addictive nature. To control your 'chocoholism', drink a tall glass of water."

LEFT: A deeply indulgent chocolate experience.

Linda Henly, a contemporary American writer, positively recommends that addictive personalities should use chocolate to satisfy their needs, stating that its advantages vastly outweigh those of other substances: "Chocolate doesn't make you stupid and clumsy. It doesn't render you incapable of operating heavy machinery... You don't have to smuggle chocolate across the border...Possession, even possession with intent to sell, is perfectly legal."

Some medical experts believe that the theobromine and caffeine in chocolate are the cause of its so-called addictive properties, but it may well be the presence of another substance called phenylethylamine. This is one of a group of chemicals known as endorphins, which have an effect similar to amphetamine, to which phenylethylamine is related. When released into the bloodstream, endorphins lift the mood, creating positive energy and feelings ranging from happiness to euphoria, as experienced in the runner's "high" or the aerobic exerciser's "burn". Phenylethylamine is also naturally present in the human body. Levels in the brain have even been found to increase when we experience the state we refer to as "falling in love", which is no doubt why we experience that heady feeling when we eat good chocolate.

CRAVING AND ADDICTION

Chocolate lovers would do well to be aware of the wealth of difference there is between craving and addiction. Craving is an unmet desire for a pleasurable substance, whether it be chocolate, hot buttered toast, or a cup of coffee. The craving is usually brought on by stress, and the desired substance usually diffuses the stress more effectively than any other means, and may actually, as a result, enhance a person's performance by increasing concentration and reducing fatigue.

Addiction, on the other hand, is defined as the habitual use of a substance, such as alcohol or drugs, which becomes less and less effective at satisfying the need and results in unpleasant withdrawal symptoms should any attempt be made to give up the substance in question.

Chocolate hardly comes into the addictive category, although it has been said that the glucose in chocolate triggers a release in the production of endorphins – the body's natural opiates – which in turn can lead to a cycle of craving.

LEFT: A silver platter of gorgeous, high quality, hand-made chocolates is every chocolate lover's fantasy.

BELOW: An advertisement showing two French ladies sharing a bottle of chocolate as if it were wine. The initial effect can be very similar.

RIGHT: Dark, rich and irresistible, a slice of moist chocolate cake is both pleasure and temptation.

BELOW: French courtesan and famous chocolyte, Madame Du Barry, was well aware of the stimulating effect chocolate had on her lovers.

WOMEN'S CRAVING AND CHOCOLATE

Women are the greatest consumers of chocolate, and several studies have sought to explain why. Although some women may enjoy chocolate as a guilt-free treat or as an energy-boost, others seem almost obsessed by it. While researching her 1995 book *Why Women Need Chocolate*, Debra Waterhouse conducted a survey which revealed that of the women surveyed:

- 🍫 97 per cent reported cravings, 68 per cent of which are for chocolate
- 🍫 50 per cent would choose chocolate in preference to sex
- 🍫 22 per cent were more likely than men to choose chocolate as a mood elevator

Psychiatrists have suggested that the mechanism that regulates body levels of phenylethylamine may be faulty in some women. This may explain a tendency to binge on chocolate after an emotional upset – it is an instinctive form of self-medication to treat the imbalance of mood-controlling chemicals.

Waterhouse states that the foods we crave are defined by a multitude of factors that may include cultural influences, emotional attachments, taste and habit as well as biological, chemical and physiological factors. In the case of chocolate, the "prozac of plants", Waterhouse adds to its mood-changing components a substance called seratonin, known for its calming properties.

It must be said, however, that although statistically it may be the case that more women buy chocolate than men, it is also true that for both sexes, and for people of all ages, chocolate can be many things. There are probably many women who could instantly name a man whose chocolate consumption is more regular and compulsive than hers, and it is perhaps one of the many cultural myths that women are more addicted to it than men. What we can say is that the seduction of chocolate, and its comforting allure, is as strong in the present as it was for the Maya warrior princes and princesses of the fourth century.

Chocolate and Love

Chocolate has long been associated with passion and its reputation as an aphrodisiac can be traced back to the days of the Aztecs and the Spanish conquistadors. Conclusions were obviously drawn from the Emperor Montezuma's liking for copious flagons of chocolate before retiring to his harem. However, as observer Bernal Díaz del Castillo was careful to point out in his memoirs: "It [chocolate] was said to have aphrodisiac properties, but we did not pay any attention to this detail."

In *The True History of Chocolate* authors Sophie and Michael Coe state that the idea that Montezuma needed sexual stimulants was a Spanish obsession for which there was no factual basis. The conquistadors apparently suffered from constipation and "searched for native Mexican laxatives as avidly as they did for aphrodisiacs". However, once the rumour that chocolate was an aphrodisiac had taken root, there was no stopping it. When chocolate eventually appeared in Europe, eighteenth-century society took to it with suspicious enthusiasm.

Historical sources abound with tales of chocolate being used as an aphrodisiac. Casanova thought that hot chocolate was "the elixir of love", and drank it instead of champagne! It may well be that the unshakeable belief of the Spanish had something to do with chocolate being an ingredient in that notorious aphrodisiac "Spanish Fly". In the following tale, the Marquis de Sade uses both chocolate and Spanish fly to amuse his guests at a ball: "Into the dessert he slipped chocolate pastilles so good that a number of people devoured them … but he had mixed in some Spanish fly … those who ate the pastilles began to burn with unchaste ardor … Even the most respectable of women were unable to resist the uterine rage that stirred within them. And so it was that M. de Sade enjoyed the favors of his sister-in-law."

LEFT AND RIGHT: The images may not be as explicit as today, but advertising has always used chocolate's link with sensuality to sell its products.

RIGHT: An early Cadbury chocolate tin uses sensual imagery.

The Great Inflamer

Brandon Head, in *The Food of the Gods,* reported that even after chocolate had become widely accepted as a nourishing beverage, it was still regarded by some "as a violent inflamer of passions, which should be prohibited to the monks". In 1905 a journalist writing in the British Spectator magazine issued dire warnings: 'I shall also advise my fair readers to be in a particular manner careful how they meddle with romances, chocolates, novels, and the like inflamers, which I look upon as very dangerous to be made use of…"

Sensual Associations

Although contemporary scientific research suggests that chocolate does not contain substances of a directly aphrodisiac nature, modern advertising clearly links chocolate with sensuality and sexuality. With the exception of chunky "macho" chocolate products, or situations in which the product is being used as a healthy, energy-boosting snack, chocolate is invariably depicted as a "naughty" indulgence, appearing in scenes heavy with sexual innuendo.

Advertising also demonstrates a definite gender bias by specifically targeting women as the primary users. Most advertisements show chocolate being enjoyed by beautiful

ABOVE: A poster illustrating the link between lovers and chocolate.

advertising made much of the wholesomeness of chocolate with posters of healthy, lively children enjoying cups of chocolate in the fresh air. The first chocolate boxes showed sentimental images of pretty young girls, flowers and kittens. Chocolate plays a large part in childhood the world over. Christmas treats, Easter eggs, birthday presents, party gifts, rewards or bribes from parents coaxing their offspring to behave well. Encouraged as most of us are to be passionate about chocolate from an early age, it is no wonder we carry that ardour with us through childhood and beyond.

RIGHT: The famous Rowntree advertisement.

BELOW: A loving mother offers chocolate to her daughter.

women, or gifts of chocolate being offered to them by a man.

The association between women, sensuality and chocolate was reinforced by the cinema, too. A common image in the 1930s was the glamorous *femme fatale*, usually blonde and usually draped on satin sheets, languorously working her way through a lavish box of chocolates.

This association between chocolate and women perpetuated the association between chocolate and romantic love, as shown on Perugina's classic Baci box. *Baci* means "kisses" in Italian, and since the chocolates first appeared in 1922 they have been exchanged as gifts between lovers who look for the romantic message hidden beneath the foil wrapper of each chocolate.

CHOCOLATE AND CHILDHOOD

This association with love and nurture, but not necessarily passion, was also exploited by manufacturers. Chocolate cake mix packets carry homely scenes of mother in the kitchen; the earliest cocoa tins portrayed nursemaids or even parents serving nourishing mugs of chocolate to young children, and

THE PLEASURE OF CHOCOLATE

Research carried out by ARISE (Associates for Research Into the Science of Enjoyment) suggests that pleasure, far from being an emotion of indeterminate nature, is a distinct neuro-chemical process with its own pathway through the nervous system. Laboratory tests have shown that when we are experiencing pleasure, the body's defence system is more effective; and when we are unhappy, depressed or stressed, the system becomes less efficient, leaving us less resistant to infection.

So it seems that pleasure is good for us even if it means we indulge in "forbidden fruits" such as chocolate. The secret, it would seem, is to indulge in our "naughty" craving without feeling guilty or anxious. That said, ARISE make it clear that they are not advocating orgies of over-indulgence; the secret is to eat better chocolate, not more chocolate.

SENSORY PLEASURE

One of the reasons we love chocolate so much is the pure unmatched physical pleasure we get not just from eating it, but also from unwrapping it, smelling it, looking at it and feeling it. When we slip the wrapper off a slim bar of dark chocolate or open up the softly padded papers of a luxury box, our sense of anticipation is already at work. The pure chocolatey smell is like perfume and the chocolate looks so smooth and glossy we want to stroke it. Breaking off a piece, it snaps cleanly with a pleasing crack. When it finally passes the lips, chocolate melts instantly in the mouth – an exquisitely pleasurable sensation. Then the flavours come flooding through – overwhelming our taste buds with over five hundred of them, two-and-a-half times more than any other food. With such a wealth of sensory pleasure in store, no wonder chocolate should be eaten slowly.

Whether or not we choose to share our pleasure with others by attempting to describe the complex flavours is another matter. The current passion for chocolate indicates that perhaps a tasting language will evolve along the same lines as that used for wine and, more recently, olive oil. At the moment, fellow chocolate lovers get by without a specialized vocabulary – they just know when it is good and a roll of the eyes or a deep sigh is enough to communicate this.

Elaine Sherman, a twentieth-century American writer, more than adequately sums up: "Chocolate is heavenly, mellow, sensual, deep, dark, sumptuous, gratifying, potent, dense, creamy,

BELOW: Chocolate provides unmatched sensory pleasure – a delight to look at, a pleasure to touch, wonderful to smell and pleasurable to eat.

ABOVE: Chocolate has been used as a gift since the days of the Aztecs. It speaks a thousand words and feelings.

seductive, suggestive, rich, excessive, silky, smooth, luxurious, celestial. Chocolate is downfall, happiness, pleasure, love, ecstasy, fantasy … chocolate makes us wicked, guilty, sinful, healthy, chic, happy."

A CULTURAL AND SOCIAL LUBRICANT

Chocolate has always been used as a gift. As Michel Richart, an inspired chocolate-maker in Lyon, rightly states, when we share good quality chocolate it weaves links between people on many, many levels. Chocolate also creates valuable cultural, social and even spiritual awareness.

A small box of luxury chocolates says a thousand "thank-you's" to a hostess, a mother or a lover. Chocolate also says "good luck", "congratulations", "bon voyage" and "sorry". Queen Victoria symbolically sent 5,000 lbs/2,268 kg chocolate to her loyal troops at Christmas. Sales of chocolate rocket on Mother's Day and Valentine's Day. We use it in one form or another to celebrate Easter, Christmas and weddings.

There is hardly a country in the western world that does not have chocolate as part of its culinary culture, whether it be a moist chocolate brownie from America, a chocolate-covered pancake from Hungary, a velvety square of Swiss milk fondant chocolate, or a foaming cup of thick Spanish drinking chocolate. It is these chocolate "experiences" that unite chocolate lovers throughout the world in celebration of the food of the gods.

THE RECIPES

TYPES OF CHOCOLATE

COUVERTURE (LEFT)

The professionals' choice, this is a fine-quality pure chocolate with a high percentage of cocoa butter, which gives it a high gloss. It is suitable for decorative use and for making handmade chocolates. It must generally be tempered.

PLAIN DARK CHOCOLATE (BELOW)

Often called "luxury", "bitter" or "continental" chocolate, this has a high percentage of cocoa solids — around 75 per cent — with little or no added sugar. Its rich, intense flavour and good dark colour make it an ideal ingredient in desserts and cakes.

MILK CHOCOLATE (RIGHT)

This contains powdered or condensed milk and generally around 20 per cent cocoa solids. The flavour is mild and sweet. Although this is the most popular eating chocolate, it is not as suitable as plain chocolate for melting and cooking.

PLAIN CHOCOLATE (ABOVE)

Ordinary plain chocolate is the most widely available chocolate to use in cooking. It contains anywhere between 30 per cent and 70 per cent cocoa solids, so check the label before you buy. The higher the cocoa solids, the better the chocolate flavour will be.

COCOA (LEFT)

This is made from the pure cocoa mass after most of the cocoa butter has been extracted. The mass is roasted, then ground to make a powder. It is probably the most economical way of giving puddings and baked goods a chocolate flavour.

ORGANIC CHOCOLATE (ABOVE)

This is slightly more expensive than other types of chocolate but is a quality product, high in cocoa solids, produced without pesticides and with consideration for the environment.

CHOCOLATE CHIPS (ABOVE)

These are small pieces of chocolate of uniform size. They contain fewer cocoa solids than ordinary chocolate and are available in plain dark, milk and white flavours.

CHOCOLATE-FLAVOURED CAKE COVERING (LEFT)

This is a blend of sugar, vegetable oil, cocoa and flavourings. The flavour is poor, but the high fat content makes it suitable for chocolate curls – to improve the flavour, add some plain chocolate.

CHOCOLATE POWDER (BELOW)

Chocolate powder is used in baking and for making drinks. It has lower cocoa solids than pure cocoa and has a much milder, sweeter taste.

WHITE CHOCOLATE (BELOW LEFT)

This does not contain any cocoa solids but gets its flavour from cocoa buttter. It is sweet, and the better quality white chocolate is quite rich and smooth. White chocolate must be melted with care, as it does not withstand heat as well as plain chocolate.

TECHNIQUES

MELTING CHOCOLATE

If chocolate is being melted on its own, all the equipment must be completely dry, as water may cause the chocolate to thicken and become a stiff paste. For this reason, do not cover chocolate during or after melting it, as condensation could form. If chocolate does thicken, add a little pure white vegetable fat (not butter or margarine) and mix well. If this does not work, start again. Do not discard the thickened chocolate; melt it with cream to make a sauce.

With or without liquid, chocolate should be melted very slowly. It is easily burned or scorched, and then develops a bad flavour. If any steam gets into the chocolate, it can turn into a solid mass. If this happens, stir in a little pure white vegetable fat. Dark chocolate should not be heated above 50°C/120°F. Milk and white chocolate should not be heated above 45°C/110°F. Take particular care when melting white chocolate, which clogs very easily when subjected to heat.

MELTING CHOCOLATE OVER SIMMERING WATER

1 Chop or cut the chocolate into small pieces with a sharp knife to enable it to melt quickly and evenly.

2 Put the chocolate in the top of a double boiler or in a heatproof bowl over a saucepan of barely simmering water. The bowl should not touch the water.

3 Heat gently until the chocolate is melted and smooth, stirring occasionally. Remove from the heat and stir.

MELTING CHOCOLATE OVER DIRECT HEAT

When a recipe recommends melting chocolate with a liquid such as milk, cream or even butter, this can be done over direct heat in a saucepan.

1 Choose a heavy-based saucepan. Add the chocolate and liquid and melt over a low heat, stirring frequently, until the chocolate is melted and the mixture is smooth. Remove from heat immediately. This method is also used for making sauces, icings and some sweets.

2 Chocolate can also be melted in a very low oven. Preheat oven to 110°C/225°F/Gas ¼. Put the chocolate in an ovenproof bowl and place in the oven for a few minutes. Remove the chocolate before it is completely melted and stir until smooth.

MELTING CHOCOLATE IN THE MICROWAVE

Check the chocolate at frequent intervals during the cooking time. These times are for a 650–700 W oven and are approximate, as microwave ovens vary.

1 Place 115g/4oz chopped or broken dark, bittersweet or semi-sweet chocolate in a microwave-safe bowl and microwave on Medium for about 2 minutes. The same quantity of milk or white chocolate should be melted on Low for about 2 minutes.

2 Check the chocolate frequently during the cooking time. The chocolate will not change shape, but will start to look shiny. It must then be removed from the microwave and stirred until completely melted and smooth.

TEMPERING CHOCOLATE

TEMPERING CHOCOLATE

Tempering is the process of gently heating and cooling chocolate to stabilize the emulsification of cocoa solids and butterfat. This technique is generally used by professionals handling couverture chocolate. It allows the chocolate to shrink quickly (to allow easy release from a mould, for example with Easter eggs) or to be kept at room temperature for several weeks or months without losing its crispness and shiny surface. All solid chocolate is tempered in production, but once melted loses its "temper" and must be tempered again unless it is to be used immediately. Untempered chocolate tends to "bloom" or becomes dull and streaky or takes on a cloudy appearance. This can be avoided if the melted chocolate is put in the fridge immediately: chilling the chocolate solidifies the cocoa butter and prevents it from rising to the surface and "blooming". General baking and dessert-making do not require tempering, which is a fussy procedure and takes practice. However, it is useful to be aware of the technique when preparing sophisticated decorations, moulded chocolates or coatings. Most shapes can be made without tempering if they are chilled immediately.

EQUIPMENT

To temper chocolate successfully, you will need a marble slab or similar cool, smooth surface, such as an upturned baking sheet. A flexible plastic scraper is ideal for spreading the chocolate, but you can use a palette knife. As the temperature is crucial, you will need a chocolate thermometer. Look for this at a specialist kitchen supply shop, where you may also find blocks of tempered chocolate, ready for immediate use.

1 Break up the chocolate into small pieces and place it in the top of a double boiler or a heatproof bowl over a saucepan of hot water. Heat gently until just melted.

2 Remove from the heat. Spoon about three-quarters of the melted chocolate on to a marble slab or other cool, smooth, non porous work surface.

3 With a flexible plastic scraper or palette knife, spread the chocolate thinly, then scoop it up before spreading it again. Repeat the sequence, keeping the chocolate constantly on the move, for about 5 minutes.

4 Using a chocolate thermometer, check the temperature of the chocolate as you work it. As soon as the temperature registers 28°C/82°F, tip the chocolate back into the bowl and stir into the remaining chocolate.

5 With the addition of the hot chocolate, the temperature should now be 32°C/90°F, making the chocolate ready for use. To test, drop a little of the chocolate from a spoon on to the marble; it should set very quickly.

STORING CHOCOLATE

Chocolate can be stored successfully for up to a year if the conditions are favourable. This means a dry place with a temperature of around 20°C/68°F. At higher temperatures, the chocolate may develop white streaks as the fat comes to the surface. Although this will not spoil the flavour, it will mar the appearance of the chocolate, making it unsuitable for use as a decoration. When storing chocolate, keep it cool and dry. Place inside an airtight container, away from strong smelling foods. Check the "best before" dates on the pack.

PIPING WITH CHOCOLATE

Pipe chocolate directly on to a cake, or on to non stick baking paper to make run-outs, small outlined shapes or irregular designs. After melting the chocolate, allow it to cool slightly so it just coats the back of a spoon. If it still flows freely it will be too runny to hold its shape when piped. When it is the right consistency, you then need to work fast as the chocolate will set quickly. Use a paper piping bag and keep the pressure very tight, as the chocolate will flow readily without encouragement.

MAKING A PAPER PIPING BAG

A non-stick paper cone is ideal for piping small amounts of messy liquids like chocolate as it is small, easy to handle and disposable, unlike a conventional piping bag, which will need cleaning.

1 Fold a square of non-stick baking paper in half to form a triangle. With the triangle point facing you, fold the left corner down to the centre.

2 Fold the right corner down and wrap it around the folded left corner to form a cone. Fold the ends into the cone.

3 Spoon the melted chocolate into the cone and fold the top edges over. When ready to pipe, snip off the end of the point neatly to make a tiny hole, about 3 mm/$\frac{1}{8}$ in in diameter.

4 Another method is to use a small heavy-duty freezer or plastic bag. Place a piping nozzle in one corner of the bag, so that it is in the correct position for piping. Fill as above, squeezing the filling into one corner and twisting the top to seal. Snip off the corner of the bag, if necessary, so that the tip of the nozzle emerges, and squeeze gently to pipe the design.

CHOCOLATE DRIZZLES

You can have great fun making random shapes or, with a steady hand, special designs that will look great on cakes or biscuits.

1 Melt the chocolate and pour it into a paper cone or small piping bag fitted with a very small plain nozzle. Drizzle the chocolate on to a baking sheet lined with non-stick baking paper to make small, self-contained lattice shapes, such as circles or squares. Allow to set for 30 minutes then peel off the paper.

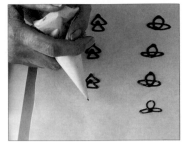

2 Chocolate can be used in many designs, such as flowers or butterflies. Use non-stick baking paper as tracing paper and pipe the chocolate over the chosen design or decorative shape.

3 For butterflies, pipe chocolate on to individually cut squares and leave until just beginning to set. Use a long, thin box (such as an egg carton) and place the butterfly shape in the box or between the cups so it is bent in the centre, creating the butterfly shape. Chill until needed.

PIPING ON TO CAKES

This looks effective on top of a cake iced with coffee glacé icing.

1 Melt 50g/2oz each of white and plain dark chocolate in separate bowls, and allow to cool slightly. Place the chocolates in separate paper piping bags. Cut a small piece off the pointed end of each bag in a straight line.

2 Hold each piping bag in turn above the surface of the cake and pipe the chocolates all over as shown in the picture. Alternatively, pipe a freehand design in one continuous curvy line, first with one bag of chocolate, then the other.

PIPING CURLS

Make lots of these curly shapes and store them in a cool place ready for using as cake decorations. Try piping the lines in contrasting colours of chocolate to vary the effect.

1 Melt 115g/4oz chocolate and allow to cool slightly. Cover a rolling pin with baking parchment and attach it with tape. Fill a paper piping bag with the chocolate and cut a small piece off the pointed end in a straight line.

2 Pipe lines of chocolate backwards and forwards over the baking parchment.

3 Leave the piped curls to set in a cool place, then carefully peel off the baking parchment. Use a palette knife to lift the curls on to the cake.

FEATHERING OR MARBLING CHOCOLATE

These two related techniques provide some of the easiest and most effective ways of decorating the top of a cake, and they are also used when making a swirled mixture for cut-outs. Chocolate sauce and double cream can also be feathered or marbled to decorate a dessert.

1 Melt two contrasting colours of chocolate and spread one over the cake or surface to be decorated.

2 Spoon the contrasting chocolate into a piping bag and pipe lines or swirls over the chocolate base.

3 Working quickly before the chocolate sets, draw a skewer or cocktail stick through the swirls to create a feathered or marbled effect.

CHOCOLATE RUN-OUTS

Try piping the outline in one colour of chocolate and filling in the middle with another. The effect can be dramatic.

1 Tape a piece of greaseproof paper to a baking sheet or flat board. Draw around a shaped biscuit cutter on to the paper several times. Secure a piece of non-stick baking paper over the top.

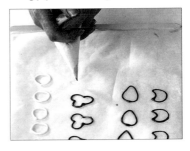

2 Pipe over the outline of your design in a continuous thread.

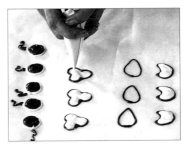

3 Cut the end off the other bag, making the hole slightly wider than before, and pipe the chocolate to fill in the outline so it looks slightly rounded. Leave the shapes to set in a cool place, then carefully lift them off the non-stick baking paper with a palette knife.

CHOCOLATE DECORATIONS

GRATED CHOCOLATE

Chocolate can be grated by hand or in a food processor. Make sure you grate it at the correct temperature.

1 Chill the chocolate and hold it with a piece of folded foil or paper towel to prevent the heat of your hand melting it. Hold a hand- or box-grater over a large plate and grate with an even pressure.

2 A food processor fitted with the metal blade can also be used to grate chocolate, but be sure the chocolate is soft enough to be pierced with a sharp knife. Cut the chocolate into small pieces and, with the machine running, drop the chocolate pieces through the feeder tube until very fine shavings are produced. Use the grater attachment and pusher to feed the chocolate through the processor for larger shavings.

COOK'S TIPS

The chocolate you use for decorating should not be too cold or it will splinter; warm chocolate will give a softer, looser curl, but do not allow it to become too soft or warm or it will be difficult to handle and may bloom. Use tempered chocolate for the best results.

COOK'S TIPS

If using a metal grater for grating chocolate, chill it in the freezer before use and the chocolate will be less likely to melt.
Experiment with different utensils when making chocolate curls. Metal palette knives, paint scrapers, tablespoons and even wide, straight pastry scrapers can be used.

MINI CHOCOLATE CURLS

Chocolate curls make an ideal decoration for many desserts and cakes, whether these are made from plain, bittersweet or white chocolate. These curls can be made very quickly using a vegetable peeler, and can be stored for several weeks in an airtight container in a cool, dry place.

1 Bring a thick piece or bar of chocolate to room temperature. (Chocolate that is too cold will "grate", or if too warm will slice.) With a swivel-bladed peeler held over a plate or baking sheet, pull the blade firmly along the edge of the chocolate and allow curls to fall on to the plate or baking sheet in a single layer.

2 Use a skewer or cocktail stick to transfer curls to the dessert or cake.

CHUNKY CHOCOLATE CURLS

These curls are best made with dark chocolate that has been melted with pure white vegetable fat (about 5ml/1tsp per 25g/1oz of chocolate), which keeps the chocolate from hardening completely.

1 Melt 175g/6oz plain or bittersweet chocolate with 30ml/2tbsp pure white vegetable fat, stirring until smooth. Pour into a small rectangular or square tin lined with foil or non-stick baking paper to produce a block about 2.5cm/1in thick. Chill until set.

2 Allow the block to come to room temperature, remove it from the tin, then hold it with a piece of folded foil or paper towel (to stop it melting) and use a swivel-bladed peeler to produce short chunky curls. The block of chocolate can also be grated.

COOK'S TIPS

The decorations on this page are useful for all kinds of cakes and desserts. When you have mastered the techniques, try marbling dark and white chocolate together for a special effect.

CHOCOLATE SCROLLS OR SHORT ROUND CURLS

Temper dark or white chocolate, or use chocolate prepared for Chunky Chocolate Curls to produce these scrolls.

1 Pour the prepared chocolate evenly on to a marble slab or the back of a baking sheet. Using a metal palette knife, spread to about 3mm/⅛in thick and allow to set for about 30 minutes until just firm.

2 To make long scrolls, use the blade of a long, sharp knife on the surface of the chocolate, and, with both hands, push away from your body at a 25–45° angle to scrape off a thin layer of chocolate. Twist the handle of the knife about a quarter of a circle to make a slightly wider scroll. Use a teaspoon to make cup-shaped curls.

3 A variety of shapes and sizes can be produced, depending on the temperature of the chocolate and the tool used.

CHOCOLATE SQUIGGLES

Melt a quantity of chocolate and spread fairly thinly over a cool, smooth surface, leave until just set, then draw a citrus zester firmly across the surface to remove curls or "squiggles" of the chocolate.

CHOCOLATE CUT-OUTS

You can make abstract shapes, or circles, squares and diamonds, by cutting them out free-hand with a sharp knife.

1 Cover a baking sheet with baking parchment and tape down at each corner. Melt 115g/4 oz dark, milk or white chocolate. Pour the chocolate on to the baking parchment.

2 Spread the chocolate evenly with a palette knife. Allow to stand until the surface is firm enough to cut, but not so hard that it will break. It should no longer feel sticky when touched lightly with your finger.

3 Press the cutter firmly through the chocolate and lift off the paper with a palette knife. Try not to touch the surface of the chocolate or you will leave marks on it and spoil its appearance.

4 The finished shapes can be left plain or piped with a contrasting chocolate for a decorative effect.

5 Abstract shapes can be cut with a knife free-hand. They look particularly effective pressed on to the sides of a cake iced with plain or chocolate buttercream.

COOK'S TIPS
If you do not feel confident about cutting chocolate cut-outs freehand, use biscuit or aspic cutters. Cut-outs look good around the sides of cakes or gâteaux. Space them at regular intervals or allow them to overlap.

Chocolate Leaves

You can use any fresh, non-toxic leaf with distinct veins, to make these decorations. Rose, bay or lemon leaves work well. If small leaves are required, for decorating petits fours, for instance, use mint or lemon balm leaves.

1 Wash and dry the leaves thoroughly. Melt plain or white chocolate and use a pastry brush or spoon to coat the veined side of each leaf completely.

2 Place the coated leaves chocolate-side up on a baking sheet lined with non-stick baking paper to set.

3 Starting at the stem end, gently peel away each leaf in turn. Store the chocolate leaves in a cool place until needed.

Chocolate Baskets

These impressive baskets make pretty, edible containers for mousse, or ice cream.

Makes 6

175g/6oz plain, milk or white chocolate
25g/1oz/2 tbsp butter

1 Cut out six 15cm/6in rounds from non-stick baking paper.

2 Melt the chocolate with the butter in a heatproof bowl over barely simmering water. Stir until smooth. Spoon one-sixth of the chocolate over each round, using a teaspoon to spread it to within 2cm/¾in of the edge.

Below: Chocolate baskets can be used to hold many kinds of delicious desserts, such as mousse, ice cream and tiramisu.

3 Carefully lift each covered paper round and drape it over an upturned cup or ramekin, curving the edges to create a frilled effect.

4 Leave until completely set, then carefully lift off the chocolate shape and peel away the paper.

5 For a different effect, brush the chocolate over, leaving the edges jagged. Invert chocolate baskets on individual dessert plates and gently peel off the paper. Add your chosen filling, taking care not to break the chocolate.

6 For a simple filling, whip cream with a little orange-flavoured liqueur, pipe the mixture in swirls in the chocolate cups and top with mandarin segments, half-dipped in chocolate.

CHOCOLATE CUPS

Large or small cupcake papers or sweet cases can be used to make chocolate cups to fill with ice cream, mousse or liqueur. Use double liners inside each other for extra support.

1 Melt the chocolate. Using a paintbrush or pastry brush, completely coat the bottom and sides of the paper cases. Allow to set, then repeat once or twice to build up the layers. Allow to set for several hours or overnight.

2 Carefully peel off the paper case, set the chocolate cups on a baking sheet and fill as desired.

CHOCOLATE SHORTCRUST PASTRY (1)

Suitable for sweet flans and tarts, this quantity will line a 23cm/9in flan tin.

115g/4oz plain chocolate, broken into squares
225g/8oz/2 cups plain flour
115g/4oz/½ cup unsalted butter
15–30ml/1–2 tbsp cold water

1 Melt the chocolate in a heatproof bowl over hot water. Remove from the heat and allow to cool, but not set.

2 Place the flour in a mixing bowl. Rub in the butter until the mixture resembles fine breadcrumbs.

3 Make a well in the centre of the rubbed-in mixture. Add the cooled chocolate and mix in together with just enough cold water to mix to a firm dough. Knead lightly, then wrap in clear film and chill before rolling out. Once you have chilled the flan tin, chill again before baking.

LEFT: These tiny chocolate cups are ideal as a container for sweets. You can also fill them with nuts and fruit for petits fours. Look out for different sizes of cases for these little cups.

CHOCOLATE SHORTCRUST PASTRY (2)

An alternative sweet chocolate pastry, this time made with cocoa. Use a 23cm/9in flan tin.

175g/6oz/1½ cups plain flour
30ml/2 tbsp cocoa powder
30ml/2 tbsp icing sugar
115g/4oz/½ cup butter
15–30ml/1–2 tbsp cold water

1 Sift the flour, cocoa powder and icing sugar into a mixing bowl.
2 Place the butter in a pan with the water and heat gently until just melted. Cool.
3 Stir into the flour to make a smooth dough. Chill until firm, then roll out and use as required.

TIPS FOR COOKING WITH CHOCOLATE

Melt chocolate slowly, as overheating will spoil both the flavour and texture.
Avoid overheating – dark chocolate should not be heated above 49°C/120°F; milk and white chocolate should not be heated above 43°C/110°F.
Never allow water or steam to come into contact with melting chocolate, as this may cause it to stiffen. If the chocolate comes into contact with steam, and forms a solid mass, add a small amount of pure vegetable oil and mix in. If this does not work you will have to start again. Don't discard spoiled chocolate, it will probably melt when added to another ingredient such as milk, butter or cream.
Remember to use high quality chocolate for the best results.
Look for the cocoa solid content on the back of the wrapper.
Do not cover chocolate after melting, as condensation could cause it to stiffen.

TEA-TIME CHOCOLATE TREATS

SIMPLE CHOCOLATE CAKE

<u>2</u> Cream the butter or margarine with the sugar in a mixing bowl until pale and fluffy. Add the eggs one at a time, beating well after each addition. Stir in the chocolate mixture until well combined.

<u>3</u> Sift the flour and cocoa over the mixture and fold in with a metal spoon until evenly mixed. Scrape into the prepared tins, smooth level and bake for 35–40 minutes or until well risen and firm. Turn out on to wire racks to cool.

<u>4</u> Sandwich the cake layers together with a thick, even layer of chocolate buttercream. Dust with a mixture of icing sugar and cocoa just before serving.

SERVES 6–8

115g/4oz plain chocolate, chopped into small pieces
45ml/3 tbsp milk
150g/5oz/⅓ cup unsalted butter or margarine, softened
150g/5oz/scant 1 cup light muscovado sugar
3 eggs
200g/7oz/1¾ cups self-raising flour
15ml/1 tbsp cocoa powder
1 quantity Chocolate Buttercream, for the filling
icing sugar and cocoa powder, for dusting

<u>1</u> Preheat oven to 180°C/350°F/Gas 4. Grease two 18 cm/7 in round sandwich cake tins and line the base of each with non-stick baking paper. Select a small saucepan and a heatproof bowl that will fit over it. Place the chocolate and the milk in the bowl. Bring a small saucepan of water to just below simmering point. Place the bowl containing the chocolate mixture on top. Leave for about 5 minutes, until the chocolate softens, then stir until smooth. Leave the bowl over the saucepan, but remove from the heat.

ONE-MIX CHOCOLATE SPONGE

SERVES 8–10

175g / 6oz / ¾ cup soft margarine, at room temperature
115g / 4oz / ½ cup caster sugar
60ml / 4 tbsp golden syrup
175g / 6oz / 1½ cups self-raising flour, sifted
30ml / 2 tbsp cocoa powder, sifted
2.5ml / ½ tsp salt
3 eggs, beaten
little milk (optional)
150ml / ¼ pint / ⅔ cup whipping cream
15–30ml / 1–2 tbsp finely shredded marmalade
sifted icing sugar, to decorate

1 Preheat the oven to 180°C/350°F/Gas 4. Grease two 18 mm/7 in sandwich cake tins. Cream the margarine, sugar, syrup, flour, cocoa, salt and eggs in a bowl.

2 If the mixture seems a little thick, stir in enough milk to give a soft dropping consistency. Spoon the mixture into the prepared tins, and bake for about 30 minutes, changing shelves if necessary after 15 minutes, until just firm and springy to the touch.

3 Leave the cakes to cool for 5 minutes, then remove from the tins and leave to cool completely on a wire rack.

4 Whip the cream and fold in the marmalade. Use the mixture to sandwich the two cakes together. Sprinkle the top with sifted icing sugar.

CHOCOLATE AND BEETROOT LAYER CAKE

SERVES 10–12

cocoa powder, for dusting
225g/8oz can cooked whole beetroot, drained
and juice reserved
115g/4oz/½ cup unsalted butter, softened
425g/15oz/2½ cups soft light brown sugar
3 eggs
15ml/1 tbsp vanilla essence
75g/3oz bittersweet chocolate, melted
225g/8oz/2 cups plain flour
10ml/2 tsp baking powder
2.5ml/½ tsp salt
120ml/4fl oz/½ cup buttermilk
chocolate curls (optional)
CHOCOLATE GANACHE FROSTING
475ml/16fl oz/2 cups whipping cream or
double cream
500g/1¼lb fine quality, bittersweet or plain
chocolate, chopped into
small pieces
15ml/1 tbsp vanilla essence

1 Preheat the oven to 180°C/350°F/ Gas 4. Grease two 23 cm/9 in cake tins and dust the base and sides with cocoa. Grate the beetroot and add to the juice. Set aside. With a hand-held electric mixer, beat the butter, brown sugar, eggs and vanilla essence in a mixing bowl until pale. Reduce the speed and beat in the melted chocolate. Sift the flour, baking powder and salt into a bowl.

2 With the mixer on low speed gradually beat the flour mixture into the butter mixture, alternately with the buttermilk. Add the beetroot and juice and beat for 1 minute. Divide between the tins and bake for 30–35 minutes or until a cake tester inserted in the centre of each cake comes out clean. Cool for 10 minutes, then turn the cakes out on a wire rack and cool completely.

3 To make the ganache frosting, heat the cream in a heavy-based saucepan over medium heat, until it just begins to boil, stirring occasionally to prevent it from scorching. Remove from the heat and stir in the chocolate, stirring constantly until melted and smooth. Stir in the vanilla essence. Strain into a bowl. Cool, then chill, stirring every 10 minutes for about 1 hour, until spreadable.

4 Assemble the cake. Place one layer on a serving plate and spread with one-third of the ganache frosting. Place the second layer on top and spread the remaining ganache over the cake, taking it down the sides. Decorate with the chocolate curls, if using. Allow the ganache frosting to set for 20–30 minutes, then chill the cake before serving.

FRENCH CHOCOLATE CAKE

SERVES 10

250g / 9oz bittersweet chocolate, chopped into small pieces
225g / 8oz / 1 cup unsalted butter, cut into small pieces
90g / 3½oz / scant ½ cup granulated sugar
30ml / 2 tbsp brandy or orange-flavoured liqueur
5 eggs
15ml / 1 tbsp plain flour
icing sugar, for dusting
whipped or soured cream, for serving

1 Preheat oven to 180°C/350°F/Gas 4. Generously grease a 23 x 5 cm/9 x 2 in springform tin. Line the base with non-stick baking paper and grease. Wrap the bottom and sides of the tin in foil to prevent water from seeping through into the cake.

2 In a saucepan, over a low heat, melt the chocolate, butter and sugar, stirring frequently until smooth. Remove from the heat, cool slightly and stir in the brandy or liqueur.

3 In a large bowl beat the eggs lightly for 1 minute. Beat in the flour, then slowly beat in the chocolate mixture until well blended. Pour into the tin.

4 Place the springform tin in a large roasting tin. Add enough boiling water to come 2 cm/¾ in up the side of the springform tin. Bake for 25–30 minutes, until the edge of the cake is set but the centre is still soft. Remove the springform tin from the roasting tin and remove the foil. Cool on a wire rack. The cake will sink in the centre and become its classic slim shape as it cools. Don't worry if the surface cracks slightly.

5 Remove the side of the springform tin and turn the cake on to a wire rack. Lift off the springform tin base and then carefully peel back the paper, so the base of the cake is now the top. Leave the cake on the rack until it is quite cold.

6 Cut 6–8 strips of non-stick baking paper 2.5 cm/1 in wide and place randomly over the cake. Dust the cake with icing sugar, then carefully remove the paper. Slide the cake on to a plate and serve with whipped or soured cream.

HAZELNUT AND CHOCOLATE CAKE

SERVES 10

115g / 4oz / ½ cup unsalted butter, softened
150g / 5oz plain chocolate
115g / 4oz / ½ cup caster sugar
4 eggs, separated
115g / 4oz / 1 cup ground lightly toasted hazelnuts
50g / 2oz / 1 cup fresh breadcrumbs
grated rind of 1½ oranges
30ml / 2 tbsp sieved marmalade, warmed
60ml / 4 tbsp chopped hazelnuts, to decorate

FOR THE ICING

150g / 5oz plain chocolate, chopped into small pieces
50g / 2oz / ¼ cup butter, diced

<u>1</u> Preheat oven to 180°C/350°F/Gas 4. Butter a 23 cm/9 in round cake tin and line the base with greaseproof paper.

<u>2</u> Melt the chocolate and set aside. Beat the butter and sugar together, then gradually add the egg yolks, beating well. The mixture may curdle slightly. Beat in the melted chocolate, then the hazelnuts, breadcrumbs and orange rind. Whisk the egg whites until stiff, then fold into the chocolate mixture. Transfer to the cake tin. Bake for 40–45 minutes, until set.

<u>3</u> Remove from the oven, cover with a damp dish towel for 5 minutes, then transfer to a wire rack until cold.

<u>4</u> Make the icing. Place the chocolate and butter in a heatproof bowl over a pan of simmering water and stir until smooth. Leave until cool and thick. Spread the cake with the marmalade, then the icing. Scatter over the nuts, then leave to set.

CHOCOLATE AND ORANGE ANGEL CAKE

SERVES 10

25g/1oz/¼ cup plain flour
30ml/2 tbsp cocoa powder
30ml/2 tbsp cornflour
pinch of salt
5 egg whites
2.5ml/½ tsp cream of tartar
115g/4oz/½ cup caster sugar
blanched and shredded rind of 1 orange,
to decorate
FOR THE ICING
200g/7oz/scant 1 cup caster sugar
75ml/5 tbsp cold water
1 egg white

1 Preheat oven to 180°C/350°F/Gas 4. Sift the flour, cocoa, cornflour and salt together three times. Beat the egg whites in a large bowl until foamy. Add the cream of tartar to the egg whites and whisk until soft peaks form.

2 Add the caster sugar to the egg whites a spoonful at a time, whisking after each addition. Add, by sifting, a third of the flour and cocoa mixture, and gently fold in. Repeat, sifting and folding in the flour and cocoa two more times. Spoon the mixture into a 20 cm/8 in non-stick ring tin and level the top. Bake for 35 minutes or until springy when lightly pressed. When cooled, turn upside-down on to a wire rack and leave to cool in the tin.

3 Make the icing. Put the sugar in a pan with the water. Stir over a low heat until dissolved. Boil until the syrup reaches a temperature of 120°C/250°F on a sugar thermometer, or when a drop of the syrup makes a soft ball when dropped into a cup of cold water. Remove the pan from the heat. Ease the cake out of the tin.

4 Whisk the egg white until stiff. Add the syrup in a thin stream, whisking all the time. Continue to whisk until the mixture is very thick and fluffy. Spread the icing over the top and sides of the cooled cake. Sprinkle the orange rind over the top of the cake and transfer it to a platter. Serve.

Chocolate and Cherry Polenta Cake

Serves 8

50g/2oz/⅓ cup quick-cook polenta
200g/7oz plain chocolate, chopped into
small pieces
5 eggs, separated
175g/6oz/¾ cup caster sugar
115g/4oz/1 cup ground almonds
75ml/5 tbsp plain flour
finely grated rind of 1 orange
115g/4oz/1 cup glacé cherries, halved
icing sugar, for dusting

1 Place the polenta in a heatproof bowl and pour over just enough boiling water to cover (about 120ml/4 fl oz/½ cup). Stir well, then cover the bowl and leave to stand for about 30 minutes, until the quick-cook polenta has absorbed all the excess moisture.

2 Preheat oven to 190°C/375°F/Gas 5. Grease a deep 22 cm/8½ in round cake tin and line the base with non-stick baking paper. Melt the chocolate.

3 Whisk the egg yolks with the sugar in a bowl until thick and pale. Beat in the chocolate, then fold in the polenta, ground almonds, flour and orange rind.

4 Whisk the egg whites in a grease-free bowl until stiff. Stir about 15ml/1 tbsp of the whites into the chocolate mixture to lighten it, then fold in the rest. Finally, fold in the cherries. Scrape the mixture into the prepared tin and bake for 45–55 minutes or until well risen and firm. Turn out and cool on a wire rack, then dust with icing sugar to serve.

MARBLED CHOCOLATE PEANUT BUTTER CAKE

SERVES 12–14

115g/4oz bittersweet chocolate, chopped into
small pieces
225g/8oz/1 cup unsalted butter, softened
225g/8oz/⅔ cup smooth or chunky
peanut butter
200g/7oz/scant 1 cup granulated sugar
225g/8 oz/1¼ cups soft light brown sugar
5 eggs
225g/8 oz/2 cups plain flour
10ml/2 tsp baking powder
2.5ml/½ tsp salt
120ml/4fl oz/½ cup milk
50g/2oz/⅓ cup chocolate chips

CHOCOLATE PEANUT BUTTER GLAZE

25g/1oz/2 tbsp butter, cut up
30ml/2 tbsp smooth peanut butter
45ml/3 tbsp golden syrup
5ml/1 tsp vanilla essence
175g/6oz plain chocolate, chopped into
small pieces
15ml/1 tbsp water

1 Preheat oven to 180°C/350°F/Gas 4. Generously grease and flour a 3 litre/ 5 pint/12 cup tube or ring tin. Melt the chocolate. In a large mixing bowl beat the butter, peanut butter and sugars until light and creamy. Add the eggs one at a time, beating well after each addition.
2 In a medium bowl, sift together the flour, baking powder and salt. Add to the butter mixture alternately with the milk until just blended. Pour half the mixture into another bowl. Stir the melted chocolate into one bowl of batter until well blended. Stir the chocolate chips into the other bowl of batter.

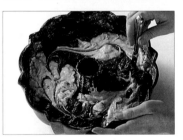

3 Using a large spoon, drop alternate spoonfuls of chocolate mixture and peanut butter mixture into the prepared tin. Using a knife, pull through the batters to create a swirled marbled effect. Bake for 50–60 minutes, until the top springs back when touched. Cool the cake in the tin for 10 minutes. Turn out on to a rack to cool completely.

4 Make the glaze. Combine all the ingredients in a small saucepan. Melt over a low heat, stirring until well blended and smooth. Cool slightly. When slightly thickened, drizzle the glaze over the cake, allowing it to run down the sides.

Chocolate-orange Battenburg

3 Fold the rest of the flour and the cocoa into the remaining bowl of mixture, with sufficient milk to give a soft dropping consistency. Fill one half of the tin with the orange mixture and the second half with the chocolate. Flatten the top with a wetted spoon. Bake for 15 minutes, then reduce the heat to 160°C/325°F/Gas 3, and bake the cake for a further 20–30 minutes or until the top is just firm. Leave to cool in the tin for a few minutes. Turn out the cakes on to a board and cut each one into two identical strips. Trim so that they are even, then leave to cool.

4 Using the chocolate and nut spread, sandwich the cakes together, chocolate and orange side by side, then orange and chocolate on top. Spread the sides with more of the chocolate and nut spread. On a board lightly dusted with cornflour, roll out the white almond paste to a rectangle 18 cm/7 in wide and long enough to wrap all around the cake. Wrap the almond paste carefully around the cake, making the join underneath. Press to seal. Mark a criss-cross pattern on the almond paste with a knife, then pinch together the corners if desired. Store in a cool place. Cut with a sharp knife into chequered slices to serve.

Serves 8

115g/4oz/½ cup soft margarine
115g/4oz/½ cup caster sugar
2 eggs, beaten
few drops of vanilla essence
115g/4oz/1 cup ground almonds
115g/4oz/1 cup self-raising flour, sifted
grated rind and juice of ½ orange
30ml/2 tbsp cocoa powder, sifted
30–45ml/2–3 tbsp milk
1 jar chocolate and nut spread
cornflour, to dust
225g/8oz white almond paste

1 Preheat oven to 180°C/350°F/Gas 4. Grease and line an 18 cm/7 in square cake tin. Arrange a double piece of foil across the middle of the tin, to divide it into two equal rectangles.

2 Cream the margarine and sugar in a mixing bowl, then beat in the eggs, vanilla essence and ground almonds. Divide the mixture evenly between two bowls. Fold half the flour into one bowl, then stir in the orange rind and sufficient juice to give a soft dropping consistency. Set the orange-flavoured mixture aside.

CHOCOLATE CHIP WALNUT LOAF

MAKES 1 LOAF

115g / 4 oz / ½ cup caster sugar
115g / 4 oz / 1 cup plain flour
5ml / 1 tsp baking powder
60ml / 4 tbsp cornflour
115g / 4 oz / ½ cup butter, softened
2 eggs, beaten
5ml / 1 tsp vanilla essence
30ml / 2 tbsp currants or raisins
25g / 1 oz / ¼ cup walnuts, finely chopped
grated rind of ½ lemon
45ml / 3 tbsp plain chocolate chips
icing sugar, for dusting

1 Preheat oven to 180°C/350°F/Gas 4. Grease and line a 22 x 12 cm/8½ x 4½ in loaf tin. Sprinkle 25ml/1½ tbsp of the caster sugar into the pan and tilt to distribute the sugar in an even layer over the bottom and sides. Shake out any excess sugar.

2 Sift the flour, baking powder and cornflour into a mixing bowl. Repeat this twice more. Set aside.

3 With an electric mixer, cream the butter until soft. Add the remaining sugar and continue beating until light and fluffy. Add the eggs, one at a time, beating after each addition.

4 Gently fold the dry ingredients into the butter mixture, in three batches; do not overmix.

5 Fold in the vanilla essence, currants or raisins, walnuts, lemon rind and chocolate chips until just blended.

6 Pour the mixture into the prepared tin and bake for 45–50 minutes. Cool in the tin for 5 minutes before transferring to a rack to cool completely. Place on a serving plate and dust over an even layer of icing sugar before serving. Alternatively, top with glacé icing and decorate with walnut halves.

BITTER MARMALADE CHOCOLATE LOAF

SERVES 8

*115g/4oz plain chocolate, chopped into
small pieces*
3 eggs
200g/7oz/scant 1 cup caster sugar
175ml/6fl oz/¾ cup soured cream
200g/7oz/1¾ cups self-raising flour

FOR THE FILLING AND GLAZE

175g/6oz/⅔ cup bitter orange marmalade
*115g/4oz plain chocolate, chopped into
small pieces*
60ml/4 tbsp soured cream
shredded orange rind, to decorate

<u>1</u> Preheat oven to 180°C/350°F/Gas 4.
Grease a 900g/2lb loaf tin lightly, then
line it with non-stick baking paper. Melt
the chocolate.

<u>2</u> Combine the eggs and sugar in a mixing
bowl. Using a hand-held electric mixer,
whisk the mixture until it is thick and
creamy, then stir in the soured cream and
chocolate. Fold in the self-raising flour
evenly, using a metal spoon and a figure-
of-eight action.

<u>3</u> Scrape the mixture into the prepared
tin and bake for about 1 hour or until
well risen and firm to the touch. Cool for
a few minutes in the tin, then turn out on
to a wire rack and leave the loaf to cool
completely.

<u>4</u> Make the filling. Spoon two-thirds of
the marmalade into a small saucepan and
melt over a gentle heat. Melt the
chocolate and stir it into the marmalade
with the soured cream.

<u>5</u> Slice the cake across into three layers
and sandwich back together with about
half the marmalade filling. Spread the rest
over the top of the cake and leave to set.
Spoon the remaining marmalade over the
cake and scatter with shredded orange
rind, to decorate.

CHOCOLATE CHIP MARZIPAN LOAF

MAKES 1 LOAF

115g / 4oz / ½ cup unsalted butter, softened
150g / 5oz / scant 1 cup light muscovado sugar
2 eggs, beaten
45ml / 3 tbsp cocoa powder
150g / 5oz / 1¼ cups self-raising flour
130g / 3½ oz marzipan
60ml / 4 tbsp plain chocolate chips

1 Preheat oven to 180°C / 350°F / Gas 4. Grease a 900g / 2lb loaf tin and line the base with non-stick baking paper. Cream the butter and sugar in a mixing bowl until light and fluffy.

2 Add the eggs to the creamed mixture one at a time, beating well after each addition to combine.

3 Sift the cocoa and flour over the mixture and fold in evenly.

4 Chop the marzipan into small pieces with a sharp knife. Tip into a bowl and mix with the chocolate chips. Set aside about 60ml / 4 tbsp and fold the rest evenly into the cake mixture.

5 Scrape the mixture into the prepared tin, level the top and scatter with the reserved marzipan and chocolate chips.

6 Bake for 45–50 minutes or until the loaf is risen and firm. Cool for a few minutes in the tin, then turn out on to a wire rack to cool completely.

CHOCOLATE COCONUT ROULADE

4 Scrape the mixture into the prepared tin, taking it right into the corners. Smooth the surface with a palette knife, then bake for 20–25 minutes or until well risen and springy to the touch.

5 Turn the cooked roulade out on to the sugar-dusted greaseproof paper and carefully peel off the lining paper. Cover with a damp, clean dish towel and leave to cool completely.

6 Make the filling. Whisk the cream with the whisky in a bowl until the mixture just holds it shape, grate the creamed coconut and stir in with the sugar.

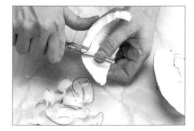

7 Uncover the sponge and spread about three-quarters of the cream mixture to the edges. Roll up carefully from a long side. Transfer to a plate, pipe or spoon the remaining cream mixture on top. Use a vegetable peeler to make coconut and chocolate curls and pile on the cake.

SERVES 8

115g / 4oz / ½ cup caster sugar
5 eggs, separated
50g / 2oz / ½ cup cocoa powder
FOR THE FILLING
300ml / ½ pint / 1¼ cups double cream
45ml / 3 tbsp whisky
or brandy
50g / 2oz piece solid creamed
coconut
30ml / 2 tbsp caster sugar
FOR THE TOPPING
a piece of fresh coconut
dark chocolate for curls

1 Preheat oven to 180°C/350°F/Gas 4. Grease a 33 x 23 cm/13 x 9 in Swiss roll tin. Lay a large sheet of greaseproof paper or non-stick baking paper on the work surface and dust it evenly with 30ml/ 2 tbsp of the caster sugar.

2 Place the egg yolks in a heatproof bowl. Add the remaining caster sugar and whisk with a hand-held electric mixer until the mixture is thick enough to leave a trail. Sift the cocoa over, then fold in carefully and evenly with a metal spoon.

3 Whisk the egg whites in a clean, grease-free bowl until they form soft peaks. Fold about 15ml/1 tbsp of the whites into the chocolate mixture to lighten it, then fold in the rest evenly.

CHOCOLATE CHESTNUT ROULADE

SERVES 10–12

175g/6oz bittersweet chocolate, chopped into small pieces
30ml/2 tbsp cocoa powder, sifted
60ml/4 tbsp hot strong coffee or espresso
6 eggs, separated
75g/3oz/6 tbsp caster sugar
pinch of cream of tartar
5ml/1 tsp pure vanilla essence
cocoa powder, for dusting
glacé chestnuts, to decorate

CHESTNUT CREAM FILLING

475ml/16fl oz/2 cups double cream
30ml/2 tbsp rum or coffee-flavoured liqueur
350g/12oz/1½ cups canned sweetened chestnut purée
115g/4oz bittersweet chocolate, grated

1 Preheat oven to 180°C/350°F/Gas 4. Lightly grease the base and sides of a 39 x 27 x 2.5 cm/15½ x 10½ x 1 in Swiss roll tin. Line with non-stick baking paper, allowing a 2.5 cm/1 in overhang. Melt the chocolate. Dissolve the cocoa in the hot coffee to make a paste. Set aside.

2 Using a hand-held mixer, beat the egg yolks with half the sugar in a mixing bowl until pale and thick. Slowly beat in the melted chocolate and cocoa-coffee paste until just blended. In a separate bowl, beat the egg whites and cream of tartar until stiff peaks form. Sprinkle the remaining sugar over the whites in two batches and beat until the whites are stiff and glossy, then beat in the vanilla essence.

3 Stir a spoonful of the whites into the chocolate mixture to lighten it, then fold in the rest. Spoon into the tin. Bake for 20–25 minutes or until the cake springs back when touched with a fingertip.

4 Dust a dish towel with cocoa. Turn the cake out on to the towel immediately and remove the paper. Trim off any crisp edges. Starting at a narrow end, roll the cake and towel together Swiss roll fashion. Cool completely.

5 Make the filling. Whip the cream and rum or liqueur until soft peaks form. Beat a spoonful of cream into the chestnut purée to lighten it, then fold in the remaining cream and grated chocolate. Set aside a quarter of this mixture for the decoration. Unroll the cake and spread chestnut cream to within 2.5 cm/1 in of the edge.

6 Using a dish towel to lift the cake, carefully roll it up again. Place seam-side down on a serving plate. Spread some of the reserved chestnut cream over the top and use the rest for piped rosettes. Decorate with the glacé chestnuts.

MARBLED SWISS ROLL

SERVES 6–8

90g/3½oz/scant 1 cup plain flour
15ml/1 tbsp cocoa powder
25g/1oz plain chocolate, grated
25g/1oz white chocolate, grated
3 eggs
115g/4oz/½ cup caster sugar
30ml/2 tbsp boiling water

FOR THE FILLING

1 quantity Chocolate Buttercream
45ml/3 tbsp chopped walnuts

<u>1</u> Preheat oven to 200°C/400°F/Gas 6. Grease a 30 x 20 cm/12 x 8 in Swiss roll tin and line with non-stick baking paper. Sift half the flour with the cocoa into a bowl. Stir in the grated plain chocolate. Sift the remaining flour into another bowl. Stir in the grated white chocolate.

<u>2</u> Whisk the eggs and sugar in a heatproof bowl set over a saucepan of hot water until it holds its shape when the whisk is lifted and a ribbon trail remains.

<u>3</u> Remove the bowl from the heat and tip half the mixture into a separate bowl. Fold the plain chocolate mixture into one portion, then fold the white chocolate mixture into the other. Stir 15ml/1 tbsp boiling water into each half to soften.

BAKED ALASKA

For a delicious dessert that takes only minutes to prepare, make individual Baked Alaskas by topping slices of the roll with chocolate ice cream, covering both cake and ice cream thickly with meringue mixture and baking at 230°C/450°F/Gas 8 for 2–3 minutes, watching carefully, until the meringue is tinged with brown.

<u>4</u> Place alternate spoonfuls of mixture in the prepared tin and swirl lightly together with a knife or slim metal skewer for a marbled effect. Bake for about 12–15 minutes or until the cake is firm and the surface springs back when touched with a fingertip. Turn the cake out on to a sheet of non-stick baking paper placed flat on the work surface.

<u>5</u> Trim the edges to neaten and cover with a damp, clean dish towel. Cool.

<u>6</u> For the filling, mix the chocolate buttercream and walnuts in a bowl. Uncover the sponge, lift off the lining paper and spread the surface with the buttercream. Roll up carefully from a long side and place on a serving plate. Slice to serve, and store in an airtight container.

CHOCOLATE CHRISTMAS LOG

SERVES 12-14

*1 chocolate Swiss roll, see Chocolate
Chestnut Roulade*
*1 quantity of Chocolate Ganache or
Buttercream*
**FOR THE WHITE CHOCOLATE
CREAM FILLING**
*200g/7oz fine quality white chocolate,
chopped into small pieces*
475ml/16fl oz/2 cups double cream
*30ml/2 tbsp brandy or chocolate-flavoured
liqueur (optional)*
FOR THE CRANBERRY SAUCE
*450g/1lb fresh or frozen cranberries, rinsed
and picked over*
*275g/10oz/1 cup seedless raspberry
preserve, melted*
*115g/4oz/½ cup granulated sugar, or
to taste*

1 Make the cranberry sauce. Process the
cranberries in a food processor fitted with
a metal blade, until liquid. Press through
a sieve into a small bowl, and discard
pulp. Stir in the melted raspberry
preserve and the sugar to taste. If the
sauce is too thick, add a little water to
thin. Cover and place in the fridge.

2 Make the filling. In a small pan, heat the
chocolate with 120ml/4 fl oz/½ cup of
the cream until melted, stirring. Strain
into a bowl and cool to room
temperature. In a separate bowl, beat the
remaining cream with the brandy or
liqueur until soft peaks form; fold into
the chocolate mixture.

3 Unroll the Swiss roll, spread with the
mixture and roll up again from a long
end. Cut off a quarter of the roll at an
angle and arrange both pieces on a cake
board to resemble a log.
4 If using chocolate ganache for the
topping, allow it to soften to room
temperature, then beat to a soft,
spreading consistency. Cover the log with
ganache or buttercream and mark it with
a fork to resemble bark. Dust lightly with
icing sugar and top with a sprig of holly
or similar Christmas decoration. Serve
with the cranberry sauce.

MERINGUE MUSHROOMS
Small, decorative mushrooms are
traditionally used to decorate the
yule log. Using meringue mix, pipe
the "caps" and "stems" separately, dry
out in a low oven, then sandwich
together with ganache or chocolate
buttercream. Dust with cocoa, if you
like. Alternatively, shape mushrooms
from marzipan.

RICH CAKES AND GATEAUX

CHOCOLATE DATE TORTE

SERVES 8

4 egg whites
115g/4oz/½ cup caster sugar
200g/7oz plain chocolate
*175g/6oz/scant 1 cup Medjool dates, pitted
and finely chopped*
*175g/6oz/1½ cups walnuts or pecan
nuts, chopped*
5ml/1 tsp vanilla essence
FOR THE FROSTING
200g/7oz/scant 1 cup fromage frais
200g/7oz/scant 1 cup mascarpone
few drops of vanilla essence
icing sugar, to taste

<u>1</u> Preheat oven to 180°C/350°F/Gas 4.
Grease a round 20 cm/8 in springform
cake tin. Line the base of the tin with
non-stick baking paper.

<u>2</u> Make the frosting. Mix together the
fromage frais and mascarpone, add a few
drops of vanilla essence and icing sugar to
taste, then set aside.

<u>3</u> Whisk the egg whites in a bowl until
they form stiff peaks. Whisk in 30ml/
2 tbsp of the caster sugar until the
meringue is thick and glossy, then fold in
the remainder.

<u>4</u> Chop 175g/6 oz of the chocolate, then
carefully fold into the meringue with the
dates, nuts and vanilla essence. Pour into
the prepared tin, spread level and bake
for about 45 minutes, until risen around
the edges.

<u>5</u> Allow the cake to cool in the tin for
10 minutes, then invert on a wire rack.
Peel off the lining paper and leave until
completely cold.

<u>6</u> Swirl the frosting over the top of the
torte. Melt the remaining chocolate. Use
a small paper piping bag to drizzle the
chocolate over the torte. Work quickly
and keep up an even pressure on the
piping bag. Chill the torte before serving,
then cut into wedges. This torte is best
eaten on the day it is made.

CHOCOLATE REDCURRANT TORTE

SERVES 8–10

115g/4oz/½ cup unsalted butter, softened
115g/4oz/⅔ cup dark muscovado sugar
2 eggs
150ml/¼ pint/⅔ cup soured cream
150g/5oz/1¼ cups self-raising flour
5ml/1 tsp baking powder
50g/2oz/½ cup cocoa powder
75g/3oz/¾ cup stemmed redcurrants, plus
115g/4oz/1 cup redcurrant sprigs, to decorate

FOR THE ICING

150g/5oz plain chocolate, chopped into small pieces
45ml/3 tbsp redcurrant jelly
30ml/2 tbsp dark rum
120ml/4fl oz/½ cup double cream

1 Preheat oven to 180°C/350°F/Gas 4. Grease a 1.2 litre/2 pint/5 cup ring tin and dust lightly with flour. Cream the butter with the sugar in a mixing bowl until pale and fluffy. Beat in the eggs and soured cream until thoroughly mixed.

2 Sift the flour, baking powder and cocoa over the mixture, then fold in lightly and evenly. Fold in the stemmed redcurrants. Spoon the mixture into the prepared tin and smooth the surface level. Bake for 40–50 minutes or until well risen and firm. Turn out on to a wire rack and leave to cool completely.

3 Make the icing. Mix the chocolate, redcurrant jelly and rum in a heatproof bowl. Set the bowl over simmering water and heat gently, stirring occasionally, until melted. Remove from the heat and cool to room temperature, then add the double cream, a little at a time. Mix well.
4 Transfer the cooked cake to a serving plate. Spoon the icing evenly over the cake, allowing it to drizzle down the sides. Decorate with redcurrant sprigs just before serving.

COOK'S TIP

Use a decorative gugelhupf tin or mould, if you have one. When preparing it, add a little cocoa powder to the flour used for dusting the greased tin, as this will prevent the cooked chocolate cake from being streaked with white.

SACHERTORTE

SERVES 10–12

*225g/8oz plain dark chocolate, chopped into
small pieces
150g/5oz/²⁄₃ cup butter, softened
115g/4oz/½ cup caster sugar
8 eggs, separated
115g/4oz/1 cup plain flour*

FOR THE GLAZE

*225g/8oz/scant 1 cup apricot jam
15ml/1 tbsp lemon juice*

FOR THE ICING

*225g/8oz plain dark chocolate, cut into
small pieces
200g/7oz/scant 1 cup caster sugar
15ml/1 tbsp golden syrup
250ml/8fl oz/1 cup double cream
5ml/1 tsp vanilla essence
plain chocolate leaves, to decorate*

5 Make the glaze. Heat the apricot jam with the lemon juice in a small saucepan until melted, then strain through a sieve into a bowl. Once the cake is cold, slice in half across the middle to make two even-size layers.

6 Brush the top and sides of each layer with the apricot glaze, then sandwich them together. Place on a wire rack.

1 Preheat oven to 180°C/350°F/Gas 4. Grease a 23 cm/9 in round springform cake tin and line with non-stick baking paper. Melt the chocolate in a heatproof bowl over barely simmering water, then set the bowl aside.

2 Cream the butter with the sugar in a mixing bowl until pale and fluffy, then add the egg yolks, one at a time, beating after each addition. Beat in the melted chocolate, then sift the flour over the mixture and fold it in evenly.

3 Whisk the egg whites in a clean, grease-free bowl until stiff, then stir about a quarter of the whites into the chocolate mixture to lighten it. Fold in the remaining whites.

4 Tip the chocolate mixture into the prepared cake tin and smooth level. Bake for about 50–55 minutes or until firm. Cool in the tin for 5 minutes, then turn out carefully on to a wire rack and leave to cool completely.

7 Make the icing. Mix the chocolate, sugar, golden syrup, cream and vanilla essence in a heavy saucepan. Heat gently, stirring constantly, until the mixture is thick and smooth. Simmer gently for 3–5 minutes, without stirring, until the mixture registers 95°C/200°F on a sugar thermometer. Pour the icing quickly over the cake, spreading to cover the top and sides completely. Leave to set, decorate with chocolate leaves, then serve with whipped cream, if wished.

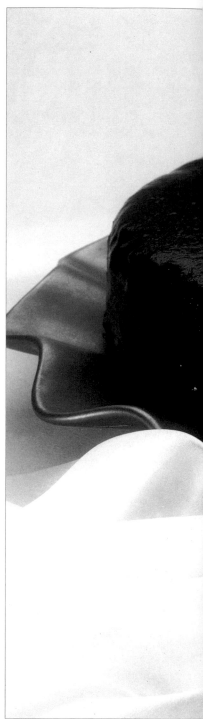

QUEEN OF SHEBA CAKE

SERVES 8–10

100g / 3½oz / scant 1 cup whole blanched
almonds, lightly toasted
115g / 4oz / ½ cup caster sugar
40g / 1½oz / ⅓ cup plain flour
115g / 4oz / ½ cup unsalted butter, softened
150g / 5oz plain chocolate, melted
3 eggs, separated
30ml / 2 tbsp almond liqueur (optional)
chopped toasted almonds, to decorate

FOR THE CHOCOLATE GLAZE

175ml / 6fl oz / ¾ cup whipping cream
225g / 8oz plain chocolate, chopped
25g / 1oz / 2 tbsp unsalted butter
30ml / 2 tbsp almond liqueur (optional)

1 Preheat oven to 180°C / 350°F / Gas 4.
Grease and base-line a 20–23 cm / 8–9 in
springform cake tin. Dust the tin lightly
with flour.

2 In the bowl of a food processor fitted
with a metal blade, process the almonds
and 30ml / 2 tbsp of the sugar until very
fine. Transfer to a bowl and sift over the
flour. Stir to mix, then set aside.

3 Beat the butter until creamy, then add
half of the remaining sugar and beat for
about 1–2 minutes until very light.
Gradually beat in the melted chocolate,
then add the egg yolks one at a time,
beating well after each addition. Beat in
the liqueur, if using.

4 In another bowl, beat the egg whites
until soft peaks form. Add the remaining
sugar and beat until the whites are stiff
and glossy, but not dry. Fold a quarter of
the whites into the chocolate mixture to
lighten it, then alternately fold in the
almond mixture and the remaining whites
in three batches. Spoon the mixture into
the prepared tin and spread evenly.

5 Bake for 30–35 minutes, until the edges
are puffed but the centre is still soft. Cool
in the tin for 15 minutes, then remove
the sides and invert the cake on a wire
rack. When quite cold, lift off the base of
the tin and the paper.

6 To make the chocolate glaze, bring the
cream to the boil in a saucepan. Remove
from the heat and add the chocolate,
stirring gently until it has melted and the
mixture is smooth. Beat in the butter and
almond liqueur, if using. Cool for about
20–30 minutes, until slightly thickened,
stirring occasionally.

7 Place the cake on the wire rack over a
baking sheet and pour over most of the
warm glaze to cover completely. Cool
slightly, then press the nuts on to the
sides of the cake. Use the remaining glaze
for a piped decoration. Transfer to a plate
and chill until ready to serve.

STICKY CHOCOLATE, MAPLE AND WALNUT SWIRLS

SERVES 12

450g / 1lb / 4 cups strong white flour
2.5ml / ½ tsp ground cinnamon
50g / 2oz / ¼ cup unsalted butter, cut into
small pieces
50g / 2oz / ¼ cup caster sugar
1 sachet easy-blend dried yeast
1 egg yolk
120ml / 4fl oz / ½ cup water
60ml / 4 tbsp milk
45ml / 3 tbsp maple syrup, to finish

FOR THE FILLING

40g / 1½oz / 3 tbsp unsalted butter, melted
50g / 2oz / ⅓ cup light muscovado sugar
175g / 6oz / 1 cup plain chocolate chips
75g / 3oz / ¾ cup chopped walnuts

1 Grease a deep 23 cm/9 in springform cake tin. Sift the flour and cinnamon into a bowl, then rub in the butter until the mixture resembles coarse breadcrumbs.

2 Stir in the sugar and yeast. In a jug or bowl, beat the egg yolk with the water and milk, then stir into the dry ingredients to make a soft dough.
3 Knead the dough on a lightly floured surface until smooth, then roll out to a rectangle measuring about 40 x 30 cm/ 16 x 12 in.

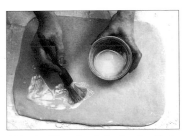

4 For the filling, brush the dough with the melted butter and sprinkle with the sugar, chocolate chips and nuts.

5 Roll up the dough from one long side like a Swiss roll, then cut into 12 thick even-size slices. Pack close together in the tin, cut sides up. Cover and leave in a warm place for about 1½ hours, until well risen and springy. Meanwhile, preheat oven to 220°C/425°F/Gas 7.
6 Bake for 30–35 minutes, until golden brown. Remove from the tin and cool on a wire rack. Brush with maple syrup while still warm. Pull swirls apart to serve.

WHITE CHOCOLATE MOUSSE AND STRAWBERRY LAYER CAKE

<u>4</u> Make the mousse filling. In a medium saucepan over a low heat, melt the chocolate and cream until smooth, stirring frequently. Stir in the rum or strawberry-flavoured liqueur and pour into a bowl. Chill until just set. With a wire whisk, whip lightly.

SERVES 10

115g/4oz fine white chocolate, chopped into small pieces
120ml/4fl oz/½ cup double cream
120ml/4fl oz/½ cup milk
15ml/1 tbsp rum or vanilla essence
115g/4oz/½ cup unsalted butter, softened
175g/6oz/¾ cup granulated sugar
3 eggs
225g/8oz/2 cups plain flour
10ml/2 tsp baking powder
pinch of salt
675g/1½lb fresh strawberries, sliced, plus extra for decoration
750ml/1¼ pints/3 cups whipping cream
30ml/2 tbsp rum or strawberry-flavoured liqueur

WHITE CHOCOLATE MOUSSE FILLING

250g/9oz white chocolate, chopped into small pieces
350ml/12fl oz/1½ cups double cream
30ml/2 tbsp rum or strawberry-flavoured liqueur

<u>1</u> Preheat oven to 180°C/350°F/Gas 4. Grease and flour two 23 x 5 cm/9 x 2 in cake tins. Line the base of the tins with non-stick baking paper. Melt the chocolate and cream in a double boiler over a low heat, stirring until smooth. Stir in the milk and rum or vanilla essence, and set aside to cool.

<u>2</u> In a large mixing bowl, beat the butter and sugar with a hand-held electric mixer for 3–5 minutes, until light and creamy, scraping the sides of the bowl occasionally. Add the eggs one at a time, beating well after each addition. In a small bowl, stir together the flour, baking powder and salt. Alternately add flour and melted chocolate to the egg mixture in batches, until just blended. Pour the mixture into the tins and spread evenly.

<u>3</u> Bake for 20–25 minutes, until a skewer inserted in the cake comes out clean. Cool in the tin for 10 minutes, then turn cakes out on to a wire rack, peel off the paper and cool completely.

<u>5</u> Assemble the cake. With a serrated knife, slice both cake layers in half, making four layers. Place one layer on the plate and spread one third of the mousse on top. Arrange one third of the sliced strawberries over the mousse. Place the second layer on top and spread with another third of the mousse. Arrange another third of the sliced strawberries over the mousse. Place the third layer on top and spread with the remaining mousse. Cover with the remaining sliced strawberries. Top with the last cake layer.

<u>6</u> Whip the cream with the rum or liqueur until firm peaks form. Spread about half the whipped cream over the top and the sides of the cake. Spoon the remaining cream into a decorating bag fitted with a medium star tip and pipe scrolls on top of the cake. Decorate with the remaining sliced strawberries, pressing half of them into the cream on the side of the cake and arranging the rest on top.

CHOCOLATE GINGER CRUNCH CAKE

SERVES 6

150g/5oz plain chocolate, chopped into small pieces
50g/2oz/¼ cup unsalted butter
115g/4oz ginger nut biscuits
4 pieces of preserved stem ginger
30ml/2 tbsp stem ginger syrup
45ml/3 tbsp desiccated coconut

TO DECORATE

25g/1oz milk chocolate, chopped into small pieces
pieces of crystallized ginger

1 Grease a 15 cm/6 in flan ring and place it on a sheet of non-stick baking paper. Melt the plain chocolate with the butter in a heatproof bowl over barely simmering water. Remove from the heat and set aside.

2 Crush the biscuits into small pieces. Tip them into a bowl.

3 Chop the stem ginger fairly finely and mix with the crushed ginger nut biscuits.

4 Stir the biscuit mixture, ginger syrup and coconut into the melted chocolate and butter, mixing well until evenly combined.

5 Tip the mixture into the prepared flan ring and press down firmly and evenly. Chill in the fridge until set.

6 Remove the flan ring and slide the cake on to a plate. Melt the milk chocolate, drizzle it over the top and decorate with the pieces of crystallized ginger.

FROSTED CHOCOLATE FUDGE CAKE

SERVES 6–8

115g/4oz plain chocolate, chopped into small pieces
175g/6oz/¾ cup unsalted butter or margarine, softened
200g/7oz/generous 1 cup light muscovado sugar
5ml/1 tsp vanilla essence
3 eggs, beaten
150ml/¼ pint/⅔ cup Greek-style yogurt
150g/5oz/1¼ cups self-raising flour
icing sugar and chocolate curls, to decorate

FOR THE FROSTING

115g/4 oz plain dark chocolate, chopped into small pieces
50g/2oz/¼ cup unsalted butter
350g/12oz/2¼ cups icing sugar
90ml/6 tbsp Greek-style yogurt

1 Preheat oven to 190°C/375°F/Gas 5. Lightly grease two 20 cm/8 in round sandwich cake tins and line the base of each with non-stick baking paper. Melt the chocolate.

2 In a mixing bowl, cream the butter or margarine with the sugar until light and fluffy. Beat in the vanilla essence, then gradually add the beaten eggs, beating well after each addition.

3 Stir in the melted plain chocolate and yogurt evenly. Fold in the flour with a metal spoon.

4 Divide the mixture between the prepared tins. Bake for 25–30 minutes or until the cakes are firm to the touch. Turn out and cool on a wire rack.

5 Make the frosting. Melt the chocolate and butter in a saucepan over a low heat. Remove from the heat and stir in the icing sugar and yogurt. Mix with a rubber spatula until smooth, then beat until the frosting begins to cool and thicken slightly. Use about a third of the mixture to sandwich the cakes together.

6 Working quickly, spread the remainder over the top and sides. Sprinkle with icing sugar and decorate with chocolate curls.

RICH CHOCOLATE LEAF GATEAU

SERVES 8

*75g / 3oz plain dark chocolate, broken
into squares
150ml / ¼ pint / ⅔ cup milk
175g / 6oz / ¾ cup unsalted butter, softened
250g / 9oz / 1⅓ cups light muscovado sugar
3 eggs
250g / 9oz / 2¼ cups plain flour
10ml / 2 tsp baking powder
75ml / 5 tbsp single cream*

FOR THE FILLING AND TOPPING

*60ml / 4 tbsp raspberry conserve
1 quantity Chocolate Ganache
dark and white chocolate leaves*

<u>1</u> Preheat oven to 190°C / 375°F / Gas 5.
Grease and base-line two 22 cm / 8½ in
sandwich cake tins. Melt the chocolate
with the milk over a low heat and allow
to cool slightly.

<u>2</u> Cream the butter with the light
muscovado sugar in a mixing bowl until
light and fluffy. Add the eggs, one at a
time, beating well after each addition.
<u>3</u> Sift the flour and baking powder over
the mixture and fold in gently but
thoroughly. Stir in the chocolate mixture
and the cream, mixing until smooth.
Divide between the prepared tins and
level the tops.

<u>4</u> Bake the cakes for 30–35 minutes or
until they are well risen and firm to the
touch. Cool in the tins for a few minutes,
then turn out on to wire racks.

<u>5</u> Sandwich the cake layers together with
the raspberry conserve. Spread the
chocolate ganache over the cake and
swirl with a knife. Place the cake on a
serving plate, then decorate with the
chocolate leaves.

CHOCOLATE ALMOND MOUSSE CAKE

SERVES 8

*50g/2oz plain dark chocolate, broken
into squares*
200g/7oz marzipan, grated or chopped
200ml/7fl oz/scant 1 cup milk
115g/4oz/1 cup self-raising flour
2 eggs, separated
*75g/3oz/⅓ cup light muscovado
sugar*

FOR THE MOUSSE FILLING

*115g/4oz plain chocolate, chopped into
small pieces*
50g/2oz/¼ cup unsalted butter
2 eggs, separated
*30ml/2 tbsp Amaretto di Saronno
liqueur*

FOR THE TOPPING

*1 quantity Chocolate Ganache
toasted flaked almonds, to decorate*

1 Preheat oven to 190°C/375°F/Gas 5. Grease a deep 17 cm/6½ in square cake tin and line with non-stick baking paper. Combine the chocolate, marzipan and milk in a saucepan and heat gently without boiling, stirring until smooth.
2 Sift the flour into a bowl and add the chocolate mixture and egg yolks, beating until evenly mixed.

3 Whisk the egg whites in a clean, grease-free bowl until stiff enough to hold firm peaks. Whisk in the sugar gradually. Stir about 15ml/1 tbsp of the whites into the chocolate mixture to lighten it, then fold in the rest.
4 Spoon the mixture into the tin, spreading it evenly. Bake for 45–50 minutes, until well risen, firm and springy to the touch. Leave to cool on a wire rack.
5 Make the mousse filling. Melt the chocolate with the butter in a small saucepan over a low heat, then remove from the heat and beat in the egg yolks and Amaretto. Whisk the egg whites in a clean, grease-free bowl until stiff, then fold into the chocolate mixture.

6 Slice the cold cake in half across the middle to make two even layers. Return one half to the clean cake tin and pour over the chocolate mousse. Top with the second layer of cake and press down lightly. Chill until set.

7 Turn the cake out on to a serving plate. Allow the chocolate ganache to soften to room temperature, then beat it to a soft, spreading consistency. Spread the chocolate ganache over the top and sides of the cake, then press toasted flaked almonds over the sides. Serve chilled.

DEATH BY CHOCOLATE

SERVES 16–20

*225g/8oz plain dark chocolate, chopped into
small pieces
115g/4 oz/½ cup unsalted butter
150ml/¼ pint/⅔ cup milk
225g/8oz/1¼ cups light muscovado sugar
10ml/2 tsp vanilla essence
2 eggs, separated
150ml/¼ pint/⅔ cup soured cream
225g/8oz/2 cups self-raising flour
5ml/1 tsp baking powder*

FOR THE FILLING AND TOPPING

*60ml/4 tbsp seedless raspberry jam
60ml/4 tbsp brandy
400g/14oz plain dark chocolate, chopped
into small pieces
200g/7oz/scant 1 cup unsalted butter
1 quantity Chocolate Ganache
plain chocolate curls, to decorate*

1 Preheat oven to 180°C/350°F/Gas 4.
Grease and base-line a deep 23 cm/9 in
springform cake tin. Place the chocolate,
butter and milk in a saucepan. Stir over a
low heat until smooth. Remove from the
heat, beat in the sugar and vanilla essence,
then leave to cool slightly.

2 Beat the egg yolks and cream in a bowl,
then beat into the chocolate mixture. Sift
the flour and baking powder over the
surface and fold in.

3 Whisk the egg whites in a grease-free
bowl until stiff. Stir about 30ml/2 tbsp of
the whites into the chocolate cake
mixture, to lighten it. Fold in the
remaining whites, using a metal spoon.

4 Scrape the mixture into the prepared
tin and bake for about 45–55 minutes or
until firm to the touch. Cool in the tin for
15 minutes, then invert the cake on to a
wire rack, remove the tin and set aside
until completely cold.

5 Slice the cold cake across the middle to
make three even layers. Make the filling.
In a small saucepan, warm the raspberry
jam with 15ml/1 tbsp of the brandy, then
brush over two of the layers. Leave to set.

6 Place the remaining brandy in a
saucepan with the chocolate and butter.
Heat gently, stirring, until the mixture is
smooth. Pour into a bowl and cool until it
begins to thicken.

7 Spread the bottom layer of the cake
with half the chocolate filling, taking care
not to disturb the jam. Top with a second
layer, jam side up, and spread with the
remaining filling. Top with the final layer
and press lightly.

8 Leave to set, then spread the top and
sides of the cake with the chocolate
ganache. Decorate with chocolate curls
and then dust the top of the cake with
cocoa powder.

VEGAN CHOCOLATE GATEAU

SERVES 8–10

*275g / 10oz / 2½ cups self-raising
wholemeal flour
50g / 2oz / ½ cup cocoa powder
45ml / 3 tbsp baking powder
225g / 8oz / 1¼ cups caster sugar
few drops of vanilla essence
135ml / 9 tbsp sunflower oil
350ml / 12fl oz / 1½ cups water
sifted cocoa powder, for sprinkling
25g / 1oz / ¼ cup chopped nuts, to decorate*

FOR THE CHOCOLATE FUDGE

*50g / 2oz / ¼ cup vegan (soya) margarine
45ml / 3 tbsp water
250g / 9oz / 2 cups icing sugar
30ml / 2 tbsp cocoa powder
15–30ml / 1–2 tbsp hot water*

1 Preheat oven to 160°C / 325°F / Gas 3. Grease a deep 20 cm / 8 in round cake tin, line with non-stick baking paper and grease the paper lightly with a little sunflower oil.

2 Sift the flour, cocoa and baking powder into a large mixing bowl. Add the caster sugar and vanilla essence, then gradually beat in the sunflower oil. Add the water in the same way, beating constantly to produce a smooth mixture with the consistency of a thick batter.

3 Pour the cake mixture into the prepared tin and smooth the surface with the back of a spoon.

4 Bake the cake for about 45 minutes or until a cake tester or fine metal skewer inserted in the centre comes out clean. Remove from the oven but leave in the tin for about 5 minutes, before turning out on to a wire rack. Peel off the lining paper and leave to cool. Cut the cake in half to make two equal layers.

5 Make the chocolate fudge. Place the margarine and water in a pan and heat gently until the margarine has melted. Remove from the heat and add the sifted icing sugar and cocoa powder, beating until shiny, adding more hot water if needed. Pour into a bowl and cool until firm enough to spread and pipe.

6 Place the bottom layer of the cake on a serving plate and spread over two-thirds of the chocolate fudge mixture. Top with the other layer. Fit a piping bag with a star nozzle, fill with the remaining chocolate fudge and pipe stars over the cake. Sprinkle with cocoa powder and decorate with the chopped nuts.

BLACK FOREST GATEAU

4 Prick each layer all over with a skewer or fork, then sprinkle with Kirsch. Using a hand-held electric mixer, whip the cream in a bowl until it starts to thicken, then gradually beat in the icing sugar and vanilla essence until the mixture begins to hold its shape.

5 To assemble, spread one cake layer with a thick layer of flavoured cream and top with about half the cherries. Spread a second cake layer with cream, top with the remaining cherries, then place it on top of the first layer. Top with the final cake layer.

6 Spread the remaining cream all over the cake. Dust a plate with icing sugar, and position the cake carefully in the centre. Press grated chocolate over the sides and decorate the cake with the chocolate curls and fresh or drained cherries.

SERVES 8–10

6 eggs
200g/7oz/scant 1 cup caster sugar
5ml/1 tsp vanilla essence
50g/2oz/½ cup plain flour
50g/2oz/½ cup cocoa powder
115g/4oz/½ cup unsalted butter, melted

FOR THE FILLING AND TOPPING
60ml/4 tbsp Kirsch
600ml/1 pint/2½ cups double cream
30ml/2 tbsp icing sugar
2.5ml/½ tsp vanilla essence
675g/1½lb jar stoned morello cherries,
well drained

TO DECORATE
icing sugar, for dusting
grated chocolate
Chocolate Curls
fresh or drained canned morello cherries

1 Preheat oven to 180°C/350°F/Gas 4. Grease three 19 cm/7½ in sandwich cake tins. Line the bottom of each with non-stick baking paper. Combine the eggs with the sugar and vanilla essence in a bowl and beat with a hand-held electric mixer until pale and very thick.
2 Sift the flour and cocoa powder over the mixture and fold in lightly and evenly with a metal spoon. Gently stir in the melted butter.
3 Divide the mixture among the prepared cake tins, smoothing them level. Bake for 15–18 minutes, until the cakes have risen and are springy to the touch. Leave them to cool in the tins for about 5 minutes, then turn out on to wire racks and leave to cool completely. Remove the lining paper from each cake layer.

WHITE CHOCOLATE CAPPUCCINO GATEAU

SERVES 8

4 eggs
115g/4oz/½ cup caster sugar
15ml/1 tbsp strong black coffee
2.5ml/½ tsp vanilla essence
115g/4oz/1 cup plain flour
75g/3oz white chocolate, coarsely grated

FOR THE FILLING

120ml/4fl oz/½ cup double cream or
whipping cream
15ml/1 tbsp coffee liqueur

FOR THE FROSTING AND TOPPING

15ml/1 tbsp coffee liqueur
1 quantity White Chocolate Frosting
white chocolate curls
cocoa powder or ground cinnamon,
for dusting

<u>1</u> Preheat oven to 180°C/350°F/Gas 4. Grease two 18 cm/7 in round sandwich cake tins and line the base of each with non-stick baking paper.

<u>2</u> Combine the eggs, caster sugar, coffee and vanilla essence in a large heatproof bowl. Place over a saucepan of hot water and whisk until pale and thick.

<u>3</u> Sift half the flour over the mixture; fold in gently and evenly. Fold in the remaining flour with the grated white chocolate.

<u>4</u> Divide the mixture between the prepared tins and smooth level. Bake for 20–25 minutes, until firm and golden brown, then turn out on wire racks and leave to cool completely.

<u>5</u> Make the filling. Whip the cream with the coffee liqueur in a bowl until it holds its shape. Spread over one of the cakes, then place the second layer on top.

<u>6</u> Stir the coffee liqueur into the frosting. Spread over the top and sides of the cake, swirling with a palette knife. Top with curls of white chocolate and dust with cocoa or cinnamon. Transfer the cake to a serving plate and set aside until the frosting has set. Serve the gâteau on the day it was made, if possible.

CHOCOLATE BRANDY SNAP GATEAU

SERVES 8

225g/8oz plain dark chocolate, chopped
225g/8oz/1 cup unsalted butter, softened
200g/7oz/generous 1 cup dark
muscovado sugar
6 eggs, separated
5ml/1 tsp vanilla essence
150g/5oz/1¼ cups ground hazelnuts
60ml/4 tbsp fresh white breadcrumbs
finely grated rind of 1 large orange
1 quantity Chocolate Ganache, for filling
and frosting
icing sugar, for dusting
FOR THE BRANDY SNAPS
50g/2oz/¼ cup unsalted butter
50g/2oz/¼ cup caster sugar
75g/3oz/⅓ cup golden syrup
50g/2oz/½ cup plain flour
5ml/1 tsp brandy

1 Preheat oven to 180°C/350°F/Gas 4.
Grease two 20 cm/8 in sandwich cake
tins and line the base of each with non-
stick baking paper. Melt the chocolate
and set aside to cool slightly.

2 Cream the butter with the sugar in a
mixing bowl until pale and fluffy. Beat in
the egg yolks and vanilla essence. Add the
chocolate and mix thoroughly.

3 In a clean, grease-free bowl, whisk the
egg whites to soft peaks, then fold them
into the chocolate mixture with the
ground hazelnuts, breadcrumbs and
orange rind.

4 Divide the cake mixture between the
prepared tins and smooth the tops. Bake
for 25–30 minutes or until well risen and
firm. Turn out on to wire racks. Leave
the oven on.

5 Make the brandy snaps. Line two baking
sheets with non-stick baking paper. Melt
the butter, sugar and syrup together.

6 Stir the butter mixture until smooth.
Remove from the heat and stir in the
flour and brandy.

7 Place small spoonfuls of the mixture
well apart on the baking sheets and bake
for 8–10 minutes, until golden. Cool for
a few seconds until firm enough to lift on
to a wire rack.

8 Immediately pinch the edges of each
brandy snap to create a frilled effect. If
the biscuits become too firm, soften them
briefly in the oven.

9 Sandwich the cake layers together with
half the chocolate ganache, transfer to a
plate and spread the remaining ganache
on the top. Arrange the brandy snaps over
the gâteau and dust with icing sugar.

COOK'S TIP
To save time, you could use ready-
made brandy snaps. Simply warm
them for a few minutes in the oven
until they are pliable enough to
shape. Or use as they are, filling
them with cream, and arranging
them so that they fan out from the
centre of the gâteau.

MERINGUE GATEAU WITH CHOCOLATE MASCARPONE

SERVES ABOUT 10
4 egg whites
pinch of salt
175g/6oz/¾ cup caster sugar
5ml/1 tsp ground cinnamon
75g/3oz plain dark chocolate, grated
icing sugar and rose petals, to decorate
FOR THE FILLING
115g/4oz plain chocolate, chopped into
small pieces
5ml/1 tsp vanilla essence or rosewater
115g/4oz/½ cup mascarpone cheese

<u>1</u> Preheat oven to 150°C/300°F/Gas 2.
Line two large baking sheets with non-
stick baking paper. Whisk the egg whites
with the salt in a clean, grease-free bowl
until they form stiff peaks.
<u>2</u> Gradually whisk in half the sugar, then
add the rest and whisk until the meringue
is very stiff and glossy. Add the cinnamon
and chocolate and whisk lightly to mix.

<u>3</u> Draw a 20 cm/8 in circle on the lining
paper on one of the baking sheets, replace
it upside down and spread the marked
circle evenly with about half the
meringue. Spoon the remaining meringue
in 28–30 small neat heaps on both baking
sheets. Bake for 1½ hours, until crisp.

<u>4</u> Make the filling. Melt the chocolate in a
heatproof bowl over hot water. Cool
slightly, then add the vanilla essence or
rosewater and cheese. Cool the mixture
until it holds it shape.

<u>5</u> Spoon the chocolate mixture into a
large piping bag and sandwich the
meringues together in pairs, reserving a
small amount of filling for assembling
the gâteau.
<u>6</u> Arrange the filled meringues on a
serving platter, piling them up in a
pyramid. Keep them in position with a
few well-placed dabs of the reserved
filling. Dust the pyramid with icing sugar,
sprinkle with the rose petals and serve at
once, while the meringues are crisp.

CARIBBEAN CHOCOLATE RING WITH RUM SYRUP

SERVES 8–10

115g / 4oz / ½ cup unsalted butter
115g / 4oz / ¾ cup light muscovado sugar
2 eggs, beaten
2 ripe bananas, mashed
30ml / 2 tbsp desiccated coconut
30ml / 2 tbsp soured cream
115g / 4oz / 1 cup self-raising flour
45ml / 3 tbsp cocoa powder
2.5ml / ½ tsp bicarbonate of soda

FOR THE SYRUP

115g / 4oz / ½ cup caster sugar
30ml / 2 tbsp dark rum
50g / 2oz plain dark chocolate, chopped

TO DECORATE

mixture of tropical fruits, such as mango,
pawpaw, starfruit and cape gooseberries
chocolate shapes or curls

1 Preheat oven to 180°C/350°F/Gas 4. Grease a 1.5 litre/2½ pint/6¼ cup ring tin with butter.

2 Cream the butter and sugar in a bowl until light and fluffy. Add the eggs gradually, beating well, then mix in the bananas, coconut and soured cream.

3 Sift the flour, cocoa and bicarbonate of soda over the mixture and fold in thoroughly and evenly.

4 Tip into the prepared tin and spread evenly. Bake for 45–50 minutes, until firm to the touch. Cool for 10 minutes in the tin, then turn out to finish cooling on a wire rack.

5 For the syrup, place the sugar in a small pan. Add 60ml/4 tbsp water and heat gently, stirring occasionally until dissolved. Bring to the boil and boil rapidly, without stirring, for 2 minutes. Remove from the heat.

6 Add the rum and chocolate to the syrup and stir until the mixture is melted and smooth, then spoon evenly over the top and sides of the cake.

7 Decorate the ring with tropical fruits and chocolate shapes or curls.

SPECIAL OCCASION AND NOVELTY CAKES

STRAWBERRY CHOCOLATE VALENTINE GATEAU

SERVES 8

175g / 6oz / 1½ cups self-raising flour
10ml / 2 tsp baking powder
75ml / 5 tbsp cocoa powder
115g / 4oz / ½ cup caster sugar
2 eggs, beaten
15ml / 1 tbsp black treacle
150ml / ¼ pint / ⅔ cup sunflower oil
150ml / ¼ pint / ⅔ cup milk

FOR THE FILLING

45ml / 3 tbsp strawberry jam
150ml / ¼ pint / ⅔ cup double cream or
whipping cream
115g / 4oz strawberries, sliced

TO DECORATE

1 quantity Chocolate Fondant
chocolate hearts
icing sugar, for dusting

1 Preheat oven to 160°C / 325°F / Gas 3. Grease a deep 20 cm / 8 in heart-shaped cake tin and line the base with non-stick baking paper. Sift the self-raising flour, baking powder and cocoa powder into a large mixing bowl. Stir in the sugar, then make a well in the centre of the dry ingredients.

2 Add the eggs, treacle, oil and milk to the well. Mix with a spoon to incorporate the dry ingredients, then beat with a hand-held electric mixer until the mixture is smooth and creamy.

3 Spoon the mixture into the prepared cake tin and spread evenly. Bake for about 45 minutes, until well risen and firm to the touch. Cool in the tin for a few minutes, then turn out on to a wire rack to cool completely.

4 Using a sharp knife, slice the cake neatly into two layers. Place the bottom layer on a board or plate. Spread with the strawberry jam.

5 Whip the cream in a bowl. Stir in the strawberries, then spread over the jam. Top with the remaining cake layer.

6 Roll out the chocolate fondant and cover the cake. Decorate with chocolate hearts and dust with icing sugar.

COOK'S TIP

If you do not have a heart-shaped cake tin, consider hiring one from a kitchen shop. All sorts of sizes are available, often for a modest fee.

DOUBLE HEART ENGAGEMENT CAKE

SERVES 20
double quantity One-Mix Chocolate
Sponge mixture
double quantity Chocolate Buttercream
icing sugar, for sifting
chocolate curls and fresh raspberries,
to decorate

VARIATIONS
Use plain buttercream, tinted to a
delicate shade of rose. Decorate with
strawberries, half-dipped in melted
chocolate.
Cover the cakes with Chocolate
Ganache and drizzle melted
chocolate over the top. Arrange
chocolate-dipped fruit on top.
Cover both the cakes with Chocolate
Fondant and top with pale apricot or
cream sugar roses and chocolate
leaves. Trim each cake with a narrow
apricot or cream ribbon.

1 Preheat oven to 160°C/325°F/Gas 3.
Grease and base-line with greaseproof
paper two 20 cm/8 in heart-shaped cake
tins. Divide the one-mix chocolate
sponge cake mixture evenly between the
tins and smooth the surfaces. Bake for 30
minutes. Turn on to a wire rack, peel off
the lining paper and leave to cool.

2 Cut each cake in half horizontally. Use
about one-third of the buttercream to fill
both cakes, then sandwich them together
to make two. Cover the tops of the cakes
with buttercream.

3 Arrange on a cake board. Use the
remaining icing to coat the sides of the
cakes. Make sure it is thickly covered.

4 Generously cover the tops and sides
of both the cakes with the chocolate
curls, beginning from the top of the heart
and arranging them as shown, and
pressing them gently into the
buttercream as you go.
5 Dust a little icing sugar over the top of
each cake and decorate with raspberries.
Chill until ready to serve.

WHITE CHOCOLATE CELEBRATION CAKE

SERVES 40–50

900g / 2lb / 8 cups plain flour
2.5ml / ½ tsp salt
20ml / 4 tsp bicarbonate of soda
450g / 1lb white chocolate, chopped
475ml / 16fl oz / 2 cups whipping cream
450g / 1lb / 2 cups unsalted butter, softened
900g / 2lb / 4 cups caster sugar
12 eggs
20ml / 4 tsp lemon essence
grated rind of 2 lemons
335ml / 11fl oz / 1⅓ cups buttermilk
lemon curd, for filling
chocolate leaves, to decorate

FOR THE LEMON SYRUP

200g / 7oz / scant 1 cup granulated sugar
250ml / 8fl oz / 1 cup water
60ml / 4 tbsp lemon juice

FOR THE BUTTERCREAM

675g / 1½lb white chocolate chopped
1kg / 2¼lb cream cheese, softened
500g / 1¼lb / 2½ cups unsalted butter, at room temperature
60ml / 4 tbsp lemon juice
5ml / 1 tsp lemon essence

1 Divide all the ingredients into two equal batches, so that the quantities are more manageable. Use each batch to make one cake. Preheat oven to 180°C/350°F/Gas 4. Grease a 30 cm/12 in round cake tin. Base-line with non-stick baking paper. Sift the flour, salt and bicarbonate of soda into a bowl and set aside. Melt the chocolate and cream in a saucepan over a medium heat, stirring until smooth. Set aside to cool to room temperature.

VARIATION

For a summer celebration, decorate the cake with raspberries and white chocolate petals. To make the petals, you will need about 20 x 7.5 cm/3 in foil squares. Spread melted white chocolate thinly over each piece of foil, so that it resembles a rose petal. Before the chocolate sets, bend the foil up to emphasize the petal shape. When set, peel away the foil.

2 Beat the butter until creamy, then add the sugar and beat for 2–3 minutes. Beat in the eggs, then slowly beat in the melted chocolate, lemon essence and rind. Gradually add the flour mixture, alternately with the buttermilk, to make a smooth pouring mixture. Pour into the tin and bake for 1 hour or until a skewer inserted in the cake comes out clean.
3 Cool in the tin for 10 minutes, then invert the cake on a wire rack and cool completely. Wrap in clear film until ready to assemble. Using the second batch of ingredients, make another cake in the same way.
4 Make the lemon syrup. In a small saucepan, combine the sugar and water. Over a medium heat, bring to the boil, stirring until the sugar dissolves. Remove from the heat, stir in the lemon juice and cool completely. Store in an airtight container until required.

5 Make the buttercream. Melt the chocolate. Cool slightly. Beat the cream cheese in a bowl until smooth. Gradually beat in the cooled white chocolate, then the butter, lemon juice and essence. Chill.
6 Split each cake in half. Spoon syrup over each layer, let it soak in, then repeat. Spread the bottom half of each cake with lemon curd and replace the tops.

7 Gently beat the buttercream in a bowl until creamy. Spread a quarter over the top of one of the filled cakes. Place the second filled cake on top. Spread a small amount of softened butter over the top and sides of the cake to create a smooth, crumb-free surface. Chill for 15 minutes, so that the buttercream sets a little.

8 Place the cake on a serving plate. Set aside a quarter of the remaining buttercream for piping, then spread the rest evenly over the top and sides of the filled cake.

9 Spoon the reserved buttercream into a large icing bag fitted with a small star tip. Pipe a shell pattern around the rim of the cake. Decorate with chocolate leaves, made with dark or white chocolate (or a mixture) and fresh flowers.

CHOCOLATE BOX WITH CARAMEL MOUSSE AND BERRIES

SERVES 8–10

275g / 10oz plain chocolate, chopped into
small pieces

FOR THE CARAMEL MOUSSE

4 x 50g / 2oz chocolate-coated caramel bars,
coarsely chopped

25ml / 1½ tbsp milk or water

350ml / 12fl oz / 1½ cups double cream

1 egg white

FOR THE CARAMEL SHARDS

115g / 4oz / ½ cup granulated sugar

60ml / 4 tbsp water

FOR THE TOPPING

115g / 4oz fine quality white chocolate,
chopped into small pieces

350ml / 12fl oz / 1½ cups double cream

450g / 1lb mixed berries or cut up fruits such
as raspberries, strawberries, blackberries or
sliced nectarine and orange segments

1 Prepare the chocolate box. Turn a 23 cm / 9 in square baking tin bottom-side up. Mould a piece of foil around the tin, then turn it right side up and line it with the foil, pressing against the edges to make the foil as smooth as possible.

2 Place the plain chocolate in a heatproof bowl over a saucepan of simmering water. Stir until the chocolate has melted and is smooth. Immediately pour the melted chocolate into the lined tin. Tilt to coat the bottom and sides evenly, keeping the top edges of the sides as straight as possible. As the chocolate coats the sides, tilt the pan again to coat the corners and sides once more. Chill until firm.

3 Place the caramel bars and milk or water in a heatproof bowl. Place over a pan of simmering water and stir until melted. Remove the bowl from the heat and cool for 10 minutes, stirring occasionally.

4 Using a hand-held electric mixer, whip the cream in a bowl until soft peaks form. Stir a spoonful of the whipped cream into the caramel mixture to lighten it, then fold in the remaining cream. In another bowl beat the egg white until just stiff. Fold the egg white into the mousse mixture. Pour into the box. Chill for several hours or overnight, until set.

5 Meanwhile, make the caramel shards. Lightly oil a baking sheet. In a small pan over a low heat, dissolve the sugar in the water, swirling the pan gently. Increase the heat and boil the mixture for 4–5 minutes, until the sugar begins to turn a pale golden colour. Protecting your hand with an oven glove, immediately pour the mixture on to the oiled sheet. Tilt the sheet to distribute the caramel in an even layer. (Do not touch – caramel is dangerously hot.) Cool completely, then using a metal palette knife, lift the caramel off the baking sheet and break into pieces.

6 Make the topping. Combine the white chocolate and 120ml / 4fl oz / ½ cup of the cream in a small pan and melt over a low heat until smooth, stirring frequently. Strain into a medium bowl and cool to room temperature, stirring occasionally. In another bowl, beat the remaining cream with a hand-held electric mixer, until firm peaks form. Stir a spoonful of cream into the white chocolate mixture, then gently fold in the remaining whipped cream.

7 Using the foil as a guide, remove the mousse-filled box from the tin and peel the foil carefully from the sides, then the bottom. Slide the box gently on to a serving plate.

8 Spoon the chocolate-cream mixture into a piping bag fitted with a medium star tip. Pipe a decorative design of rosettes or shells over the surface of the set mousse. Decorate the cream-topped box with the mixed berries or cut up fruits and the caramel shards.

PUPPIES IN LOVE

SERVES 8–10

1 chocolate Swiss roll
115g/4oz yellow marzipan
60ml/4 tbsp Chocolate Buttercream
115g/4oz/1⅓ cups desiccated coconut
green, brown, pink and red food colourings
450g/1lb bought sugarpaste
icing sugar, for dusting
60ml/4 tbsp apricot jam, warmed and sieved

1 Cut the Swiss roll in half. Each half will form the body of one of the puppies. To make the faces, cut the marzipan in half and roll each portion into a ball, then into a squat cone shape. Use the buttercream to stick the faces on to the bodies.

2 Place the desiccated coconut in a bowl. Add a few drops of green food colouring and a few drops of water and stir until the coconut is flecked with green and white. Scatter it over a cake board, then position the two puppy shapes on the board.

3 Cut off about 25g/1oz of the sugarpaste and set aside, wrapped in clear film. Colour half the remaining icing brown and half pink. Cut off about 50g/2oz from each colour, wrap in clear film and set aside.

4 Lightly dust the work surface with icing sugar and roll out the larger portions of brown and pink paste into rectangles large enough to wrap each piece of Swiss roll. Cut each portion of paste in half widthways and trim the edges. Cover all four sections with clear film and set aside.

5 Roll out the reserved pieces of brown and white paste, then use a small round cutter to stamp out several circles. Gather up the paste trimmings and set aside, wrapped in clear film. Stick the white circles on to one of the brown rectangles, then the brown circles on to one of the pink rectangles, using a little water. Use a rolling pin to press them in slightly.

6 Use a sharp knife to slash all four paste rectangles along the two short edges. Brush each half of Swiss roll with jam, then lay the brown paste without spots over one body, and the pink paste without spots over the other. Place a little water on the back of each, then put the brown spotty paste over the brown dog and the pink spotty paste over the pink dog.

7 Roll half of the reserved trimmings, pink and brown, in your hands to make the tails. Stick them in place with a little jam. Make a fringe from the brown icing for the brown puppy, and tie a few strands of pink icing together with ribbon to make a fringe for the pink puppy. Stick them in place with a dab of water.

8 Use the remaining pieces of sugarpaste to shape eyes, a nose and a mouth for each puppy. Stick them on to the faces.

PORCUPINE

SERVES 15

1 quantity One-mix Chocolate Sponge Cake
1½ quantity Chocolate Buttercream
5–6 chocolate flake bars
60g / 2oz white marzipan
cream, black, green, red, brown food
colourings
9 cocktail sticks

1 Preheat the oven to 180°C / 350°F / Gas 4. Grease and line the bottoms of a 900ml / 1½ pint / 3¾ cup and a 600ml / 1 pint / 2½ cup pudding basin (deep bowl). Spoon the cake mixture into both basins (bowls) to two-thirds full. Bake in a preheated oven allowing 55 mins–1 hour for the larger basin (bowl) and 35–40 mins for the smaller basin (bowl). Turn out and allow to cool on a wire rack.

2 When they are completely cool, place both cakes on a surface so the widest ends are underneath. Take the smaller cake and, holding a sharp knife at an angle, slice off a piece from one side, cutting down towards the middle of the cake. Then make a corresponding cut on the other side to make a pointed nose shape at one end.

3 Place the larger cake on the cake board behind the smaller one. Cut one of the cut-off slices in half and position either side, between the larger and smaller cake, to fill in the side gaps. Place the other cut-off piece on top to fill in the top gap, securing all with a little buttercream.

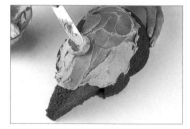

4 Spread the remaining buttercream over the cake. On the pointed face part, make markings with a cocktail stick.

5 Break or cut the flake bars into thin strips and stick at an angle into the buttercream over the body of the porcupine to represent spikes.

6 Reserve a small portion of marzipan. Divide the remainder into three and colour one portion black, one green and one cream. Colour a tiny portion of the reserved, white marzipan brown for the apple stems.

7 With the cream coloured marzipan, shape the ears and feet, using black and white make the eyes, and with the rest of the black shape the nose and the claws for the feet. With the green marzipan make the apples, painting on red markings with a fine paintbrush. Position the stems. Place everything except the apples in its proper place on the porcupine cake. Finally, place the apples on the board by the front of the porcupine.

APPLE TREE

SERVES 10–12

1 chocolate Swiss Roll
225g/8oz/1 cup Buttercream, tinted with
pale green food colouring
½ quantity Chocolate Buttercream
One-mix Chocolate Sponge Cake, baked in a
450g/1lb fluted round cake tin
225g/8oz marzipan
red and green food colouring
florist's tape and florist's wire, for the apples
green-coloured desiccated coconut (see Puppies
in Love, step 2)
tiny fresh flowers, to decorate (optional)

3 Twist the florist's tape around the florist's wire, then cut it into 7.5 cm/3 in lengths. Press the lengths of wire through most of the apples, bending the ends so the apples cannot fall off when hanging. Press the hanging apples into the tree, reserving the remaining apples.

4 Fill a piping bag with the remaining green buttercream. Pipe leaves all over the tree top. Scatter the green coconut around the base of the tree and pipe a few extra leaves. Add a few tiny fresh flowers for effect, if liked. Remove the wires from the cake before serving.

1 Stand the Swiss roll upright on a cake board, trimming it, if necessary. Anchor it on the board with a dab of the buttercream. Spread with chocolate buttercream, swirling the icing. Using about three-quarters of the green buttercream, thickly cover the round sponge cake. Draw the icing into peaks and swirls. Position the cake on top of the trunk to make the top of the tree.

2 Colour about 25g/1oz of the marzipan green. Colour the remainder red, then roll it into cherry-size apples. Roll the green marzipan into tiny sausage shapes and shape the stalks and leaves. Use a cocktail stick to make tiny holes in the tops of the apples, then insert a stalk and leaf into each.

HOT DESSERTS

CHOCOLATE CINNAMON CAKE WITH BANANA SAUCE

6 Fold a dollop of whites into the chocolate mixture to lighten it. Fold in the remaining whites in three batches, alternating with the sifted flour mixture.

7 Pour the mixture into the prepared tin. Bake for 40-50 minutes or until a skewer inserted in the centre comes out clean. Turn the cake out on to a wire rack. Preheat the grill.

8 Make the sauce. Slice the bananas into a shallow, flameproof dish. Stir in the brown sugar and lemon juice. Place under the grill for 8 minutes, stirring occasionally, until caramelized.
9 Mash the banana mixture until almost smooth. Tip into a bowl and stir in the cream and rum, if using. Slice the cake and serve with the sauce.

SERVES 6
25g/1oz plain chocolate, chopped into small pieces
115g/4oz/½ cup unsalted butter, at room temperature
15ml/1 tbsp instant coffee powder
5 eggs, separated
225g/8oz/1 cup granulated sugar
115g/4oz/1 cup plain flour
10ml/2 tsp ground cinnamon
FOR THE SAUCE
4 ripe bananas
45ml/3 tbsp soft light brown sugar
15ml/8oz/1 tbsp fresh lemon juice
175ml/6fl oz/¾ cup whipping cream
15ml/1 tbsp rum (optional)

1 Preheat oven to 180°C/350°F/Gas 4. Grease a 20 cm/8 in round cake tin.
2 Combine the chocolate and butter in the top of a double boiler or in a heatproof bowl set over a saucepan of simmering water. Stir until melted. Remove from the heat and stir in the coffee. Set aside.
3 Beat the egg yolks with the granulated sugar until thick and lemon-coloured. Add the chocolate mixture and beat on low speed until just blended.
4 Stir the flour and cinnamon together in a bowl.
5 In another bowl, beat the egg whites until they hold stiff peaks.

RICH CHOCOLATE AND COFFEE PUDDING

SERVES 6

75g / 3oz / ¾ cup plain flour
10ml / 2 tsp baking powder
pinch of salt
50g / 2oz / ¼ cup butter or margarine
25g / 1oz plain chocolate, chopped into
small pieces
115g / 4oz / ½ cup caster sugar
75ml / 3fl oz / 5 tbsp milk
1.5ml / ¼ tsp vanilla essence
whipped cream, for serving

FOR THE TOPPING

30ml / 2 tbsp instant coffee powder
325ml / 11fl oz / generous ½ pint hot water
90g / 3½oz / 7 tbsp soft dark brown sugar
65g / 2½oz / 5 tbsp caster sugar
30ml / 2 tbsp unsweetened cocoa powder

1 Preheat oven to 180°C/350°F/Gas 4. Grease a 23 cm/9 in square non-stick baking tin.

2 Sift the flour, baking powder and salt into a small bowl. Set aside.

3 Melt the butter or margarine, chocolate and caster sugar in a heatproof bowl set over a saucepan of simmering water, or in a double boiler, stirring occasionally. Remove the bowl from the heat.

4 Add the flour mixture and stir well. Stir in the milk and vanilla essence. Mix with a wooden spoon, then pour the mixture into the prepared baking tin.

5 Make the topping. Dissolve the coffee in the water in a bowl. Allow to cool.

6 Mix the brown sugar, caster sugar and cocoa powder in a bowl. Sprinkle the mixture over the pudding mixture.

7 Pour the coffee evenly over the surface. Bake for 40 minutes or until the pudding is risen and set on top. The coffee mixture will have formed a delicious creamy sauce underneath. Serve immediately with whipped cream.

HOT CHOCOLATE CAKE

MAKES 10–12 SLICES

*200g/7oz/1¾ cups self-raising wholemeal
flour*
25g/1oz/¼ cup cocoa powder
pinch of salt
175g/6oz/¾ cup soft margarine
175g/6oz/1 cup soft light brown sugar
few drops of vanilla essence
4 eggs
75g/3oz white chocolate, roughly chopped
chocolate leaves and curls, to decorate

FOR THE WHITE CHOCOLATE SAUCE

*75g/3oz white chocolate chopped into
small pieces*
150ml/¼ pint/⅔ cup single cream
30–45ml/2–3 tbsp milk

1 Preheat oven to 160°C/325°F/Gas 3.
Sift the flour, cocoa and salt into a bowl,
then tip in the bran remaining in the
sieve. Cream the margarine, sugar and
vanilla essence until fluffy, then gently
beat in 1 egg.

2 Gradually stir in the remaining eggs,
one at a time, alternately with the flour
mixture, to make a smooth mixture.

3 Stir in the white chocolate and spoon
into a 675–900g/1½–2lb loaf tin or a
18 cm/7 in greased cake tin. Bake for
30–40 minutes or until just firm to the
touch and shrinking away from the sides
of the tin.

4 To make the sauce, heat the chocolate
and cream very gently in a pan until the
chocolate is melted. Add the milk and stir
until cool. Spoon a little sauce on to each
plate and add a slice of cake. Decorate
with chocolate leaves and curls. Do this
just before you are ready to serve.

STEAMED CHOCOLATE AND FRUIT PUDDINGS WITH CHOCOLATE SYRUP

SERVES 4

115g / 4oz / ⅔ cup dark muscovado sugar
1 eating apple
75g / 3oz / ¾ cup cranberries, thawed if frozen
115g / 4oz / ½ cup soft margarine
2 eggs
115g / 4oz / ½ cup self-raising flour
45ml / 3 tbsp cocoa powder

FOR THE CHOCOLATE SYRUP

115g / 4oz plain chocolate, chopped
30ml / 2 tbsp clear honey
15ml / ½oz / 1 tbsp unsalted butter
2.5ml / ½ tsp vanilla essence

1 Prepare a steamer or half fill a saucepan with water and bring it to the boil. Grease four individual pudding basins and sprinkle each one with a little of the muscovado sugar to coat well all over.

2 Peel and core the apple. Dice it into a bowl, add the cranberries and mix well. Divide the fruit among the prepared pudding basins.

3 Place the remaining muscovado sugar in a mixing bowl. Add the margarine, eggs, flour and cocoa. Beat until combined and smooth.

4 Spoon the mixture into the basins and cover each with a double thickness of foil. Steam for about 45 minutes, topping up the boiling water as required, until the puddings are well risen and firm.

5 Make the syrup. Mix the chocolate, honey, butter and vanilla essence in a small saucepan. Heat gently, stirring until melted and smooth.

6 Run a knife around the edge of each pudding to loosen it, then turn out on to individual plates. Serve at once, with the chocolate syrup.

Chocolate, Date and Walnut Pudding

Serves 4

25g/1oz/¼ cup chopped walnuts
25g/1oz/2 tbsp chopped dates
2 eggs
5ml/1 tsp vanilla essence
30ml/2 tbsp golden caster sugar
45ml/3 tbsp plain wholemeal flour
15ml/1 tbsp cocoa powder
30ml/2 tbsp skimmed milk

1 Preheat oven to 180°C/350°F/Gas 4. Grease and base-line with greaseproof paper a 1.2 litre/2 pint/5 cup pudding basin. Spoon in the walnuts and dates.
2 Combine the egg yolks, vanilla essence and sugar in a heatproof bowl. Place over a pan of hot water.

3 Whisk the egg whites to soft peaks. Whisk the egg yolk mixture until it is thick and pale, then remove the bowl from the heat. Sift the flour and cocoa over the mixture and fold them in with a metal spoon. Stir in the milk, to soften the mixture, then fold in the egg whites.

4 Spoon the mixture over the walnuts and dates in the basin and bake for 40–45 minutes or until the pudding is well risen and firm to the touch. Run a knife around the pudding to loosen it from the basin, and then turn it out on to a plate and serve immediately.

MAGIC CHOCOLATE MUD PUDDING

SERVES 4

50g / 2oz / 4 tbsp butter, plus extra for greasing
90g / 3½oz / scant 1 cup self-raising flour
5ml / 1 tsp ground cinnamon
75ml / 5 tbsp cocoa powder
200g / 7oz / generous 1 cup light muscovado or demerara sugar
475ml / 16fl oz / 2 cups milk
crème fraîche, Greek-style yogurt or vanilla ice cream, to serve

1 Preheat oven to 180°C/350°F/Gas 4. Prepare the dish: use the extra butter to grease a 1.5 litre/2½ pint/6¼ cup ovenproof dish. Place the dish on a baking sheet and set aside.

2 Sift the flour and ground cinnamon into a bowl. Sift in 15ml/1 tbsp of the cocoa and mix well.

3 Place the butter in a saucepan. Add 115g/4oz/½ cup of the sugar and 150ml/¼ pint/⅔ cup of the milk. Heat gently without boiling, stirring from time to time, until the butter has melted and all the sugar has dissolved. Remove the pan from the heat.

4 Stir in the flour mixture, mixing evenly. Pour the mixture into the prepared dish and level the surface.

5 Mix the remaining sugar and cocoa in a bowl, then sprinkle over the pudding mixture.

6 Pour the remaining milk evenly over the pudding.

7 Bake for 45–50 minutes or until the sponge has risen to the top and is firm to the touch. Serve hot, with the crème fraîche, yogurt or ice cream.

CHOCOLATE CHIP AND BANANA PUDDING

SERVES 4

200g / 7oz / 1¾ cups self-raising flour
75g / 3oz / 6 tbsp unsalted butter or margarine
2 ripe bananas
75g / 3oz / 6 tbsp caster sugar
60ml / 4 tbsp milk
1 egg, beaten
60ml / 4 tbsp plain chocolate chips or chopped chocolate
Glossy Chocolate Sauce, to serve

1 Prepare a steamer or half fill a saucepan with water and bring it to the boil. Grease a 1 litre / 1¼ pint / 4 cup pudding basin. Sift the flour into a bowl and rub in the unsalted butter or margarine until the mixture resembles coarse breadcrumbs.

2 Mash the bananas in a bowl. Stir them into the flour and butter mixture, then add the caster sugar and mix well.

3 Whisk the milk with the egg in a jug or small bowl, then beat into the pudding mixture. Stir in the chocolate chips or chopped chocolate.

4 Spoon the mixture into the prepared basin, cover closely with a double thickness of foil, and steam for 2 hours, topping up the water as required.

5 Run a knife around the top of the pudding to loosen it, then turn it out on to a serving dish. Serve hot, with the sauce.

DARK CHOCOLATE RAVIOLI WITH WHITE CHOCOLATE AND CREAM CHEESE FILLING

SERVES 4

175g / 6oz / 1½ cups plain flour
25g / 1oz / ¼ cup cocoa powder
salt
30ml / 2 tbsp icing sugar
2 large eggs, beaten
15ml / 1 tbsp olive oil
single cream and grated chocolate, to serve

FOR THE FILLING

175g / 6oz white chocolate, chopped
350g / 12oz / 3 cups cream cheese
1 egg, plus 1 beaten egg to seal

1 Make the pasta. Sift the flour with the cocoa, salt and icing sugar on to a work surface. Make a well in the centre and pour the eggs and oil in. Mix together with your fingers. Knead until smooth. Alternatively, make the dough in a food processor, then knead by hand. Cover and rest for at least 30 minutes.

2 To make the filling, melt the white chocolate in a heatproof bowl placed over a pan of simmering water. Cool slightly. Beat the cream cheese in a bowl, then beat in the chocolate and eggs. Spoon into a piping bag fitted with a plain nozzle.

3 Cut the dough in half and wrap one portion in clear film. Roll the pasta out thinly to a rectangle on a lightly floured surface, or use a pasta machine. Cover with a clean damp dish towel and repeat with the remaining pasta.

4 Pipe small mounds (about 5ml / 1 tsp) of filling in even rows, spacing them at 4 cm / 1½ in intervals across one piece of the dough. Using a pastry brush, brush the spaces of dough between the mounds with beaten egg.

5 Using a rolling pin, lift the remaining sheet of pasta over the dough with the filling. Press down firmly between the pockets of filling, pushing out any trapped air. Cut the filled chocolate pasta into rounds with a serrated ravioli cutter or sharp knife. Transfer to a floured dish towel. Leave for 1 hour to dry out, ready for cooking.

6 Bring a frying pan of water to the boil and add the ravioli a few at a time, stirring to prevent them sticking together. (Adding a few drops of a bland oil to the water will help, too.) Simmer gently for 3–5 minutes, remove with a perforated spoon and serve with a generous splash of single cream and grated chocolate.

HOT MOCHA RUM SOUFFLES

SERVES 6

25g/1oz/2 tbsp unsalted butter, melted
65g/2½ oz/generous ½ cup cocoa powder
75g/3oz/6 tbsp caster sugar
60ml/4 tbsp strong black coffee
30ml/2 tbsp dark rum
6 egg whites
icing sugar, for dusting

1 Preheat oven to 190°C/375°F/Gas 5. Grease six 250ml/
8fl oz/1 cup soufflé dishes with melted butter.
2 Mix 15ml/1 tbsp of the cocoa powder with 15ml/1 tbsp of
the caster sugar in a bowl. Tip the mixture into each of the
dishes in turn, rotating them so that they are evenly coated.
3 Mix the remaining cocoa powder with the coffee and rum in a
medium bowl.
4 Whisk the egg whites in a clean, grease-free bowl until they
form firm peaks. Whisk in the remaining caster sugar. Stir a
generous spoonful of the whites into the cocoa mixture to
lighten it, then fold in the remaining whites.
5 Spoon the mixture into the prepared dishes, smoothing the
tops. Place on the hot baking sheet, and bake for 12–15 minutes
or until well risen. Serve immediately, dusted with icing sugar.

EASY CHOCOLATE AND ORANGE SOUFFLES

SERVES 4

600ml/1 pint/2½ cups milk
50g/2oz/generous ¼ cup semolina
50g/2oz/⅓ cup soft light brown sugar
grated rind of 1 orange
90ml/6 tbsp fresh orange juice
3 eggs, separated
65g/2½ oz plain chocolate, grated
icing sugar, for sprinkling
single cream, to serve

1 Preheat oven to 200°C/400°F/Gas 6. Butter a shallow
1.75 litre/3 pint/7½ cup ovenproof dish. Place a baking sheet
in the oven to heat up.
2 Pour the milk into a heavy-based saucepan, sprinkle over the
semolina and brown sugar, then heat, stirring the mixture all the
time, until boiling and thickened. Remove the pan from the
heat. Cool slightly, then beat in the orange rind and juice, egg
yolks and all but 15ml/1 tbsp of the grated chocolate.
3 In a clean, grease-free bowl, whisk the egg whites until stiff
but not dry, then lightly fold into the semolina mixture in three
batches. Spoon the mixture into the dish. Place the dish on the
baking sheet and bake for about 30 minutes, until just set in the
centre and risen. Sprinkle the top with the reserved chocolate
and dust with the icing sugar. Serve with cream.

CHOCOLATE AMARETTI PEACHES

SERVES 4

115g/4oz amaretti biscuits, crushed
50g/2oz plain chocolate, chopped
grated rind of ½ orange
15ml/1 tbsp clear honey
1.5ml/¼ tsp ground cinnamon
1 egg white, lightly beaten
4 firm ripe peaches
150ml/¼ pint/⅔ cup white wine
15ml/1 tbsp caster sugar
whipped cream, to serve

1 Preheat oven to 190°C/375°F/Gas 5. Mix together the crushed amaretti biscuits, chocolate, orange rind, honey and cinnamon in a bowl. Add the beaten egg white and mix to bind the mixture.

2 Halve and stone the peaches and fill the cavities with the chocolate mixture, mounding it up slightly.

3 Arrange the stuffed peaches in a lightly buttered, shallow ovenproof dish, which will just hold the peaches comfortably. Mix the wine and sugar in a jug.

4 Pour the wine mixture around the peaches. Bake for 30–40 minutes, until the peaches are tender when tested with a slim metal skewer and the filling is golden. Serve at once with a little of the cooking juices spooned over. Offer the whipped cream separately.

Peachy Chocolate Bake

Serves 6

*200g / 7oz plain dark chocolate, chopped into
small pieces
115g / 4oz / ½ cup unsalted butter
4 eggs, separated
115g / 4oz / ½ cup caster sugar
425g / 15oz can peach slices, drained
whipped cream or Greek-style yogurt,
to serve*

1 Preheat oven to 160°C/325°F/Gas 3.
Butter a wide ovenproof dish. Melt the
chocolate with the butter in a heatproof
bowl over barely simmering water.
Remove from the heat.

2 Whisk the egg yolks with the sugar
until thick and pale. In a clean, grease-
free bowl, whisk the whites until stiff.

3 Beat the chocolate into the egg yolk
mixture. Fold in the whites lightly.

4 Fold the peach slices into the mixture,
then tip into the prepared dish. Bake for
35–40 minutes or until risen and just
firm. Serve hot, with cream or Greek-
style yogurt if liked.

PUFFY PEARS

SERVES 4

225g / 8oz puff pastry, thawed if frozen
2 pears, peeled
2 squares plain chocolate, roughly chopped
15ml / 1 tbsp lemon juice
1 egg, beaten
15ml / 1 tbsp caster sugar

1 Roll the pastry into a 25 cm / 10 in square on a lightly floured surface. Trim the edges, then cut it into four equal smaller squares. Cover with clear film and set aside.
2 Remove the core from each pear half and pack the gap with the chopped chocolate. Place a pear half, cut-side down, on each piece of pastry and brush them with the lemon juice, to prevent them from going brown.
3 Preheat oven to 190°C / 375°F / Gas 5. Cut the pastry into a pear shape, by following the lines of the fruit, leaving a 2.5 cm / 1 in border. Use the trimmings to make leaves and brush the pastry border with the beaten egg.
4 Arrange the pastry and pears on a baking sheet. Make deep cuts in the pears, taking care not to cut right through the fruit, and sprinkle them with the sugar. Cook for 20–25 minutes, until lightly browned. Serve hot or cold.

VARIATION

Use apples instead of pears, if preferred. Cut the pastry into 10 cm / 4 in rounds. Slice 2 peeled and cored eating apples. Toss with a little lemon juice, drain and arrange on the pastry. Dot with 25g / 1oz / 2 tbsp butter and chopped milk chocolate. Bake as for Puffy Pears. While still hot, brush the apple slices with warmed redcurrant jelly.

PEARS IN CHOCOLATE FUDGE BLANKETS

SERVES 6

6 ripe eating pears
30ml / 2 tbsp lemon juice
75g / 3oz / 6 tbsp caster sugar
300ml / ½ pint / 1¼ cups water
1 cinnamon stick
FOR THE SAUCE
200ml / 7fl oz / scant 1 cup double cream
150g / 5oz / scant 1 cup light muscovado sugar
25g / 1oz / 2tbsp unsalted butter
25g / 1oz / 2 tbsp golden syrup
120ml / 4fl oz / ½ cup milk
200g / 7oz plain dark chocolate, broken into squares

1 Peel the pears thinly, leaving the stalks on. Scoop out the cores from the base. Brush the cut surfaces with lemon juice to prevent them from browning.
2 Place the sugar and water in a large saucepan. Heat gently until the sugar dissolves. Add the pears and cinnamon stick with any remaining lemon juice, and, if necessary, a little more water, so that the pears are almost covered.
3 Bring to the boil, then lower the heat, cover the pan and simmer the pears gently for 15–20 minutes or until they are just tender when pierced with a slim skewer.
4 Meanwhile, make the sauce. Place the cream, sugar, butter, golden syrup and milk in a heavy-based saucepan. Heat gently until the sugar has dissolved and the butter and syrup have melted, then bring to the boil. Boil, stirring constantly, for about 5 minutes or until the sauce is thick. Remove from the heat and stir in the chocolate, a few squares at a time, until melted.
5 Using a slotted spoon, transfer the poached pears to a dish. Keep hot. Boil the syrup rapidly to reduce to about 45–60ml / 3–4 tbsp. Remove the cinnamon stick and stir the syrup into the chocolate sauce. Serve poured over the pears in individual bowls.

PRUNE BEIGNETS IN CHOCOLATE ARMAGNAC SAUCE

SERVES 4

75g/3oz/¾ cup plain flour
45ml/3 tbsp ground almonds
45ml/3 tbsp oil or melted butter
1 egg white
60ml/4 tbsp water
oil, for deep frying
175g/6oz/1 cup ready-to-eat
stoned prunes
45ml/3 tbsp vanilla sugar
15ml/1 tbsp cocoa powder

FOR THE SAUCE

200g/7oz milk chocolate, chopped into
small pieces
120ml/4fl oz/½ cup crème fraîche
30ml/2 tbsp Armagnac or brandy

1 Start by making the sauce. Melt the chocolate, remove from the heat, stir in the crème fraîche until smooth, then add the Armagnac or brandy. Replace the bowl over the water, off the heat, so that the sauce stays warm.

2 Beat the flour, almonds, oil or butter and egg white in a bowl, then beat in enough of the water to make a smooth thick batter.

3 Heat the oil for deep frying to 180°C/350°F or until a cube of dried bread browns in 30–45 seconds. Dip the prunes into the batter and fry a few at a time until the beignets rise to the surface of the oil and are golden brown and crisp.

4 Remove each successive batch of beignets with a slotted spoon, drain on kitchen paper and keep hot. Mix the vanilla sugar and cocoa in a bowl or stout paper bag, add the drained beignets and toss well to coat.

5 Serve in individual bowls, with the chocolate sauce poured over the top of each serving.

COOK'S TIPS

Vanilla sugar is sold commercially in many European countries but is very easy to make. Simply store a vanilla pod in a jar of granulated or caster sugar for a few weeks, until the sugar has taken on the vanilla flavour. Shake the jar occasionally. Used in cakes, biscuits and puddings, vanilla sugar imparts a delicate flavour. If you do not have any vanilla sugar for tossing the beignets, use plain granulated or caster sugar and add a pinch of ground cinnamon, if you like.
Serve the beignets as soon as possible after cooking, as they do not keep well. Use stoned dates or dried apricots as a substitute for the prunes if you prefer.

CHOCOLATE, DATE AND ALMOND FILO COIL

SERVES 6

275g / 10oz pack filo pastry, thawed if frozen
50g / 2oz / 4 tbsp unsalted butter, melted
icing sugar, cocoa powder and ground
cinnamon, for dusting

FOR THE FILLING

75g / 3oz / 6 tbsp unsalted butter
115g / 4oz plain dark chocolate, chopped into
small pieces
115g / 4oz / 1 cup ground almonds
115g / 4oz / ⅔ cup chopped dates
75g / 3oz / ½ cup icing sugar
10ml / 2 tsp rosewater
2.5ml / ½ tsp ground cinnamon

1 Preheat oven to 180°C / 350°F / Gas 4. Grease a 22 cm / 8½ in round cake tin. Make the filling. Melt the butter with the chocolate, then stir in the other ingredients to make a paste. Leave to cool.

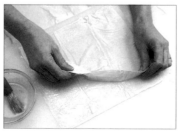

2 Lay one sheet of filo on a clean work surface. Brush it lightly with melted butter, then lay a second sheet on top and brush that with melted butter too.

3 Roll a handful of the chocolate almond mixture into a long sausage shape and place along one long edge of the layered filo. Roll the pastry tightly around the filling to make a roll. Keep the roll even, shaping it with your hands.

4 Place the roll in the tin, coiling it around against the sides. Make enough rolls to fill the tin and fit them in place.

5 Brush the coil with the remaining melted butter. Bake in the oven for 30–35 minutes, until the pastry is golden brown and crisp.

6 Remove the coil from the tin, and place it on a plate. Serve warm, dusted with icing sugar, cocoa and cinnamon.

CHOCOLATE ALMOND MERINGUE PIE

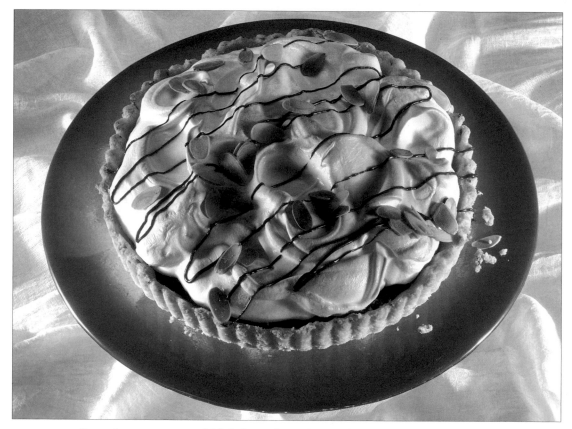

SERVES 6

175g/6oz/1½ cups plain flour
50g/2oz/½ cup ground rice
150g/5oz/⅔ cup unsalted butter
finely grated rind of 1 orange
1 egg yolk
flaked almonds and melted plain dark
chocolate, to decorate

FOR THE FILLING

150g/5oz plain dark chocolate, chopped into
small pieces
50g/2oz/4 tbsp unsalted butter, softened
75g/3oz/6 tbsp caster sugar
10ml/2 tsp cornflour
4 egg yolks
75g/3oz/¾ cup ground almonds

FOR THE MERINGUE

3 egg whites
150g/5oz/⅔ cup caster sugar

1 Sift the flour and ground rice into a bowl. Rub in the butter until the mixture resembles breadcrumbs. Stir in the orange rind. Add the egg yolks; bring the dough together. Roll out and use to line a 23 cm/9 in round flan tin. Chill.

2 Preheat oven to 190°C/375°F/Gas 5. Prick the pastry base, cover with grease-proof paper weighed down with baking beans and bake blind for 10 minutes.

3 Make the filling. Melt the chocolate, then cream the butter with the sugar in a bowl, and beat in the cornflour and egg yolks. Fold in the almonds, then the melted chocolate. Remove the paper and beans from the pastry case and add the filling. Bake for a further 10 minutes.

4 Make the meringue. Whisk the egg whites in a clean, grease-free bowl until stiff, then gradually whisk in about half the caster sugar. Fold in the remaining sugar with a metal spoon.

5 Spoon the meringue over the chocolate filling, lifting it up with the back of the spoon to form peaks. Reduce the oven temperature to 180°C/350°F/Gas 4 and bake the pie for 15–20 minutes or until the topping is pale gold. Serve warm, scattered with the almonds and drizzled with the melted chocolate.

CHOCOLATE PECAN PIE

SERVES 6

200g / 7oz / 1¾ cups plain flour
75ml / 5 tbsp caster sugar
90g / 3½oz / scant ½ cup unsalted butter,
softened
1 egg, beaten
finely grated rind of 1 orange

FOR THE FILLING

200g / 7oz / ¾ cup golden syrup
45ml / 3 tbsp soft light muscovado sugar
150g / 5oz plain chocolate, chopped into
small pieces
50g / 2oz / ¼ cup butter
3 eggs, beaten
5ml / 1 tsp vanilla essence
175g / 6oz / 1½ cups pecan nuts

1 Sift the flour into a bowl and stir in the sugar. Work in the butter evenly with your fingertips until combined.

2 Beat the egg and orange rind in a bowl, then stir into the mixture to make a firm dough. Add a little water if the mixture is too dry, and knead briefly.

3 Roll out the pastry on a lightly floured surface and use to line a deep, 20 cm/8 in loose-based flan tin. Chill for 30 minutes.

4 Preheat oven to 180°C/350°F/Gas 4. Make the filling. Melt the syrup, sugar, chocolate and butter in a small saucepan.

5 Remove the saucepan from the heat and beat in the eggs and vanilla essence. Sprinkle the pecan nuts into the pastry case and carefully pour over the chocolate mixture.

6 Place the tin on a baking sheet and bake the pie for 50–60 minutes or until the filling is set. Leave in the tin for 10 minutes, then remove the sides to serve. Serve plain, or with a little single cream.

BAKED CHOCOLATE AND RAISIN CHEESECAKE

SERVES 8–10

75g/3oz/¾ cup plain flour
45ml/3 tbsp cocoa powder
75g/3oz/½ cup semolina
50g/2oz/¼ cup caster sugar
115g/4oz/½ cup unsalted butter, softened

FOR THE FILLING

225g/8oz/1 cup cream cheese
120ml/4fl oz/½ cup natural yogurt
2 eggs, beaten
75g/3oz/6 tbsp caster sugar
finely grated rind of 1 lemon
75g/3oz/½ cup raisins
45ml/3 tbsp plain chocolate chips

FOR THE TOPPING

75g/3oz plain chocolate, chopped into
small pieces
30ml/2 tbsp golden syrup
40g/1½oz/3 tbsp butter

1 Preheat oven to 150°C/300°F/Gas 2. Sift the flour and cocoa into a mixing bowl and stir in the semolina and sugar. Using your fingertips, work the butter into the flour mixture until it makes a firm dough.

2 Press the dough into the base of a 22 cm/8½ in springform tin. Prick all over with a fork and bake in the oven for 15 minutes. Remove the tin but leave the oven on.

RUM AND RICOTTA CHEESECAKE

Use ricotta instead of cream cheese in the filling. Omit the lemon rind. Soak the raisins in 30ml/2 tbsp rum before stirring them in with the chocolate chips. Add 5ml/1 tsp rum to the topping.

3 Make the filling. In a large bowl, beat the cream cheese with the yogurt, eggs and sugar until evenly mixed. Stir in the lemon rind, raisins and chocolate chips.

4 Smooth the cream cheese mixture over the chocolate shortbread base and bake for a further 35–45 minutes or until the filling is pale gold and just set. Cool in the tin on a wire rack.

5 To make the topping, combine the chocolate, syrup and butter in a heatproof bowl. Set over a saucepan of simmering water and heat gently, stirring occasionally, until melted. Pour the topping over the cheesecake and leave until set. Remove the sides of the tin and carefully slide the chocolate and raisin cheesecake on to a serving plate. Serve sliced, with single cream, if you like.

CHOCOLATE AND ORANGE SCOTCH PANCAKES

SERVES 4

115g / 4oz / 1 cup self-raising flour
30ml / 2 tbsp cocoa powder
2 eggs
50g / 2oz plain chocolate, chopped into
small pieces
200ml / 7fl oz / scant 1 cup milk
finely grated rind of 1 orange
30ml / 2 tbsp orange juice
butter or oil, for frying
chocolate curls, to decorate

FOR THE SAUCE

2 large oranges
25g / 1oz / 2 tbsp unsalted butter
45ml / 3 tbsp light muscovado sugar
250ml / 8fl oz / 1 cup crème fraîche
30ml / 2 tbsp Grand Marnier or
Cointreau

1 Sift the flour and cocoa into a bowl and make a well in the centre. Add the eggs and beat well, gradually incorporating the surrounding dry ingredients to make a smooth mixture.

2 Mix the chocolate and milk in a saucepan. Heat gently until the chocolate has melted, then beat into the mixture until smooth and bubbly. Stir in the orange rind and juice to make a batter.

3 Heat a large heavy-based frying pan or griddle. Grease with a little butter or oil. Drop large spoonfuls of batter on to the hot surface, leaving room for spreading. Cook over a moderate heat. When the pancakes are lightly browned underneath and bubbly on top, flip over to cook the other side. Slide on to a plate and keep hot, then make more in the same way.

4 Make the sauce. Grate the rind of 1 orange into a bowl and set aside. Peel both oranges, taking care to remove all the pith, then slice the flesh fairly thinly.
5 Heat the butter and sugar in a wide, shallow pan over a low heat, stirring until the sugar dissolves. Stir in the crème fraîche and heat gently.
6 Add the pancakes and orange slices to the sauce, heat gently for 1–2 minutes, then spoon over the liqueur. Sprinkle with the reserved orange rind. Scatter over the chocolate curls and serve the pancakes at once.

CHOCOLATE CHIP BANANA PANCAKES

MAKES 16

2 ripe bananas
2 eggs
200ml / 7fl oz / scant 1 cup milk
150g / 5oz / 1¼ cups self-raising flour, sifted
25g / 1oz / ⅓ cup ground almonds
15ml / 1 tbsp caster sugar
pinch of salt
15ml / 1 tbsp plain chocolate chips
butter, for frying
50g / 2oz / ½ cup toasted flaked almonds

FOR THE TOPPING

150ml / ¼ pint / ⅔ cup double cream
15ml / 1 tbsp icing sugar

1 Mash the bananas in a bowl. Beat in the eggs and half the milk. Mix in the flour, ground almonds, sugar and salt. Add the remaining milk and the chocolate chips.

2 Stir the mixture well until it makes a thick batter. Heat a knob of butter in a non-stick frying pan. Spoon the pancake mixture into heaps, allowing room for them to spread. When the pancakes are lightly browned underneath, flip them over to cook the other side. Slide on to a plate and keep hot, then make more pancakes in the same way.

3 Make the topping. Pour the cream into a bowl. Add the icing sugar, to sweeten it slightly, and whip to soft peaks. Spoon the cream on to the pancakes and decorate with flaked almonds. Serve at once.

Chocolate Crepes with Plums and Port

2 Meanwhile, make the filling. Halve and stone the plums. Place them in a saucepan and add the sugar and water. Bring to the boil, then lower the heat, cover, and simmer for about 10 minutes or until the plums are tender. Stir in the port, taking care not to break up the plums, then simmer for a further 30 seconds. Remove from the heat and keep warm.

3 Have ready a sheet of non-stick baking paper. Heat a crêpe pan, grease it lightly with a little oil, then pour in just enough batter to cover the base of the pan, swirling to coat evenly. Cook until the crêpe has set, then flip it over to cook the other side. Slide the crêpe out on to the sheet of paper, then cook 9–11 more crêpes in the same way. It should not be necessary to add more oil to the pan, but if the crêpes start to stick, add a very light coating.

4 Make the sauce. Combine the chocolate and cream in a saucepan. Heat gently, stirring until smooth. Add the port and heat gently, stirring, for 1 minute.

5 Divide the plum filling among the crêpes, add a dollop of crème fraîche or Greek-style yogurt to each and roll them up carefully. Serve in individual bowls, with the chocolate sauce spooned over the top of each portion.

Serves 6

*50g/2oz plain chocolate, chopped into
small pieces*
200ml/7fl oz/scant 1 cup milk
120ml/4fl oz/½ cup single cream
30ml/2 tbsp cocoa powder
115g/4oz/1 cup plain flour
2 eggs
oil, for frying

For the Filling

500g/1¼lb red or golden plums
50g/2oz/¼ cup caster sugar
30ml/2 tbsp water
30ml/2 tbsp port
*150g/5oz/¾ cup crème fraîche or
Greek-style yogurt*

For the Sauce

*150g/5oz plain chocolate, chopped into
small pieces*
175ml/6fl oz/¾ cup double cream
15ml/1 tbsp port

1 Make the crêpe batter. Place the chocolate in a saucepan with the milk. Heat gently, stirring occasionally, until the chocolate has dissolved. Pour the chocolate and milk mixture into a blender or food processor and add the cream, cocoa, flour and eggs. (If the blender or food processor is a small one, it may be necessary to do this in batches.) Process until smooth, then tip into a jug and chill for 30 minutes.

RICH CHOCOLATE BRIOCHE BAKE

SERVES 4

40g / 1½oz / 3 tbsp unsalted butter, plus extra for greasing
200g / 7oz plain chocolate, chopped into small pieces
60ml / 4 tbsp bitter marmalade
4 individual brioches, cut into halves, or 1 large brioche loaf, cut into thick slices
3 eggs
300ml / ½ pint / 1¼ cups milk
300ml / ½ pint / 1¼ cups single cream
30ml / 2 tbsp demerara sugar

1 Preheat oven to 180°C/350°F/Gas 4. Using the extra butter, lightly grease a shallow ovenproof dish.

2 Melt the chocolate with the marmalade and butter in a heatproof bowl over just simmering water, stirring the mixture occasionally, until smooth.

3 Spread the melted chocolate mixture over the brioche slices. Arrange them in the dish so that the slices overlap.

4 Beat the eggs in a large bowl, then add the milk and cream and mix well. Transfer to a jug and pour evenly over the slices. Sprinkle with the demerara sugar and bake for 40–50 minutes, until the custard has set lightly and the brioche slices are golden brown. Serve hot.

Chocolate Souffle Crepes

Makes 12 crepes

75g/3oz/¾ cup plain flour
15ml/1 tbsp cocoa powder
5ml/1 tsp caster sugar
pinch of salt
5ml/1 tsp ground cinnamon
2 eggs
175ml/6fl oz/¾ cup milk
5ml/1 tsp vanilla essence
50g/2oz/4 tbsp unsalted butter,
melted
raspberries, pineapple and mint sprigs,
to decorate

For the Pineapple Syrup

½ medium pineapple, peeled, cored and
finely chopped
120ml/4fl oz/½ cup water
30ml/2 tbsp natural maple syrup
5ml/1 tsp cornflour
½ cinnamon stick
30ml/2 tbsp rum

For the Souffle Filling

250g/9oz bittersweet chocolate, chopped into
small pieces
75ml/3fl oz/⅓ cup double cream
3 eggs, separated
25g/1oz/2 tbsp caster sugar

1 Prepare the syrup. In a saucepan over a medium heat, bring the pineapple, water, maple syrup, cornflour and cinnamon stick to the boil. Simmer for 2–3 minutes, until the sauce thickens, whisking frequently. Remove from the heat and discard the cinnamon. Pour into a bowl, and stir in the rum. Cool, then chill.

Cook's Tip

You might be able to find ready-made crêpes in the shops, which will save time.

2 Prepare the crêpes. Sift the flour, cocoa, sugar, salt and cinnamon into a bowl. Stir, then make a well in the centre. In a bowl, beat the eggs, milk and vanilla. Gradually add to the well in the flour mixture, whisking in flour from the side of the bowl to form a smooth batter. Stir in half the melted butter and pour into a jug. Allow to stand for 1 hour.

3 Heat an 18–20 cm/7–8 in crêpe pan. Brush with butter. Stir the batter. Pour 45ml/3 tbsp batter into the pan; swirl the pan to cover the bottom. Cook over a medium-high heat for 1–2 minutes until the bottom is golden. Turn over and cook for 30–45 seconds, then turn on to a plate. Stack between sheets of non-stick baking paper and set aside.

4 Prepare the filling. In a saucepan over a medium heat, melt the chocolate and cream until smooth, stirring frequently.

5 In a bowl, with a hand-held electric mixer, beat the yolks with half the sugar for 3–5 minutes, until light and creamy. Gradually beat in the chocolate mixture. Allow to cool. In a separate bowl with cleaned beaters, beat the egg whites until soft peaks form. Gradually beat in the remaining sugar until stiff peaks form. Beat a large spoonful of whites in to the chocolate mixture to lighten it, then fold in the remaining whites.

6 Preheat oven to 200°C/400°F/Gas 6. Lay a crêpe on a plate, bottom side up. Spoon a little soufflé mixture on to the crêpe, spreading it to the edge. Fold the bottom half over the soufflé mixture, then fold in half again to form a filled triangle. Place on a buttered baking sheet. Repeat with the remaining crêpes. Brush the tops with melted butter and bake for 15–20 minutes, until the filling has souffléd. Decorate with raspberries, pineapple pieces and mint and serve with the syrup.

Variation

For a simpler version of the crêpes, just serve with a spoonful of maple syrup rather than making the pineapple syrup.

CHOCOLATE ORANGE MARQUISE

SERVES 6–8

200g / 7oz / scant 1 cup caster sugar
60ml / 4 tbsp freshly squeezed orange juice
350g / 12oz plain dark chocolate, chopped
into small pieces
225g / 8oz / 1 cup unsalted butter, cubed
5 eggs
finely grated rind of 1 orange
45ml / 3 tbsp plain flour
icing sugar and finely pared strips of orange
rind, to decorate

<u>1</u> Preheat oven to 180°C / 350°F / Gas 4.
Grease a 23 cm / 9 in round cake tin with
a depth of 6 cm / 2½ in. Line the base
with non-stick baking paper.
<u>2</u> Place 115g / 4oz / ½ cup of the sugar in a
saucepan. Add the orange juice and stir
over a gentle heat until the sugar has
dissolved completely.

<u>3</u> Remove from the heat and stir in the
chocolate until melted, then add the
butter, cube by cube, until thoroughly
melted and evenly mixed.
<u>4</u> Whisk the eggs with the remaining
sugar in a large bowl until pale and very
thick. Add the orange rind. Then, using a
metal spoon, fold the chocolate mixture
lightly and evenly into the egg mixture.
Sift the flour over the top and fold in.

<u>5</u> Scrape the mixture into the prepared
tin. Place in a roasting pan, transfer to
the oven, then carefully pour hot water
into the roasting pan to come about
halfway up the sides of the cake tin.
<u>6</u> Bake for about 1 hour or until the cake
is firm to the touch. Remove the cake tin
from the water bath and place on a wire
rack to cool for 15–20 minutes. To turn
out, invert the cake on a baking sheet,
place a serving plate upside down on top,
then turn plate and baking sheet over
together so that the cake is transferred to
the plate.
<u>7</u> Dust with icing sugar, decorate with
strips of pared orange rind and serve still
warm. This cake is wonderfully rich and
moist and really doesn't need an
accompaniment, but you could offer
single cream, if you wish.

Hot Chocolate Zabaglione

SERVES 6
6 egg yolks
150g / 5oz / ⅔ cup caster sugar
45ml / 3 tbsp cocoa powder
200ml / 7fl oz / scant 1 cup Marsala
cocoa powder or icing sugar, for dusting

1 Half fill a medium saucepan with water and bring to simmering point. Select a heatproof bowl that will fit over the pan, place the egg yolks and sugar in it, and whisk until the mixture is pale and all the sugar has dissolved.

CHOCOLATE FONDUE
SERVES 4-6

225g / 8oz plain chocolate, chopped into small pieces
300ml / ½ pint / 1¼ cups double cream
30ml / 2 tbsp Grand Marnier (optional)
25g / 1oz / 2 tbsp butter, diced
cherries, strawberries, sliced bananas,
mandarin segments and cubes of sponge cake, for dipping

1 Combine the chocolate, cream and Grand Marnier (if using) in a fondue pan or small heavy-based saucepan. Heat gently until melted, stirring frequently.
2 Arrange the fruit and cake for dipping on a large platter. Stir the butter into the fondue until melted. Place the fondue pot or pan over a lighted spirit burner.
3 Guests spear the items of their choice on fondue forks and swirl them in the dip until coated. Anyone who loses his or her dipper pays a forfeit.

2 Add the cocoa and Marsala, then place the bowl over the simmering water. Whisk with a hand-held electric mixer until the mixture is thick and foamy.

3 Pour quickly into tall heatproof glasses, dust lightly with cocoa or icing sugar and serve immediately with chocolate cinnamon tuiles or amaretti biscuits.

CHOCOLATE TARTS, PIES AND CHEESECAKES

GREEK CHOCOLATE MOUSSE TARTLETS

SERVES 6

1 quantity Chocolate Shortcrust Pastry
chocolate shapes, to decorate

FOR THE FILLING

200g/7oz white chocolate, chopped into
small pieces
120ml/4fl oz/½ cup milk
10ml/2 tsp powdered gelatine
30ml/2 tbsp caster sugar
5ml/1 tsp vanilla essence
2 eggs, separated
250ml/8fl oz/1 cup Greek-style yogurt

1 Preheat oven to 190°C/375°F/Gas 5. Roll out the pastry and line six deep 10 cm/4 in loose-based flan tins.

2 Prick the pastry with a fork, cover with greaseproof paper weighed down with baking beans and bake blind for 10 minutes. Remove the baking beans and paper, return to the oven and bake a further 15 minutes. Cool in the tins.

3 Make the filling. Melt the chocolate. Pour the milk into a saucepan, sprinkle over the powdered gelatine and heat gently, stirring until the gelatine has dissolved completely. Remove from the heat and stir in the chocolate.

4 Whisk the sugar, vanilla essence and egg yolks in a large bowl, then beat in the chocolate mixture. Beat in the yogurt until evenly mixed.

5 Whisk the egg whites in a clean, grease-free bowl until stiff, then fold into the mixture. Divide among the pastry cases and chill for 2–3 hours, until set. Decorate with chocolate shapes, and dust with icing sugar if wished.

CHOCOLATE AND PINE NUT TART

SERVES 8

200g/7oz/1¾ cups plain flour
50g/2oz/¼ cup caster sugar
pinch of salt
grated rind of ½ orange
115g/4oz/½ cup unsalted butter, cut into
small pieces
3 egg yolks, lightly beaten
15–30 ml/1–2 tbsp iced water

FOR THE FILLING

2 eggs
45ml/3 tbsp caster sugar
grated rind of 1 orange
15ml/1 tbsp orange-flavoured liqueur
250ml/8fl oz/1 cup whipping cream
115g/4oz plain chocolate, chopped into
small pieces
75g/3oz/1 cup pine nuts, toasted

FOR THE DECORATION

1 orange
50g/2oz/¼ cup granulated sugar
120ml/4fl oz/½ cup water

1 In a food processor fitted with a metal blade, process the flour, sugar, salt and orange rind. Add the butter and process for 20–30 seconds, until the mixture looks like coarse crumbs. Add the yolks and pulse until the dough begins to stick together. If the dough appears dry, add the iced water, little by little, until the mixture just holds together. Knead the dough gently, then wrap in clear film. Chill for 2–3 hours or overnight.

2 Lightly grease a 23 cm/9 in tart tin with a removable base. Let the dough soften briefly, then roll out on a well-floured surface into a 28 cm/11 in round. Ease the dough into the tin and press the overhang down slightly with floured fingers, to make the top edge thicker.

3 Roll a rolling pin over the top edge to cut off excess dough. Press the thicker top edge against the sides of the tin to form a raised rim. Prick the base with a fork. Chill for 1 hour. Preheat oven to 200°C/400°F/Gas 6. Line the tart shell with greaseproof paper; fill with baking beans and bake blind for 5 minutes. Lift out the foil and beans, then return the tart shell to the oven and bake for 5 minutes more, until set. Cool in the tin on a wire rack. Lower the oven temperature to 180°C/350°F/Gas 4.

4 Prepare the filling. Beat the eggs, sugar, orange rind and liqueur in a bowl. Stir in the cream. Sprinkle the chocolate evenly over the base of the tart shell, then sprinkle with the pine nuts.

5 Gently pour the filling into the tart shell. Bake for 20–30 minutes, until the pastry is golden and the custard is set. Cool slightly in the tin on a wire rack.

6 Prepare the decoration. Peel the orange thinly, avoiding the pith, then cut the rind into thin strips. Dissolve the sugar in the water in a pan over a medium heat, then add the orange rind strips. Boil for about 5 minutes, until the syrup is thick and has begun to caramelize. Off the heat, stir in about 15ml/1 tbsp cold water to prevent the mixture from darkening further.

7 Brush the orange syrup over the tart and decorate with the caramelized strips. Remove the side of the tin and slide the tart on to a plate. Serve warm.

CHOCOLATE TRUFFLE TART

SERVES 12

115g / 4oz / 1 cup plain flour
30g / 1¼oz / ⅓ cup cocoa powder
50g / 2oz / ¼ cup caster sugar
2.5ml / ½ tsp salt
*115g / 4oz / ½ cup unsalted butter, cut
into pieces*
1 egg yolk
15–30ml / 1–2 tbsp iced water
*25g / 1oz fine quality white or milk chocolate,
melted*
whipped cream for serving (optional)
FOR THE TRUFFLE FILLING
350ml / 12fl oz / 1½ cups double cream
*350g / 12oz couverture or fine quality
bittersweet chocolate, chopped*
*50g / 2oz / 4 tbsp unsalted butter, cut into
small pieces*
30ml / 2 tbsp brandy or liqueur

1 Prepare the pastry. Sift the flour and cocoa into a bowl. In a food processor fitted with a metal blade, process the flour mixture with the sugar and salt. Add the butter and process for 15–20 seconds, until the mixture resembles coarse breadcrumbs.

2 In a bowl, lightly beat the yolk with the iced water. Add to the flour mixture and pulse until the dough begins to stick together. Turn out the dough on to a sheet of clear film. Use the film to help shape the dough into a flat disc. Wrap tightly. Chill for 1–2 hours, until firm.

3 Lightly grease a 23 cm/9 in tart tin with a removable base. Let the dough soften briefly, then roll it out between sheets of waxed paper or clear film to a 28 cm/11 in round, about 5 mm/¼ in thick. Peel off the top sheet and invert the dough into a tart tin. Remove the bottom sheet. Ease the dough into the tin. Prick with a fork. Chill for 1 hour.

4 Preheat oven to 180°C/350°F/Gas 4. Line the tart with foil or non-stick baking paper; fill with baking beans. Bake blind for 5–7 minutes. Lift out the foil with the beans, return the pastry case to the oven and bake for a further 5–7 minutes, until the pastry is just set. Cool completely in the tin on a rack.

5 Prepare the filling. In a medium pan over a medium heat, bring the cream to the boil. Remove the pan from the heat and stir in the chocolate until melted and smooth. Stir in the butter and brandy or liqueur. Strain into the prepared tart shell, tilting the tin slightly to level the surface. Do not touch the surface of the filling or it will spoil the glossy finish.

6 Spoon the melted chocolate into a paper piping bag and cut off the tip. Drop rounds of chocolate over the surface of the tart and use a skewer or toothpick to draw a point gently through the chocolate to produce a marbled effect. Chill for 2–3 hours, until set. To serve, allow the tart to soften slightly at room temperature.

CHOCOLATE TIRAMISU TART

SERVES 12–16

115g/4oz/½ cup unsalted butter
15ml/1 tbsp coffee-flavoured liqueur or water
175g/6oz/1½ cups plain flour
25g/1oz/¼ cup cocoa powder
25g/1oz/¼ cup icing sugar
pinch of salt
2.5ml/½ tsp vanilla essence
cocoa powder, for dusting

FOR THE CHOCOLATE LAYER

350ml/12fl oz/1½ cups double cream
15ml/1 tbsp golden syrup
115g/4oz bittersweet chocolate, chopped into
small pieces
25g/1oz/2 tbsp unsalted butter, cut into
small pieces
30ml/2 tbsp coffee-flavoured liqueur

FOR THE FILLING

250ml/8fl oz/1 cup whipping cream
350g/12oz/1½ cups mascarpone cheese, at
room temperature
45ml/3 tbsp icing sugar
45ml/3 tbsp cold espresso or strong black
coffee
45ml/3 tbsp coffee-flavoured liqueur
90g/3½oz plain chocolate, grated

1 Make the pastry. Lightly grease a 23 cm/9 in springform tin. In a saucepan, heat the butter and liqueur or water until the butter has melted. Sift the flour, cocoa, icing sugar and salt into a bowl. Remove the butter mixture from the heat, stir in the vanilla essence and gradually stir into the flour mixture until a soft dough forms.

2 Knead lightly until smooth. Press on to the base and up the sides of the tin to within 2 cm/¾ in of the top. Prick the dough. Chill for 40 minutes. Preheat oven to 190°C/375°F/Gas 5. Bake the pastry case for 8–10 minutes. If the pastry puffs up, prick it with a fork and bake for 2–3 minutes more until set. Cool in the tin on a rack.

3 Prepare the chocolate layer. Bring the cream and syrup to a boil in a pan over a medium heat. Off the heat, add the chocolate, stirring until melted. Beat in the butter and liqueur and pour into the pastry case. Cool completely, then chill.

4 Prepare the filling. Using a hand-held electric mixer, whip the cream in a bowl until soft peaks form. In another bowl, beat the cheese until soft, then beat in the icing sugar until smooth and creamy. Gradually beat in the cold coffee and liqueur; gently fold in the whipped cream and chocolate. Spoon the filling into the pastry case, on top of the chocolate layer. Level the surface. Chill until ready to serve.

5 To serve, run a sharp knife around the side of the tin to loosen the tart shell. Remove the side of the tin and slide the tart on to a plate. Sift a layer of cocoa powder over the tart to decorate, or pipe rosettes of whipped cream around the rim and top each with a chocolate-coated coffee bean. Chocolate Tiramisu Tart is very rich, so serve it in small wedges, with cups of espresso.

WHITE CHOCOLATE AND MANGO CREAM TART

SERVES 8

175g/6oz/1½ cups plain flour
75g/3oz/1 cup sweetened, desiccated coconut
115g/4oz/½ cup butter, softened
30ml/2 tbsp caster sugar
2 egg yolks
2.5ml/½ tsp almond essence
600ml/1 pint/2½ cups whipping cream
1 large ripe mango
50g/2oz/½ cup toasted flaked almonds,
to decorate

FOR THE WHITE CHOCOLATE
CUSTARD FILLING

150g/5oz fine quality white chocolate,
chopped into small pieces
120ml/4fl oz/½ cup whipping cream or
double cream
75ml/5 tbsp cornflour
15ml/1 tbsp plain flour
50g/2oz/¼ cup granulated sugar
350ml/12fl oz/1½ cups milk
5 egg yolks

1 Using a hand-held electric mixer at low speed, beat the flour, coconut, butter, sugar, egg yolks and almond essence in a deep bowl until the mixture forms a soft dough. Lightly grease a 23 cm/9 in tart tin with a removable base. Press the pastry on to the bottom and sides. Prick the pastry case with a fork. Chill the case for 30 minutes.

COOK'S TIP

Choose a mango that is a rich yellow in colour, with a pink or red blush. It should just yield to the touch, but should not be too soft. Peel it carefully, then cut it in half around the stone. Cut each piece in half again, then in neat slices.

2 Preheat oven to 180°C/350°F/Gas 4. Line the pastry case with non-stick baking paper; fill with baking beans and bake blind for 10 minutes. Remove the paper and beans and bake for a further 5–7 minutes, until golden. Cool the cooked pastry in the tin on a wire rack.

3 Prepare the custard filling. In a small saucepan over a low heat, melt the white chocolate with the cream, stirring until smooth. Set aside. Combine the cornflour, plain flour and sugar in a medium saucepan. Stir in the milk gradually. Place over a medium heat and cook, stirring constantly, until the mixture has thickened.

4 Beat the egg yolks in a small bowl. Slowly add about 250ml/8fl oz/1 cup of the hot milk mixture, stirring constantly. Return the yolk mixture to the rest of the sauce in the pan, stirring constantly.

5 Bring the custard filling to a gentle boil, stirring constantly until thickened. Stir in the melted white chocolate until well blended. Cool to room temperature, stirring frequently to prevent a skin from forming on the surface. Beat the whipping cream in a medium-sized bowl until soft peaks form. Fold approximately 120ml/4fl oz/½ cup of the whipped cream into the white chocolate custard and spoon half the custard into the base. Peel and slice the mango thinly.

6 With the aid of a slim metal spatula or palette knife, arrange the mango slices over the custard in concentric circles, starting at the rim and then filling in the centre. Try to avoid moving the mango slices once in position. Carefully pour the remaining custard over the mango slices, smoothing the surface evenly. Remove the side of the tin and slide the tart carefully on to a serving plate.

7 Spoon the remaining flavoured cream into a large piping bag fitted with a medium star tip. Pipe the cream in a scroll pattern in parallel rows on top of the tart, keeping the rows about 1 cm/½ in apart. Carefully sprinkle the toasted flaked almonds between the rows. Serve the tart chilled.

CHOCOLATE PECAN TORTE

SERVES 16

200g / 7oz bittersweet or plain chocolate,
chopped into small pieces
150g / 5oz / 10 tbsp unsalted butter,
cut into pieces
4 eggs
90g / 3½oz / scant ½ cup caster sugar
10ml / 2 tsp vanilla essence
115g / 4oz / 1 cup ground pecan nuts
10ml / 2 tsp ground cinnamon
24 toasted pecan halves, to decorate

FOR THE CHOCOLATE HONEY GLAZE
115g / 4oz bittersweet or plain chocolate,
chopped into small pieces
50g / 2oz / ¼ cup unsalted butter,
cut into pieces
30ml / 2 tbsp clear honey
pinch of ground cinnamon

1 Preheat oven to 180°C / 350°F / Gas 4. Grease a 20 x 5 cm / 8 x 2 in springform tin; line with non-stick baking paper. Wrap the tin in foil to prevent water from seeping in. Melt the chocolate and butter, stirring until smooth. Beat the eggs, sugar and vanilla essence in a mixing bowl until the mixture is frothy. Stir in the melted chocolate, ground nuts and cinnamon. Pour into the tin.

2 Place the tin in a roasting pan. Pour in boiling water to come 2 cm / ¾ in up the side of the springform tin. Bake for 25–30 minutes, until the edge of the cake is set but the centre is still soft. Remove the tin from the water bath and lift off the foil. Cool the cake in the tin on a wire rack.

3 Prepare the glaze. Heat all the ingredients in a small pan until melted, stirring until smooth. Off the heat, half-dip the toasted pecan halves in the glaze and place on a baking sheet lined with non-stick baking paper until set.

4 Remove the cake from the tin, place it on the rack and pour the remaining glaze over. Decorate the outside of the torte with the chocolate-dipped pecans and leave to set. Transfer to a plate when ready to serve, and slice in thin wedges.

CHOCOLATE LEMON TART

SERVES 8–10

175g / 6oz / 1½ cups plain flour
10ml / 2 tsp cocoa powder
25g / 1oz / ¼ cup icing sugar
2.5ml / ½ tsp salt
115g / 4oz / ½ cup unsalted butter or margarine
15ml / 1 tbsp water

FOR THE FILLING

225g / 8oz / 1 cup caster sugar
6 eggs
grated rind of 2 lemons
175ml / 6fl oz / ¾ cup fresh lemon juice
175ml / 6fl oz / ¾ cup double or whipping cream
chocolate curls, for decorating

1 Grease a 25 cm / 10 in flan tin. Sift the flour, cocoa, icing sugar and salt into a bowl. Set aside. Melt the butter or margarine and water in a saucepan over a low heat. Pour over the flour mixture and stir until the flour has absorbed all the liquid and the dough is smooth.

2 Press the dough evenly over the base and side of the prepared tin. Chill the pastry case.

3 Preheat oven to 190°C / 375°F / Gas 5, and place a baking sheet inside to heat up. Prepare the filling. Whisk the sugar and eggs in a bowl until the sugar has dissolved. Add the lemon rind and juice and mix well. Stir in the cream. Taste and add more lemon juice or sugar if needed, for a sweet taste with a touch of tartness.

4 Pour the filling into the tart shell and place the tin on the hot baking sheet. Bake for 20–25 minutes or until the filling is set. Cool on a rack, then decorate with the chocolate curls.

CHOCOLATE APRICOT LINZER TART

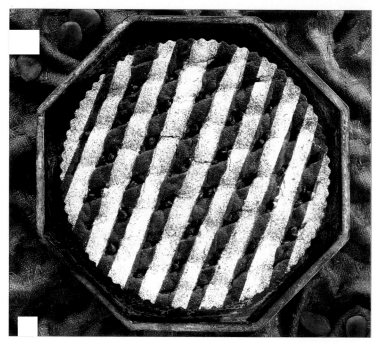

3 Turn the dough on to a flour-dusted work surface and knead lightly until just blended. Divide the dough in half. With floured fingers, press half the dough on to the bottom and sides of the tin. Prick the base of the dough with a fork. Chill for 20 minutes. Roll out the rest of the dough between two sheets of non-stick baking paper or clear film to a 28 cm/ 11 in round; slide on to a baking sheet and chill for 30 minutes.

SERVES 10–12

50g/2oz/½ cup whole blanched almonds
115g/4oz/½ cup caster sugar
175g/6oz/1½ cups plain flour
30ml/2 tbsp cocoa powder
5ml/1 tsp ground cinnamon
2.5ml/½ tsp salt
5ml/1 tsp grated orange rind
225g/8oz/1 cup unsalted butter, cut into
small pieces
45–60ml/3–4 tbsp iced water
75g/3oz/½ cup plain mini chocolate chips
icing sugar, for dusting

FOR THE APRICOT FILLING

350g/12oz/1½ cups dried apricots
120ml/4fl oz/½ cup orange juice
175ml/6fl oz/¾ cup water
45ml/3 tbsp granulated sugar
50g/2oz/2 tbsp apricot jam
2.5ml/½ tsp almond essence

1 Prepare the filling. In a pan, simmer the apricots, orange juice and water until the liquid is absorbed, stirring often. Stir in the remaining ingredients. Strain into a bowl, cool, cover and chill.

2 Prepare the pastry. Lightly grease a 28 cm/11 in tart tin with removable base. In a food processor with a metal blade, process the almonds with half the sugar until finely ground. Into a bowl, sift the flour, cocoa, cinnamon and salt. Stir in the remaining caster sugar. Add to the food processor and process to blend. Add the rind and butter and process for 15–20 seconds until the mixture resembles coarse crumbs. Add about 30ml/2 tbsp iced water and pulse until the dough just begins to stick together. If the dough appears too dry, add 15–30ml/1–2 tbsp more iced water, little by little, until the dough just holds together.

4 Preheat oven to 180°C/350°F/Gas 4. Spread the filling on to the base of the pastry-lined tin. Sprinkle with chocolate chips. Set aside. Slide the dough round on to a lightly floured surface and cut into 1 cm/½ in strips; allow the strips to soften for 3–5 minutes so that they will be easier to work with.

5 Place half the dough strips over the filling, spacing them about 1 cm/½ in apart. Place the rest of the strips at an angle on top, as shown. With your fingertips, press down on both sides of each crossing to stress the lattice effect. Press the ends on to the side of the tart, cutting off any excess. Bake for 35–40 minutes, until the strips are golden and the filling bubbles. Cool on a rack. To serve, remove the side of the tin, then dust icing sugar over the top pastry strips.

RICH CHOCOLATE BERRY TART WITH BLACKBERRY SAUCE

SERVES 10

115g/4oz/½ cup unsalted butter, softened
115g/4oz/½ cup caster sugar
2.5ml/½ tsp salt
15ml/1 tbsp vanilla essence
50g/2oz/½ cup cocoa powder
175g/6oz/1½ cups plain flour
450g/1 lb fresh berries, for topping

FOR THE CHOCOLATE GANACHE FILLING

475ml/16fl oz/2 cups double cream
150g/5oz/½ cup blackberry or raspberry jelly
225g/8oz bittersweet chocolate, chopped into small pieces
25g/1oz/2 tbsp unsalted butter, cut into small pieces

FOR THE BLACKBERRY SAUCE

225g/8oz fresh or frozen blackberries or raspberries
15ml/1 tbsp lemon juice
30ml/2 tbsp caster sugar
30ml/2 tbsp blackberry- or raspberry-flavoured liqueur

1 In a food processor fitted with a metal blade, process the butter, sugar, salt and vanilla essence until creamy. Add the cocoa and process for 1 minute. Add the flour all at once, then pulse for 10–15 seconds. Place a piece of clear film on the work surface. Turn the dough out on to this, shape into a flat disc and wrap tightly. Chill for 1 hour.

2 Lightly grease a 23 cm/9 in flan tin with a removable base. Let the dough soften for 5–10 minutes, then roll out between two sheets of clear film to a 28 cm/11 in round, about 5 mm/¼ in thick. Peel off the top sheet of clear film and invert the dough into the prepared tin. Ease the dough into the tin, and when in position lift off the clear film.

3 With floured fingers, press the dough on to the base and sides of the tin, then roll the rolling pin over the edge to cut off any excess dough. Prick the base of the dough with a fork. Chill for 1 hour. Preheat oven to 180°C/350°F/Gas 4. Line the pastry case with non-stick baking paper; fill with baking beans and bake blind for 10 minutes. Remove the paper and beans and bake for 5 minutes more, until the pastry is just set. Cool in the tin on a wire rack.

4 Prepare the ganache filling. In a medium saucepan over a medium heat, bring the cream and berry jelly to the boil. Remove from the heat and add the chocolate all at once, stirring until melted and smooth. Stir in the butter until melted, then strain into the cooled tart shell, smoothing the top. Cool the tart completely.

5 Prepare the sauce. Process the berries, lemon juice and sugar in a food processor until smooth. Strain into a small bowl and add the liqueur.

6 To serve, remove the tart from the tin. Place on a serving plate and arrange the berries on top of the tart. With a pastry brush, brush the berries with a little of the blackberry sauce to glaze lightly. Serve the remaining sauce separately.

HAZELNUT CHOCOLATE MERINGUE TORTE WITH PEARS

SERVES 8–10

175g/6oz/¾ cup granulated sugar
1 vanilla pod, split
475ml/6fl oz/2 cups water
4 ripe pears, peeled, halved and cored
*30ml/2 tbsp hazelnut- or pear-flavoured
liqueur*
150g/5oz/1¼ cups hazelnuts, toasted
6 egg whites
pinch of salt
350g/12oz/2¼ cups icing sugar
5ml/1 tsp vanilla essence
50g/2oz plain chocolate, melted

FOR THE CHOCOLATE CREAM

*275g/10oz fine quality bittersweet or plain
chocolate, chopped into small pieces*
475ml/16fl oz/2 cups whipping cream
*60ml/4 tbsp hazelnut- or pear-flavoured
liqueur*

1 In a saucepan large enough to hold the pears in a single layer combine the sugar, vanilla pod and water. Over a high heat, bring to the boil, stirring until the sugar dissolves. Lower the heat, add the pears to the syrup, cover and simmer gently for 12–15 minutes until tender. Remove the pan from the heat and allow the pears to cool in their poaching liquid. Carefully lift the pears out of the liquid and drain on kitchen paper. Transfer them to a plate, sprinkle with liqueur, cover and chill overnight.

2 Preheat oven to 180°C/350°F/Gas 4. With a pencil draw a 23 cm/9 in circle on each of two sheets of non-stick baking paper. Turn the paper over on to two baking sheets (so that the pencil marks are underneath). Crumb the toasted hazelnuts in a food processor fitted with a metal blade.

3 In a large bowl, beat the whites with a hand-held electric mixer until frothy. Add the salt and beat on high speed until soft peaks form. Reduce the mixer speed and gradually add the icing sugar, beating well after each addition until all the sugar has been added and the whites are stiff and glossy; this will take 12–15 minutes. Gently fold in the nuts and vanilla essence and spoon the meringue on to the circles on the baking sheets, smoothing the top and sides.

4 Bake for 1 hour until the tops are dry and firm. Turn off the oven and allow to cool in the oven for 2–3 hours or overnight, until completely dry.

5 Prepare the chocolate cream. Melt the chocolate in a heatproof bowl set over a saucepan of simmering water. Stir the chocolate until melted and smooth. Cool to room temperature. Using a hand-held electric mixer beat the cream in a bowl to form soft peaks. Quickly fold the cream into the melted chocolate; fold in the liqueur. Spoon about one third of the chocolate cream into an icing bag fitted with a star tip. Set aside.

6 Thinly slice each pear half lengthwise with a sharp knife. Place one meringue layer on a serving plate. Spread with half the chocolate cream and arrange half the sliced pears evenly over the cream. Pipe a border of rosettes around the edge.

7 Top with the second meringue layer and spread with the remaining chocolate cream. Arrange the remaining pear slices in an attractive pattern over the chocolate cream. Pipe a border of rosettes around the edge. Spoon the melted chocolate into a small paper cone and drizzle the chocolate over the pears. Chill for at least 1 hour before serving.

CHILLED CHOCOLATE AND DATE SLICE

SERVES 6–8

115g / 4oz / ½ cup unsalted butter, melted
225g / 8oz ginger biscuits, finely crushed
50g / 2oz / ⅔ cup stale sponge cake crumbs
75ml / 5 tbsp orange juice
115g / 4oz / ⅔ cup stoned dates
25g / 1oz / ¼ cup finely chopped nuts
175g / 6oz bittersweet chocolate
300ml / ½ pint / 1¼ cups whipping cream
grated chocolate and icing sugar, to decorate

1 Mix the butter and ginger biscuit crumbs in a bowl, then press the mixture on to the sides and base of an 18 cm / 7 in loose-based flan tin. Chill the crust while making the filling.

2 Put the sponge cake crumbs into a bowl. Pour over 60ml / 4 tbsp of the orange juice, stir well with a wooden spoon and leave to soak. Put the dates in a saucepan and add the remaining orange juice. Warm the mixture over a low heat. Mash the warm dates thoroughly and stir in the cake crumbs, with the finely chopped nuts.

3 Mix the chocolate with 60ml / 4 tbsp of the cream in a heatproof bowl. Place the bowl over a saucepan of barely simmering water and stir occasionally until melted. In a separate bowl, whip the rest of the cream to soft peaks, then fold in the melted chocolate.

4 Add the cooled date, crumb and nut mixture to the cream and chocolate and mix lightly but thoroughly. Pour into the crumb crust. Using a spatula, level the mixture. Chill until just set, then mark the tart into portions, using a sharp knife dipped in hot water. Return the tart to the fridge and chill until firm. To decorate, scatter the grated chocolate over the surface and dust with icing sugar. Serve in wedges, with single cream, if desired. Fresh orange segments make an excellent accompaniment.

CHOCOLATE MARSHMALLOW PIE

Make the crumb crust as for the main recipe, but add a delicious marshmallow filling. Melt 275g / 10oz / 3 cups white marshmallows with 30ml / 2 tbsp milk or single cream in the top of a double boiler over simmering water. Alternatively, use a deep bowl and microwave the mixture on High for about 4 minutes, stirring often. Off the heat, stir in 90g / 3½oz grated chocolate until melted, then add 30ml / 2 tbsp brandy. Tip the mixture into a clean bowl, cool, then chill until beginning to set. Fold in 250ml / 8fl oz / 1 cup whipped cream, pour into the crumb crust and return to the fridge until completely set. Decorate with chocolate curls.

BAKED CHOCOLATE CHEESECAKE

SERVES 10–12

*275g / 10oz plain chocolate, chopped into
small pieces*

*1.2kg / 2½lb / 5 cups cream cheese, at room
temperature*

200g / 7oz / scant 1 cup granulated sugar

10ml / 2 tsp vanilla essence

4 eggs, at room temperature

175ml / 6fl oz / ¾ cup soured cream

15ml / 1 tbsp cocoa powder

FOR THE BASE

200g / 7oz chocolate biscuits, crushed

75g / 3oz / 6 tbsp butter, melted

2.5ml / ½ tsp ground cinnamon

<u>1</u> Preheat oven to 180°C / 350°F / Gas 4.
Lightly grease the base and sides of a
23 x 7.5 cm / 9 x 3 in springform tin.

<u>2</u> To make the base, mix the crushed
biscuits with the butter and cinnamon.
Press the mixture evenly on to the base of
the tin to make a crust. Melt the
chocolate and set it aside.

<u>3</u> Beat the cream cheese until smooth,
then beat in the sugar and vanilla essence.
Add the eggs, one at a time.

<u>4</u> Stir the soured cream into the cocoa
powder to form a paste. Add to the
cream cheese mixture. Stir in the melted
chocolate and mix until smooth.

<u>5</u> Pour the filling on to the base. Bake for
1 hour. Cool in the tin, then remove the
sides of the tin and slide the cheesecake
on to a plate. Serve chilled.

MARBLED CHOCOLATE CHEESECAKE

SERVES 6

50g / 2oz / ½ cup cocoa powder
75ml / 5 tbsp hot water
900g / 2lb cream cheese, at room temperature
200g / 7oz / scant 1 cup caster sugar
4 eggs
5ml / 1 tsp vanilla essence
75g / 3oz digestive biscuits, crushed

<u>1</u> Preheat oven to 180°C/350°F/Gas 4. Line a 20 x 8 cm/8 x 3 in cake tin with greaseproof paper. Grease the paper.
<u>2</u> Sift the cocoa powder into a bowl. Pour over the hot water and stir to dissolve.
<u>3</u> Beat the cheese until smooth, then beat in the sugar, followed by the eggs, one at a time. Do not overmix.
<u>4</u> Divide the mixture evenly between two bowls. Stir the chocolate mixture into one bowl, then add the vanilla essence to the remaining mixture.

<u>5</u> Pour a cup or ladleful of the plain mixture into the centre of the tin; it will spread out into an even layer. Slowly pour over a cupful of chocolate mixture in the centre. Continue to alternate the cake mixtures in this way until both are used up. Draw a thin metal skewer through the cake mixture for a marbled effect.
<u>6</u> Set the tin in a roasting pan and pour in hot water to come 4 cm/1½ in up the sides of the cake tin.

<u>7</u> Bake the cheesecake for about 1½ hours, until the top is golden. (The cake will rise during baking but will sink later.) Cool in the tin on a wire rack.
<u>8</u> Run a knife around the inside edge of the cake. Invert a flat plate over the tin and turn out the cake.

<u>9</u> Sprinkle the crushed biscuits evenly over the cake, gently invert another plate on top, and turn over again. Cover and chill for 3 hours, preferably overnight.

RASPBERRY, MASCARPONE AND WHITE CHOCOLATE CHEESECAKE

SERVES 8

50g / 2oz / ¼ cup unsalted butter
225g / 8oz ginger biscuits, crushed
50g / 2oz / ½ cup chopped pecan nuts
or walnuts

FOR THE FILLING

275g / 10oz / 1¼ cups mascarpone cheese
175g / 6oz / ¾ cup fromage frais
2 eggs, beaten
45ml / 3 tbsp caster sugar
250g / 9oz white chocolate, chopped into
small pieces
225g / 8oz / 1½ cups fresh or frozen raspberries

FOR THE TOPPING

115g / 4oz / ½ cup mascarpone cheese
75g / 3oz / ⅓ cup fromage frais
white chocolate curls and fresh raspberries,
to decorate

1 Preheat oven to 150°C / 300°F / Gas 2. Melt the butter in a saucepan, then stir in the crushed biscuits and nuts. Press into the base of a 23 cm / 9 in springform cake tin. Level the surface.

2 Make the filling. Using a wooden spoon, beat the mascarpone and fromage frais in a large mixing bowl, then beat in the eggs, a little at a time. Add the caster sugar. Beat until the sugar has dissolved, and the mixture is smooth and creamy.

3 Melt the white chocolate gently in a heatproof bowl over a saucepan of simmering water, then stir into the cheese mixture. Add the fresh or frozen raspberries and mix lightly.

4 Tip into the prepared tin and spread evenly, then bake for about 1 hour or until just set. Switch off the oven, but do not remove the cheesecake. Leave it until cold and completely set.

5 Remove the sides of the tin and carefully lift the cheesecake on to a serving plate. Make the topping by mixing the mascarpone and fromage frais in a bowl and spreading the mixture over the cheesecake. Decorate with chocolate curls and raspberries.

APRICOT AND WHITE CHOCOLATE CHEESECAKE

Use 225g / 8oz / 1 cup ready-to-eat dried apricots instead of the fresh or frozen raspberries in the cheesecake mixture. Slice the apricots thinly or dice them. Omit the mascarpone and fromage frais topping and serve the cheesecake with an apricot sauce, made by poaching 225g / 8oz stoned fresh apricots in 120ml / 4fl oz / ½ cup water until tender, then rubbing the fruit and liquid through a sieve placed over a bowl. Sweeten the apricot purée with caster sugar to taste, and add enough lemon juice to sharpen the flavour. Alternatively, purée drained canned apricots with a little of their syrup, then stir in lemon juice to taste.

LUXURY WHITE CHOCOLATE CHEESECAKE

SERVES 16–20

150g / 5oz (about 16–18) digestive biscuits
50g / 2oz / ½ cup blanched hazelnuts, toasted
50g / 2oz / ¼ cup unsalted butter, melted
2.5ml / ½ tsp ground cinnamon
white chocolate curls, to decorate
cocoa powder, for dusting (optional)

FOR THE FILLING

350g / 12oz fine quality white chocolate,
chopped into small pieces
120ml / 4fl oz / ½ cup whipping cream or
double cream
675g / 1½lb / 3 x 8oz packets cream
cheese, softened
50g / 2oz / ¼ cup granulated sugar
4 eggs
30ml / 2 tbsp hazelnut-flavoured liqueur or
15ml / 1 tbsp vanilla essence

FOR THE TOPPING

450ml / ¾ pint / 1¾ cups soured cream
50g / 2oz / ¼ cup granulated sugar
15ml / 1 tbsp hazelnut-flavoured liqueur or
5ml / 1 tsp vanilla essence

3 Using a hand-held electric mixer, beat the cream cheese and sugar in a large bowl until smooth. Add the eggs one at a time, beating well. Slowly beat in the white chocolate mixture and liqueur or vanilla essence. Pour the filling into the baked crust. Place the tin on the hot baking sheet. Bake for 45–55 minutes, and do not allow the top to brown. Transfer the cheesecake to a wire rack while preparing the topping. Increase the oven temperature to 200°C/400°F/Gas 6.

4 Prepare the topping. In a small bowl whisk the soured cream, sugar and liqueur or vanilla essence until thoroughly mixed. Pour the mixture over the cheesecake, spreading it evenly, and return to the oven. Bake for a further 5–7 minutes. Turn off the oven, but do not open the door for 1 hour. Serve the cheesecake at room temperature, decorated with the white chocolate curls. Dust the surface lightly with cocoa powder, if desired.

1 Preheat oven to 180°C/350°F/Gas 4. Grease a 23 x 7.5 cm/9 x 3 in springform tin. In a food processor, process the biscuits and hazelnuts until fine crumbs form. Pour in the butter and cinnamon. Process just until blended. Using the back of a spoon, press on to the base and to within 1 cm/½ in of the top of the sides of the cake tin. Bake the crumb crust for 5–7 minutes, until just set. Cool in the tin on a wire rack. Lower the oven temperature to 150°C/300°F/Gas 2 and place a baking sheet inside to heat up.

2 Prepare the filling. In a small saucepan over a low heat, melt the white chocolate and cream until smooth, stirring frequently. Set aside to cool slightly.

ITALIAN CHOCOLATE RICOTTA PIE

SERVES 6

225g / 8oz / 2 cups plain flour
30ml / 2 tbsp cocoa powder
60ml / 4 tbsp caster sugar
115g / 4oz / ½ cup unsalted butter
60ml / 4 tbsp dry sherry

FOR THE FILLING

2 egg yolks
115g / 4oz / ½ cup caster sugar
500g / 1¼lb / 2½ cups ricotta cheese
finely grated rind of 1 lemon
90ml / 6 tbsp dark chocolate chips
75ml / 5 tbsp chopped mixed peel
45ml / 3 tbsp chopped angelica

1 Sift the flour and cocoa into a bowl, then stir in the sugar. Rub in the butter using your fingertips, then work in the sherry to make a firm dough.

2 Preheat oven to 200°C / 400°F / Gas 6. Roll out three-quarters of the pastry on a lightly floured surface and line a 24 cm / 9½ in loose-based flan tin.

3 Make the filling. Beat the egg yolks and sugar in a bowl, then beat in the ricotta to mix thoroughly. Stir in the lemon rind, chocolate chips, mixed peel and angelica.

4 Scrape the ricotta mixture into the pastry case and level the surface. Roll out the remaining pastry and cut into strips. Arrange these in a lattice over the pie.

5 Bake for 15 minutes. Lower the oven temperature to 180°C / 350°F / Gas 4 and cook for a further 30–35 minutes, until golden brown and firm. Cool the pie in the tin. Serve at room temperature.

BLACK BOTTOM PIE

SERVES 6–8
250g/9oz/2¼ cups plain flour
150g/5oz/⅔ cup unsalted butter
2 egg yolks
15–30ml/1–2 tbsp iced water
FOR THE FILLING
3 eggs, separated
20ml/4 tsp cornflour
75g/3oz/6 tbsp golden caster sugar
400ml/14fl oz/1⅔ cups milk
150g/5oz plain chocolate, chopped into
small pieces
5ml/1 tsp vanilla essence
1 sachet powdered gelatine
45ml/3 tbsp water
30ml/2 tbsp dark rum
FOR THE TOPPING
175ml/6 fl oz/¾ cup double cream or
whipping cream
chocolate curls

1 Sift the flour into a bowl and rub in the butter until the mixture resembles coarse breadcrumbs. Stir in the egg yolks with just enough iced water to bind the mixture to a soft dough. Roll out on a lightly floured surface and line a deep 23 cm/9 in flan tin. Chill the pastry case for about 30 minutes.

2 Preheat oven to 190°C/375°F/Gas 5. Prick the pastry case all over with a fork, cover with greaseproof paper weighed down with baking beans and bake blind for 10 minutes. Remove the baking beans and paper, return the pastry case to the oven and bake for a further 10 minutes, until the pastry is crisp and golden. Cool in the tin.

POTS AU CHOCOLAT
The chocolate and chestnut mixture (minus the pastry) also makes delicious individual *pots au chocolat*. Make the fillings as described above, then simply pour the mixture into small ramekins that have been lightly greased with butter. Decorate with a blob of whipped cream and grated chocolate and serve with *langues de chat*.

CHOCOLATE AND CHESTNUT PIE
23 cm/9 in pastry case (see recipe
above), cooked
FOR THE FILLING
115g/4oz/½ cup butter, softened
115g/4oz/¼ cup caster sugar
425g/15oz can unsweetened chestnut
purée
225g/8oz plain chocolate, broken into
small pieces
30ml/2 tbsp brandy

1 Make the filling. Cream the butter with the caster sugar in a mixing bowl until pale and fluffy. Add the unsweetened chestnut purée, about 30ml/2 tbsp at a time, beating well after each addition.

2 Put the chocolate in a heatproof bowl. Place over a saucepan of barely simmering water until the chocolate has melted, stirring occasionally until smooth. Stir the chocolate into the chestnut mixture until combined, then add the brandy.

3 Pour the filling into the cold pastry case. Using a spatula, level the surface. Chill until set. Decorate with whipped cream and chocolate leaves, if desired, or simply add a dusting of sifted cocoa.

3 Make the filling. Mix the egg yolks, cornflour and 30ml/2 tbsp of the sugar in a bowl. Heat the milk in a saucepan until almost boiling, then beat into the egg mixture. Return to the clean pan and stir over a low heat until the custard has thickened and is smooth. Pour half the custard into a bowl.

4 Put the chocolate in a heatproof bowl. Place over a saucepan of barely simmering water until the chocolate has melted, stirring occasionally until smooth. Stir the melted chocolate into the custard in the bowl, with the vanilla essence. Spread the filling in the pastry case and cover closely with dampened greaseproof paper or clear film to prevent the formation of a skin. Allow to cool, then chill until set.

5 Sprinkle the gelatine over the water in a bowl, leave until spongy, then place the bowl over a pan of simmering water until all the gelatine has dissolved. Stir into the remaining custard, then add the rum. Whisk the egg whites in a clean, grease-free bowl until peaks form. Whisk in the remaining sugar, a little at a time, until stiff, then fold the egg whites quickly but evenly into the rum-flavoured custard.

6 Spoon the rum-flavoured custard over the chocolate layer in the pastry case. Using a spatula, level the mixture, making sure that none of the chocolate custard is visible. Return the pie to the fridge until the top layer has set, then remove the pie from the tin and place it on a serving plate. Whip the cream, spread it over the pie and sprinkle with chocolate curls, to decorate.

MISSISSIPPI MUD PIE

SERVES 8

175g/6oz/1½ cups plain flour
2.5ml/½ tsp salt
115g/4oz/½ cup butter
30–45ml/2–3 tbsp iced water

FOR THE FILLING

75g/3oz plain chocolate, broken into
small pieces
50g/2oz/¼ cup butter or margarine
45ml/3 tbsp golden syrup
3 eggs, beaten
150g/5oz/⅔ cup soft light brown
sugar
5ml/1 tsp vanilla essence

TO DECORATE

115g/4oz chocolate bar
300ml/½ pint/1¼ cups whipping cream

1 Preheat oven to 220°C/425°F/Gas 7. Sift the flour and salt into a mixing bowl. Rub in the butter until the mixture resembles coarse breadcrumbs. Sprinkle in the water, about 15ml/1 tbsp at a time, and toss the mixture lightly with your fingers or a fork until the dough forms a ball.

2 On a lightly floured surface, roll out the pastry and line a 23 cm/9 in flan tin, easing in the pastry and being careful not to stretch it. With your thumbs, make a fluted edge.

3 Using a fork, prick the base and sides of the pastry case. Bake for 10–15 minutes, until lightly browned. Cool, in the pan.

4 Make the filling. In a heatproof bowl set over a pan of barely simmering water, melt the plain chocolate with the butter or margarine and the golden syrup. Remove the bowl from the heat and stir in the eggs, sugar and vanilla essence.

5 Lower the oven temperature to 180°C/350°F/Gas 4. Pour the chocolate mixture into the pastry case. Bake for 35–40 minutes, until the filling is set. Allow to cool completely in the flan tin, on a rack.

6 Make the decoration. Use the heat of your hands to soften the chocolate bar slightly. Working over a sheet of non-stick baking paper, draw the blade of a swivel-bladed vegetable peeler across the side of the chocolate bar to shave off short, wide curls. Chill the curls until required.

7 Before serving the pie, pour the cream into a bowl and whip to soft peaks. Spread over the top of the pie, hiding the chocolate filling completely. Decorate with the chocolate curls.

CHOCOLATE, BANANA AND TOFFEE PIE

SERVES 6

65g / 2½oz / 5 tbsp unsalted butter, melted

250g / 9oz milk chocolate digestive biscuits, crushed

chocolate curls, to decorate

FOR THE FILLING

397g / 13oz can condensed milk

150g / 5oz plain chocolate, chopped

120ml / 4fl oz / ½ cup crème fraîche

15ml / 1 tbsp golden syrup

FOR THE TOPPING

2 bananas

250ml / 8fl oz / 1 cup crème fraîche

10ml / 2 tsp strong black coffee

1 Mix the butter with the biscuit crumbs. Press on to the base and sides of a 23cm/9in loose-based flan tin. Chill.

2 Make the filling. Place the unopened can of condensed milk in a deep saucepan of boiling water, making sure that it is completely covered. Lower the heat and simmer, covered for 2 hours, topping up the water as necessary. The can must remain covered at all times.

3 Remove the pan from the heat and set aside, covered, until the can has cooled down completely in the water. Do not attempt to open the can until it is completely cold.

4 Gently melt the chocolate with the crème fraîche and golden syrup in a heatproof bowl over a saucepan of simmering water. Stir in the caramelized condensed milk and beat until evenly mixed. Pour the filling into the biscuit crust and spread it evenly.

5 Slice the bananas evenly and arrange them over the chocolate filling.

6 Stir the crème fraîche and coffee together in a bowl, then spoon the mixture over the bananas. Sprinkle the chocolate curls on top. Alternatively, omit the crème fraîche topping and decorate with whipped cream and extra banana slices.

CHILLED CHOCOLATE DESSERTS

DOUBLE CHOCOLATE SNOWBALL

3 Bake for 1¼–1½ hours until the surface is firm and slightly risen, but cracked. The centre will still be wobbly, but will set on cooling. Remove the bowl to a rack to cool to room temperature; the top will sink. Cover the surface of the cake with a dinner plate (to make an even surface for unmoulding); then wrap completely with clear film or foil and chill overnight.

4 To unmould, remove the film or foil, lift off the plate, and place an upturned serving plate over the top of the mould. Invert the mould on to the plate and shake firmly to release the cake. Carefully peel off the foil used for lining the bowl. Cover until ready to decorate.

5 In a food processor fitted with a metal blade, process the white chocolate until fine. Heat 120ml/4fl oz/½ cup of the cream in a small saucepan until just beginning to simmer. With the food processor running, pour the hot cream through the feeder tube and process until the chocolate has melted completely. Strain into a medium bowl and cool to room temperature, stirring occasionally.

6 In another bowl, beat the remaining cream with the electric mixer until soft peaks form. Add the liqueur and beat for 30 seconds or until the cream holds its shape, but is not yet stiff. Fold a spoonful of cream into the chocolate mixture to lighten it, then fold in the rest. Spoon into a piping bag fitted with a star tip and pipe rosettes over the surface of the cake. Dust lightly with cocoa powder to finish the decoration.

SERVES 12–14

350g/12oz bittersweet or plain chocolate, chopped into small pieces
350g/12oz/1¾ cups caster sugar
275g/10oz/1¼ cups unsalted butter, cut into small pieces
8 eggs
60ml/4 tbsp orange-flavoured liqueur or brandy
cocoa powder, for dusting

FOR THE WHITE CHOCOLATE CREAM

200g/7oz fine quality white chocolate, chopped into small pieces
475ml/16fl oz/2 cups double or whipping cream
15ml/1 tbsp orange-flavoured liqueur (optional)

1 Preheat oven to 180°C/350°F/Gas 4. Carefully line a 1.75 litre/3 pint/7½ cup round ovenproof bowl with aluminium foil, smoothing the sides. Melt the bittersweet chocolate in a heatproof bowl over a pan of barely simmering water. Add the caster sugar and stir until the chocolate has melted and the sugar has dissolved. Strain the mixture into a medium bowl.

2 With a hand-held electric mixer at low speed, beat in the butter, then the eggs, one at a time, beating well after each addition. Stir in the liqueur or brandy and pour into the prepared bowl. Tap the sides of the bowl gently to release any large air bubbles.

CHOCOLATE AMARETTO MARQUISE

SERVES 10–12

*15ml/1 tbsp flavourless vegetable oil, such as
groundnut or sunflower*
75g/3oz/7–8 amaretti biscuits, finely crushed
*25g/1oz/¼ cup unblanched almonds, toasted
and finely chopped*
*450g/1lb fine quality bittersweet or plain
chocolate, chopped into small pieces*
75ml/5 tbsp Amaretto liqueur
75ml/5 tbsp golden syrup
475ml/16fl oz/2 cups double cream
cocoa powder, for dusting
FOR THE AMARETTO CREAM
*350ml/12fl oz/1½ cups whipping cream or
double cream for serving*
*30–45ml/2–3 tbsp Amaretto di Soronno
liqueur*

1 Lightly oil a 23 cm/9 in heart-shaped or springform cake tin. Line the bottom with non-stick baking paper and oil the paper. In a small bowl, combine the crushed amaretti biscuits and the chopped almonds. Sprinkle evenly on to the base of the tin.

2 Place the chocolate, Amaretto liqueur and golden syrup in a medium saucepan over a very low heat. Stir frequently until the chocolate is melted and the mixture is smooth. Remove from the heat and allow it to cool for about 6–8 minutes, until the mixture feels just warm to the touch.

3 Pour the cream into a bowl. Whip with a hand held electric mixer, until it just begins to hold its shape. Stir a large spoonful into the chocolate mixture, to lighten it, then quickly add the remaining cream and gently fold into the chocolate mixture. Pour into the prepared tin, on top of the amaretti and almond mixture. Level the surface. Cover the tin with clear film and chill overnight.

4 To unmould, run a thin-bladed sharp knife under hot water and dry carefully. Run the knife around the edge of the tin to loosen the dessert. Place a serving plate over the tin, then invert to unmould. Carefully peel off the paper, replacing any crust that sticks to it, and dust with cocoa powder. In a bowl, whip the cream and Amaretto liqueur to soft peaks. Serve separately.

CHOCOLATE PUFFS

SERVES 4–6

65g / 2½oz / generous ½ cup plain flour
150ml / ¼ pint / ⅔ cup water
50g / 2oz / ¼ cup butter
2 eggs, beaten

FOR THE FILLING AND ICING

150ml / ¼ pint / ⅔ cup double cream
225g / 8oz / 1½ cups icing sugar
15ml / 1 tbsp cocoa powder
30–60ml / 2–4 tbsp water

1 Preheat oven to 220°C/425°F/Gas 7. Sift the flour into a bowl. Put the water in a saucepan over a medium heat, add the butter and heat gently until it melts. Increase the heat and bring to the boil, then remove from the heat. Tip in all the flour at once and beat quickly until the mixture sticks together and becomes thick and glossy, leaving the side of the pan clean. Leave the mixture to cool slightly.

2 Add the eggs, a little at a time, to the mixture and beat by hand with a wooden spoon or with an electric whisk, until the mixture (choux pastry) is thick and glossy and drops reluctantly from a spoon. (You may not need to use all of the egg.) Spoon the choux pastry into a piping bag fitted with a 2 cm/¾ in nozzle. Dampen two baking sheets with cold water.

3 Pipe walnut-sized spoonfuls of the choux pastry on to the dampened baking sheets. Leave some space for them to rise. Cook for 25–30 minutes, until they are golden brown and well risen. Use a palette knife to lift the puffs on to a wire rack, and make a small hole in each one with the handle of a wooden spoon to allow the steam to escape. Leave to cool.

4 Make the filling and icing. Whip the cream until thick. Put it into a piping bag fitted with a plain or star nozzle. Push the nozzle into the hole in each puff and squirt a little cream inside. Put the icing sugar and cocoa in a small bowl and stir together. Add enough water to make a thick glossy icing. Spread a little icing on each puff and serve when set.

CHOCOLATE HAZELNUT GALETTES

SERVES 4

*175g/6oz plain chocolate, chopped into small
pieces
45ml/3 tbsp single cream
30ml/2 tbsp flaked hazelnuts
115g/4oz white chocolate, chopped into small
pieces
175g/6oz/¾ cup fromage frais (8% fat)
15ml/1 tbsp dry sherry
60ml/4 tbsp finely chopped hazelnuts, toasted
physalis (Cape gooseberries), dipped in white
chocolate, to decorate*

1 Melt the plain chocolate in a heatproof bowl over a saucepan of barely simmering water, then remove the pan from the heat and lift off the bowl. Stir the cream into the melted chocolate. Draw twelve 7.5 cm/3 in circles on sheets of non-stick baking paper.

2 Turn the baking paper over and spread the plain chocolate over each marked circle, covering in a thin, even layer. Scatter flaked hazelnuts over four of the circles, then leave until set.

3 Melt the white chocolate in a heatproof bowl over hot water, then stir in the fromage frais and dry sherry. Fold in the chopped, toasted hazelnuts. Leave to cool until the mixture holds its shape.

4 Remove the plain chocolate rounds carefully from the paper and sandwich them together in stacks of three, spooning the white chocolate hazelnut cream between the layers and using the hazelnut-covered rounds on top. Chill before serving.

5 To serve, place the galettes on individual plates and decorate with chocolate-dipped physalis.

CHOCOLATE PAVLOVA WITH PASSION FRUIT CREAM

SERVES 6

4 egg whites
200g / 7oz / scant 1 cup caster sugar
20ml / 4 tsp cornflour
45ml / 3 tbsp cocoa powder
5ml / 1 tsp vinegar
chocolate leaves, to decorate

FOR THE FILLING

150g / 5oz plain chocolate, chopped into small pieces
250ml / 8fl oz / 1 cup double cream
150g / 5oz / ⅔ cup Greek-style yogurt
2.5ml / ½ tsp vanilla essence
4 passion fruit

1 Preheat oven to 140°C/275°F/Gas 1. Cut a piece of non-stick baking paper to fit a baking sheet. Draw a 23 cm/9 in circle on the paper.

2 Whisk the egg whites in a clean, grease-free bowl until stiff. Gradually whisk in the sugar and continue to whisk until the mixture is stiff again. Whisk in the cornflour, cocoa and vinegar.

3 Place the baking paper upside down on the baking sheet. Spread the mixture over the marked circle, making a slight dip in the centre. Bake for 1½–2 hours.

4 Make the filling. Melt the chocolate in a heatproof bowl over barely simmering water, then remove from the heat and cool slightly. In a separate bowl, whip the cream with the yogurt and vanilla essence until thick. Fold 60ml/4 tbsp into the chocolate, then set both mixtures aside.

5 Halve all the passion fruit and scoop out the pulp. Stir half into the plain cream mixture. Carefully remove the meringue shell from the baking sheet and place it on a large serving plate. Fill with the passion fruit cream, then spoon over the chocolate mixture and the remaining passion fruit pulp.

6 Decorate with chocolate leaves and serve as soon as possible, while the meringue is still crisp on the outside and deliciously chewy within.

CHOCOLATE AND CHESTNUT POTS

SERVES 6

250g/9oz plain chocolate
60ml/4 tbsp Madeira
25g/1oz/2 tbsp butter, diced
2 eggs, separated
225g/8oz/1 cup unsweetened chestnut purée
crème fraîche and chocolate curls, to decorate

1 Make a few chocolate curls for decoration, then break the rest of the chocolate into squares and melt it with the Madeira in a heatproof bowl over a saucepan of barely simmering water. Remove from the heat and add the butter, a few pieces at a time, stirring until melted and smooth.

2 Beat the egg yolks quickly into the mixture, then beat in the chestnut purée, a little at a time, making sure that each addition is absorbed before you add the next, mixing until smooth.

3 Whisk the egg whites in a clean, grease-free bowl until stiff. Stir about 15ml/1 tbsp of the whites into the chestnut mixture to lighten it, then fold in the rest evenly.

4 Spoon the mixture into six small ramekin dishes or custard cups and chill until set. Serve the pots topped with a generous spoonful of crème fraîche or whipped double cream. Decorate with the chocolate curls.

MOCHA VELVET CREAM POTS

SERVES 8

15ml/1 tbsp instant coffee powder
475ml/16fl oz/2 cups milk
75g/3oz/6 tbsp caster sugar
225g/8oz plain chocolate, chopped into small pieces
10ml/2 tsp vanilla essence
30ml/2 tbsp coffee liqueur (optional)
7 egg yolks
whipped cream and crystallized mimosa balls, to decorate

1 Preheat oven to 160°C/325°F/Gas 3. Place eight 120ml/4fl oz/½ cup custard cups or ramekins in a roasting tin. Set the tin aside.

2 Put the instant coffee into a saucepan. Stir in the milk, then add the sugar and set the pan over a medium heat. Bring to the boil, stirring constantly, until both the coffee and the sugar have dissolved completely.

3 Remove the pan from the heat and add the chocolate. Stir until it has melted and the sauce is smooth. Stir in the vanilla essence and coffee liqueur, if using.

4 In a bowl, whisk the egg yolks to blend them lightly. Slowly whisk in the chocolate mixture until well mixed, then strain the mixture into a large jug and divide equally among the cups or ramekins. Pour enough boiling water into the roasting tin to come halfway up the sides of the cups or ramekins. Carefully place the roasting tin in the oven.

5 Bake for 30–35 minutes, until the custard is just set and a knife inserted into the custard comes out clean. Remove the cups or ramekins from the roasting tin and allow to cool. Place on a baking sheet, cover and chill completely. Decorate with whipped cream and crystallized mimosa balls, if desired.

CHOCOLATE VANILLA TIMBALES

SERVES 6

350ml / 12fl oz / 1½ cups semi-skimmed milk
30ml / 2 tbsp cocoa powder
2 eggs
10ml / 2 tsp vanilla essence
45ml / 3 tbsp granulated sweetener
15ml / 1 tbsp / 1 sachet powdered gelatine
45ml / 3 tbsp hot water
extra cocoa powder, to decorate

FOR THE SAUCE

115g / 4oz / ½ cup light Greek-style yogurt
25ml / 1½ tbsp vanilla essence

1 Place the milk and cocoa powder in a saucepan and stir until the milk is boiling. Separate the eggs and beat the egg yolks with the vanilla and sweetener in a bowl, until the mixture is pale and smooth. Gradually pour in the chocolate milk, beating well.

2 Return the mixture to the pan and stir constantly over a gentle heat, without boiling, until it is slightly thickened and smooth.

3 Remove the pan from the heat. Pour the gelatine into the hot water and stir until it is completely dissolved, then quickly stir it into the milk mixture. Put this mixture aside and allow it to cool until almost setting.

4 Whisk the egg whites until they hold soft peaks. Fold the egg whites quickly into the milk mixture. Spoon the timbale mixture into six individual moulds and chill them until set.

5 To serve, run a knife around the edge, dip the moulds quickly into hot water and turn out. Dust with cocoa. For the sauce, stir together the yogurt and vanilla and spoon on to the plates.

TIRAMISU IN CHOCOLATE CUPS

SERVES 6

1 egg yolk
30ml / 2 tbsp caster sugar
2.5ml / ½ tsp vanilla essence
250g / 9oz / generous 1 cup mascarpone cheese
120ml / 4fl oz / ½ cup strong black coffee
15ml / 1 tbsp cocoa powder
30ml / 2 tbsp coffee liqueur
16 amaretti biscuits
cocoa powder, for dusting

FOR THE CHOCOLATE CUPS
175g / 6oz plain chocolate, chopped
25g / 1oz / 2 tbsp unsalted butter

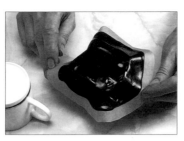

1 Make the chocolate cups. Cut out six 15 cm / 6 in rounds of non-stick baking paper. Melt the chocolate with the butter in a heatproof bowl over a saucepan of simmering water. Stir until smooth, then spread a spoonful of the chocolate mixture over each circle, to within 2 cm / ¾ in of the edge.

2 Carefully lift each paper round and drape it over an upturned teacup or ramekin so that the edges curve into frills. Leave until completely set, then carefully lift off and peel away the paper to reveal the chocolate cups.

3 Make the filling. Using a hand-held electric mixer, beat the egg yolk and sugar in a bowl until smooth, then stir in the vanilla essence. Soften the mascarpone if necessary, then stir it into the egg yolk mixture. Beat until smooth.

4 In a separate bowl, mix the coffee, cocoa and liqueur. Break up the biscuits roughly, then stir them into the mixture.

5 Place the chocolate cups on individual plates. Divide half the biscuit mixture among them, then spoon over half the mascarpone mixture.

6 Spoon over the remaining biscuit mixture (including any free liquid), top with the rest of the mascarpone mixture and dust lightly with cocoa powder. Chill for about 30 minutes before serving.

DEVILISH CHOCOLATE ROULADE

SERVES 6–8

*175g / 6oz plain dark chocolate, chopped into
small pieces*
4 eggs, separated
115g / 4oz / 1/2 cup caster sugar
cocoa powder for dusting
chocolate-dipped strawberries, to decorate

FOR THE FILLING

*225g / 8oz plain chocolate, chopped into
small pieces*
45ml / 3 tbsp brandy
2 eggs, separated
250g / 9oz / generous 1 cup mascarpone cheese

1 Preheat oven to 180°C / 350°F / Gas 4.
Grease a 33 × 23 cm / 13 × 9 in Swiss roll
tin and line with non-stick baking paper.
Melt the chocolate.

2 Whisk the egg yolks and sugar in a bowl
until pale and thick, then stir in the
melted chocolate. Place the egg whites in
a clean, grease-free bowl. Whisk them to
soft peaks, then fold lightly and evenly
into the egg and chocolate mixture.

3 Scrape into the tin and spread to the
corners. Bake for 15-20 minutes, until
well risen and firm to the touch. Dust a
sheet of non-stick baking paper with
cocoa powder. Turn the sponge out on
the paper, cover with a clean dish towel
and leave to cool.

4 Make the filling. Melt the chocolate
with the brandy in a heatproof bowl over
a saucepan of simmering water. Remove
from the heat. Beat the egg yolks
together, then beat into the chocolate
mixture. In a separate bowl whisk the
whites to soft peaks, then fold them
lightly and evenly into the filling.

5 Uncover the roulade, remove the lining
paper and spread with the mascarpone.
Spread the chocolate mixture over the
top, then roll up carefully from a long
side to enclose the filling. Transfer to a
serving plate with the join underneath,
top with fresh chocolate-dipped
strawberries and chill before serving.

COOK'S TIP

Chocolate-dipped strawberries make a
marvellous edible decoration for cakes
and desserts. Break plain, milk or
white chocolate into small pieces and
place in a small deep heatproof bowl
over a saucepan of barely simmering
water. While the chocolate melts, line
a baking sheet with non-stick baking
paper and set it aside.
Stir the melted chocolate until it is
completely smooth. Holding a
strawberry by its stalk or stalk end,
dip it partially or fully into the melted
chocolate, allowing any excess
chocolate to drip back into the bowl,
then place the fruit on the paper-lined
baking sheet. Repeat with the rest of
the fruit. Leave until the chocolate has
set. Use on the same day.
The same technique can be applied to
other relatively firm fruits, such as
cherries and orange segments.

CHOCOLATE CONES WITH APRICOT SAUCE

SERVES 6

250g / 9oz plain dark chocolate, chopped into
small pieces
350g / 12oz / 1½ cups ricotta cheese
45ml / 3 tbsp double cream
30ml / 2 tbsp brandy
30ml / 2 tbsp icing sugar
finely grated rind of 1 lemon
pared strips of lemon rind, to decorate

FOR THE SAUCE

175g / 6oz / ⅔ cup apricot jam
45ml / 3 tbsp lemon juice

1 Cut twelve 10 cm / 4 in double thickness rounds from non-stick baking paper and shape each into a cone. Secure with masking tape.

2 Melt the chocolate over a saucepan of simmering water. Cool slightly, then spoon a little into each cone, swirling and brushing it to coat the paper evenly.

3 Support each cone point downwards in a cup or glass held on its side, to keep it level. Leave in a cool place until the cones are completely set. Unless it is a very hot day, do not put the cones in the fridge, as this may mar their appearance.

4 Make the sauce. Combine the apricot jam and lemon juice in a small saucepan. Melt over a gentle heat, stirring occasionally, then press through a sieve into a small bowl. Set aside to cool.

5 Beat the ricotta cheese in a bowl until softened, then beat in the cream, brandy and icing sugar. Stir in the lemon rind. Spoon the mixture into a piping bag. Fill the cones, then carefully peel off the non-stick baking paper.

6 Spoon a pool of apricot sauce on to six dessert plates. Arrange the cones in pairs on the plates. Decorate with a scattering of pared lemon rind strips and serve immediately.

CHOCOLATE BLANCMANGE

SERVES 4

60ml / 4 tbsp cornflour
600ml / 1 pint / 2½ cups milk
45ml / 3 tbsp sugar
50–115g / 2–4oz plain chocolate, chopped
few drops of vanilla essence
white and plain chocolate curls, to decorate

1 Rinse a 750ml / 1¼ pint / 3 cup fluted mould with cold water and leave it upside down to drain. Blend the cornflour to a smooth paste with a little of the milk in a medium-sized bowl.

2 Bring the remaining milk to the boil, preferably in a non-stick saucepan, then pour on to the blended mixture stirring constantly.

3 Pour all the milk back into the saucepan and bring slowly to the boil over a low heat, stirring constantly until the mixture boils and thickens. Remove the pan from the heat, then add the sugar, chocolate and vanilla essence and stir until the sauce is smooth, all the sugar has dissolved and the chocolate pieces have melted completely.

4 Pour the chocolate mixture into the mould, cover closely with dampened greaseproof paper (to prevent the formation of a skin) and leave in a cool place for several hours to set.

5 To unmould the blancmange, place a large serving plate upside down on top of the mould. Holding the plate and mould firmly together, turn them both over. Give both plate and mould a gentle but firm shake to loosen the blancmange, then lift off the mould. Scatter the chocolate curls over the top and serve.

CHOCOLATE MANDARIN TRIFLE

SERVES 6–8

4 trifle sponges
14 amaretti biscuits
60ml/4 tbsp Amaretto di Saronno or
sweet sherry
8 mandarin oranges

FOR THE CUSTARD

200g/7oz plain chocolate, chopped into
small pieces
30ml/2 tbsp cornflour or custard powder
30ml/2 tbsp caster sugar
2 egg yolks
200ml/7fl oz/scant 1 cup milk
250g/9oz/generous 1 cup mascarpone cheese

FOR THE TOPPING

250g/9oz/generous 1 cup fromage frais
chocolate shapes
mandarin slices or segments

<u>1</u> Break up the trifle sponges and place them in a large glass serving dish. Crumble the amaretti biscuits over and then sprinkle with Amaretto or sherry.

<u>2</u> Squeeze the juice from 2 mandarins and sprinkle into the dish. Segment the rest and put in the dish.

<u>3</u> Make the custard. Melt the chocolate. In a heatproof bowl, mix the cornflour or custard powder, caster sugar and egg yolks to a smooth paste.

<u>4</u> Heat the milk in a small saucepan until almost boiling, then pour on to the egg yolk mixture, stirring constantly. Return to the clean pan and stir over a low heat until the custard has thickened slightly and is smooth.

<u>5</u> Stir in the mascarpone until melted, then mix in the melted chocolate. Spread over the sponge and biscuit, cool, then chill.

<u>6</u> To serve, spread the fromage frais over the custard, then decorate with chocolate shapes and mandarin slices or segments.

COOK'S TIP

You can use canned mandarin oranges, if you prefer. Spoon about 30ml/2 tbsp of the juice over the sponge and biscuit mixture.

CHOCOLATE PROFITEROLES

4 Beat 1 egg in a small bowl and set aside. Add the whole eggs, one at a time, to the flour mixture, beating well after each addition. Beat in just enough of the beaten egg to make a smooth, shiny dough. It should pull away and fall slowly when dropped from a spoon.

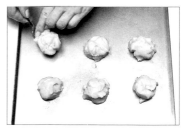

5 Using a tablespoon, ease the dough in 12 mounds on to the prepared baking sheet. Bake for 25–30 minutes, until the puffs are golden brown.

6 Remove the puffs from the oven and cut a small slit in the side of each of them to release the steam. Return the puffs to the oven, turn off the heat and leave them to dry out, with the oven door open.

7 Remove the ice cream from the freezer and allow it to soften for about 10 minutes. Split the profiteroles in half and put a small scoop of ice cream in each. Arrange on a serving platter or divide among individual plates. Pour the sauce over the profiteroles and serve at once.

SERVES 4-6

110g / 3¾oz / scant 1 cup plain flour
1.5ml / ¼ tsp salt
pinch of freshly grated nutmeg
175ml / 6fl oz / ¾ cup water
75g / 3oz / 6 tbsp unsalted butter, cut into
6 equal pieces
3 eggs
750ml / 1¼ pints / 3 cups vanilla ice cream

FOR THE CHOCOLATE SAUCE

275g / 10oz plain chocolate, chopped into
small pieces
120ml / 4fl oz / ½ cup warm water

1 Preheat oven to 200°C/400°F/Gas 6. Grease a baking sheet. Sift the flour, salt and nutmeg on to a sheet of greaseproof paper or foil.

2 Make the sauce. Melt the chocolate with the water in a heatproof bowl placed over a saucepan of barely simmering water. Stir until smooth. Keep warm until ready to serve, or reheat when required.

3 In a medium saucepan, bring the water and butter to the boil. Remove from the heat and add the dry ingredients all at once, funnelling them in from the paper or foil. Beat with a wooden spoon for about 1 minute until well blended and the mixture starts to pull away from the pan, then set the pan over a low heat and cook the mixture for about 2 minutes, beating constantly. Remove from the heat.

VARIATION

Fill the profiteroles with whipped cream, if you prefer. Spoon the cream into a piping bag and fill the slit puffs, or sandwich the halved puffs with the cream.

BITTER CHOCOLATE MOUSSE

SERVES 8

225g / 8oz plain chocolate, chopped into small pieces
60ml / 4 tbsp water
30ml / 2 tbsp orange flavoured liqueur or brandy
25g / 1oz / 2 tbsp unsalted butter, cut into small pieces
4 eggs, separated
90ml / 6 tbsp whipping cream
1.5ml / ¼ tsp cream of tartar
45ml / 3 tbsp caster sugar
crème fraîche and chocolate curls, to decorate

1 Melt the chocolate with the water in a heatproof bowl over a pan of barely simmering water, stirring until smooth. Off the heat, whisk in the liqueur or brandy and butter.

2 With a hand-held electric mixer, beat the egg yolks for 2–3 minutes until thick and creamy, then slowly beat into the melted chocolate until well blended. Set aside.

3 Whip the cream until soft peaks form and stir a spoonful into the chocolate mixture to lighten it. Fold in the remaining cream.

4 In a grease free bowl, beat the egg whites slowly until frothy. Add the cream of tartar, increase the speed and continue beating until they form soft peaks. Gradually sprinkle over the sugar and continue beating until the whites are stiff and glossy.

5 Using a rubber spatula or large metal spoon, stir a quarter of the egg whites into the chocolate mixture, then gently fold in the remaining whites, cutting down to the bottom, along the sides and up to the top in a semicircular motion until they are just combined. Gently spoon into eight individual dishes. Chill for at least 2 hours or until set.

6 Spoon a little crème fraîche over each mousse and decorate with the chocolate curls.

WHITE CHOCOLATE VANILLA MOUSSE WITH DARK CHOCOLATE SAUCE

SERVES 6–8

200g / 7 oz white chocolate, chopped into small pieces
2 eggs, separated
60ml / 4 tbsp caster sugar
300ml / ½ pint / 1¼ cups double cream
1 sachet powdered gelatine
150ml / ¼ pint / ⅔ cup Greek-style yogurt
10ml / 2 tsp vanilla essence

FOR THE SAUCE

50g / 2oz plain chocolate, chopped into small pieces
30ml / 2 tbsp dark rum
60ml / 4 tbsp single cream

1 Line a 1 litre / 1¾ pint / 4 cup loaf tin with non-stick baking paper or clear film. Melt the chocolate. Whisk the egg yolks and sugar until pale and thick, then beat in the chocolate.

2 Heat the cream in a small saucepan until almost boiling, then remove from the heat. Sprinkle the powdered gelatine over, stirring until completely dissolved. Pour on to the chocolate mixture, whisking vigorously until smooth.

3 Whisk the yogurt and vanilla essence into the mixture. In a clean, grease-free bowl, whisk the egg whites until stiff, then fold them into the mixture. Tip into the prepared loaf tin, level the surface and chill until set.

4 Make the sauce. Melt the chocolate with the rum and cream in a heatproof bowl over a saucepan of simmering water, stirring occasionally, then leave to cool completely.

5 Serve the mousse in thick slices with the cooled chocolate sauce poured around.

MANGO AND CHOCOLATE CRÈME BRULEE

SERVES 6

2 ripe mangoes, peeled, stoned and chopped
300ml/½ pint/1¼ cups double cream
300ml/½ pint/1¼ cups crème fraîche
1 vanilla pod
*115g/4oz plain dark chocolate, chopped into
small pieces*
4 egg yolks
15ml/1 tbsp clear honey
90ml/6 tbsp demerara sugar, for the topping

1 Divide the mangoes among six flameproof dishes set on a baking sheet.
2 Mix the cream, crème fraîche and vanilla pod in a large heatproof bowl. Place the bowl over a pan of barely simmering water.

3 Heat the cream mixture for 10 minutes. Do not let the bowl touch the water or the cream may overheat. Remove the vanilla pod and stir in the chocolate, a few pieces at a time, until melted. When smooth, remove the bowl, but leave the pan of water over the heat.

4 Whisk the egg yolks and clear honey in a second heatproof bowl, then gradually pour in the chocolate cream, whisking constantly. Place over the pan of simmering water and stir constantly until the chocolate custard thickens enough to coat the back of a wooden spoon.
5 Remove from the heat and spoon the custard over the mangoes. Cool, then chill in the fridge until set.
6 Preheat the grill to high. Sprinkle 15ml/1 tbsp demerara sugar evenly over each dessert and spray lightly with a little water. Grill briefly, as close to the heat as possible, until the sugar melts and caramelizes. Chill again before serving the desserts.

WHITE CHOCOLATE PARFAIT

SERVES 10

*225g/8oz white chocolate, chopped into
small pieces*
600ml/1 pint/2½ cups whipping cream
120ml/4fl oz/½ cup milk
10 egg yolks
15ml/1 tbsp caster sugar
40g/1½oz/½ cup desiccated coconut
*120ml/4fl oz/½ cup canned sweetened
coconut milk*
*150g/5oz/1¼ cups unsalted macadamia nuts
curls of fresh coconut, to decorate*

FOR THE CHOCOLATE ICING

*225g/8oz plain chocolate, chopped into
small pieces*
75g/3oz/6 tbsp butter
20ml/generous 1 tbsp golden syrup
175ml/6fl oz/¾ cup whipping cream

1 Carefully line the base and sides of a
1.4 litre/2⅓ pint/6 cup terrine mould or
loaf tin with clear film.

2 Melt the chopped white chocolate with
50ml/2fl oz/¼ cup of the cream in the
top of a double boiler or a heatproof bowl
set over a saucepan of simmering water.
Stir continually until the mixture is
smooth. Set aside.

3 Put the milk in a pan. Add 250ml/
8fl oz/1 cup of the remaining cream and
bring to boiling point over a medium heat
stirring constantly.

4 Meanwhile, whisk the egg yolks and
caster sugar together in a large bowl,
until thick and pale.

5 Add the hot cream mixture to the
yolks, whisking constantly. Pour back into
the saucepan and cook over a low heat for
2–3 minutes, until thickened. Stir
constantly and do not boil. Remove the
pan from the heat.

6 Add the melted chocolate, desiccated
coconut and coconut milk, then stir well
and leave to cool. Whip the remaining
cream in a bowl until thick, then fold into
the chocolate and coconut mixture.

7 Put 475ml/16fl oz/2 cups of the parfait
mixture in the prepared mould or tin and
spread evenly. Cover and freeze for about
2 hours, until just firm. Cover the
remaining mixture and chill.

VARIATION

White Chocolate and Ginger Parfait:
Use sliced stem ginger instead of
macadamia nuts for the central layer
of the parfait, and substitute syrup
from the jar of ginger for the golden
syrup in the icing. Leave out the
coconut, if you prefer, and use
sweetened condensed milk instead of
the coconut milk.

8 Scatter the macadamia nuts evenly over
the frozen parfait. Spoon in the remaining
parfait mixture and level the surface.
Cover the terrine and freeze for 6–8 hours
or overnight, until the parfait is firm.

9 To make the icing, melt the chocolate
with the butter and syrup in the top of a
double boiler set over hot water. Stir
occasionally.

10 Heat the cream in a saucepan, until
just simmering, then stir into the
chocolate mixture. Remove the pan from
the heat and leave the mixture to cool
until lukewarm.

11 To turn out the parfait, wrap the
terrine or tin in a hot towel and set it
upside down on a plate. Lift off the
terrine or tin, then peel off the clear film.
Place the parfait on a rack over a baking
sheet and pour the icing evenly over the
top. Working quickly, smooth the icing
down the sides with a palette knife. Leave
to set slightly, then transfer to a freezer-
proof plate and freeze for 3–4 hours
more.

12 Remove from the freezer about 15
minutes before serving, to allow the ice
cream to soften slightly. When ready to
serve, cut into slices, using a knife dipped
in hot water between each slice. Serve,
decorated with coconut curls.

CHOCOLATE ICES AND SORBETS

WHITE CHOCOLATE RASPBERRY RIPPLE ICE CREAM

2 In a saucepan, combine the milk and 250ml/8fl oz/1 cup cream and bring to the boil. In a bowl beat the yolks and sugar with a hand-held mixer for 2–3 minutes until thick and creamy. Gradually pour the hot milk mixture over the yolks and return to the pan. Cook over a medium heat until the custard coats the back of a wooden spoon, stirring constantly.

3 Remove the pan from the heat and stir in the white chocolate until melted and smooth. Pour the remaining cream into a large bowl. Strain in the hot custard, mix well, then stir in the vanilla essence. Cool, then transfer the custard to an ice-cream maker and freeze it according to the manufacturer's instructions.

4 When the mixture is frozen, but still soft, transfer one third of the ice cream to a freezerproof bowl. Set half the raspberry sauce aside. Spoon a third of the remainder over the ice cream. Cover with another third of the ice cream and more sauce. Repeat. With a knife or spoon, lightly marble the mixture. Cover and freeze. Allow the ice cream to soften for 15 minutes before serving with the remaining raspberry sauce, and the mint.

MAKES 1 LITRE/1¾ PINTS/4 CUPS
250ml/8fl oz/1 cup milk
475ml/16fl oz/2 cups whipping cream
7 egg yolks
30ml/2 tbsp granulated sugar
225g/8oz fine quality white chocolate,
chopped into small pieces
5ml/1 tsp vanilla essence
mint sprigs to decorate
FOR THE RASPBERRY RIPPLE SAUCE
275g/10oz packet frozen raspberries in light
syrup or 275g/10oz jar reduced sugar
raspberry preserve
10ml/2 tsp golden syrup
15ml/1 tbsp lemon juice
15ml/1 tbsp cornflour mixed to a paste with
15ml/1 tbsp water

1 Prepare the sauce. Press the raspberries and their syrup through a sieve into a saucepan. Add the golden syrup, lemon juice and cornflour mixture. (If using preserve, omit cornflour, but add the water.) Bring to the boil, stirring often, then simmer for 1–2 minutes. Pour into a bowl and cool, then chill.

CHOCOLATE FUDGE SUNDAES

SERVES 4

4 scoops each vanilla and coffee ice cream
2 small ripe bananas
whipped cream
toasted flaked almonds

FOR THE SAUCE

50g/2oz/⅓ cup soft light brown sugar
120ml/4fl oz/½ cup golden syrup
45ml/3 tbsp strong black coffee
5ml/1 tsp ground cinnamon
150g/5oz plain chocolate, chopped into
small pieces
75ml/3fl oz/5 tbsp whipping cream
45ml/3 tbsp coffee-flavoured liqueur
(optional)

<u>1</u> Make the sauce. Place the sugar, syrup, coffee and cinnamon in a heavy-based saucepan. Bring to the boil, then boil for about 5 minutes, stirring the mixture constantly.

<u>2</u> Turn off the heat and stir in the chocolate. When the chocolate has melted and the mixture is smooth, stir in the cream and the liqueur, if using. Leave the sauce to cool slightly. If made ahead, reheat the sauce gently until just warm.

<u>3</u> Fill four glasses with a scoop each of vanilla and coffee ice cream.

<u>4</u> Peel the bananas and slice them thinly. Scatter the sliced bananas over the ice cream. Pour the warm fudge sauce over the bananas, then top each sundae with a generous swirl of whipped cream. Sprinkle the sundaes with toasted almonds and serve at once.

CHOCOLATE ICE CREAM

SERVES 4–6
750ml / 1¼ pints / 3 cups milk
10 cm / 4 in piece of vanilla pod
4 egg yolks
115g / 4oz / ½ cup granulated sugar
225g / 8oz plain chocolate, chopped into
small pieces

<u>1</u> Heat the milk with the vanilla pod in a small saucepan. Remove from the heat as soon as small bubbles start to form on the surface. Do not let it boil. Strain the milk into a jug and set aside.

<u>2</u> Using a wire whisk or hand-held electric mixer, beat the egg yolks in a bowl. Gradually whisk in the sugar and continue to whisk until the mixture is pale and thick. Slowly add the milk to the egg mixture, whisking after each addition. When all the milk has been added, pour the mixture into a heatproof bowl.

<u>3</u> Place the heatproof bowl over a saucepan of simmering water and add the chocolate. Stir over a low heat until the chocolate melts, then raise the heat slightly and continue to stir the chocolate-flavoured custard until it thickens enough to coat the back of a wooden spoon lightly. Remove the custard from the heat, pour into a bowl and allow to cool, stirring occasionally to prevent skin forming on the surface.

<u>4</u> Freeze the chocolate mixture in an ice-cream maker, following the manufacturer's instructions, or pour it into a suitable container for freezing. Freeze for about 3 hours, or until set. Remove from the container and chop roughly into 7.5 cm / 3 in pieces. Place in a food processor and chop until smooth. Return to the freezer container and freeze again. Repeat two or three times, until the ice cream is smooth and creamy.

CHOCOLATE FLAKE ICE CREAM

SERVES 6

300ml / ½ pint / 1¼ cups whipping cream, chilled
90ml / 6 tbsp Greek-style yogurt
75–90ml / 5–6 tbsp caster sugar
few drops of vanilla essence
150g / 5oz / 10 tbsp flaked or roughly grated chocolate

COOK'S TIPS

Transfer the ice cream from the freezer to the fridge about 15 minutes before serving, so that it softens, and so that the full flavour can be appreciated.
Use a metal scoop to serve the ice cream, dipping the scoop briefly in warm water between servings. If the ice cream has been made in a loaf tin, simply slice it.

1 Have ready an ice-cream maker, or use a 600–900ml / 1–1½ pint / 2½–3¾ cup freezer-proof container, preferably with a lid. Prepare a place in the freezer so you can easily reach it. If necessary, turn the freezer to the coldest setting.

2 Softly whip the cream in a large bowl then fold in the yogurt, sugar, vanilla essence and chocolate. Stir gently to mix thoroughly, and then transfer to the ice-cream maker or freezer container.

3 Smooth the surface of the ice cream, then cover and freeze. Gently stir with a fork every 30 minutes for up to 4 hours until the ice cream is too hard to stir. If using an ice-cream maker, follow the manufacturer's instructions.

CHOCOLATE SORBET

SERVES 6

150g/5oz bittersweet chocolate, chopped
115g/4oz plain chocolate, grated
225g/8oz/1¼ cups caster sugar
475ml/16fl oz/2 cups water
chocolate curls, to decorate

1 Put all the chocolate in a food processor, fitted with the metal blade, and process for 20–30 seconds until finely chopped.
2 In a saucepan over a medium heat, bring the sugar and water to the boil, stirring until the sugar dissolves. Boil for about 2 minutes, then remove the pan from the heat.
3 With the machine running, pour the hot syrup over the chocolate in the food processor. Keep the machine running for 1–2 minutes until the chocolate is completely melted and the mixture is smooth, scraping down the bowl once.
4 Strain the chocolate mixture into a large measuring jug or bowl. Leave to cool, then chill, stirring occasionally. Freeze the mixture in an ice-cream maker. Alternatively, pour into a container suitable for use in the freezer, freeze until slushy, whisk until smooth, then freeze again. Whisk for a second time before the mixture hardens completely. Allow the sorbet to soften for 5–10 minutes at room temperature and serve in scoops, decorated with chocolate curls.

CHOCOLATE SORBET WITH RED FRUITS

SERVES 6

475ml/16fl oz/2 cups water
45ml/3 tbsp clear honey
115g/4oz/½ cup caster sugar
75g/3oz/¾ cup cocoa powder
50g/2oz plain dark or bittersweet chocolate, chopped into small pieces
400g/14oz soft red fruits, such as raspberries, redcurrants or strawberries

1 Place the water, honey, caster sugar and cocoa powder in a saucepan. Heat gently, stirring occasionally, until the sugar has completely dissolved.
2 Remove the pan from the heat, add the chocolate and stir until melted. Leave until cool.
3 Tip into an ice-cream maker and churn until frozen. Alternatively, pour into a container suitable for use in the freezer, freeze until slushy, whisk until smooth, then freeze again. Whisk for a second time before the mixture hardens completely, and cover the container.
4 Remove from the freezer 10–15 minutes before serving, so that the sorbet softens slightly. Serve in scoops in chilled dessert bowls, with the soft fruits.

ROCKY ROAD ICE CREAM

SERVES 6

*115g/4oz plain chocolate, chopped into
small pieces
150ml/¼ pint/⅔ cup milk
300ml/½ pint/1¼ cups double cream
115g/4oz/2 cups marshmallows, chopped
115g/4oz/½ cup glacé cherries, chopped
50g/2oz/½ cup crumbled shortbread biscuits
30ml/2 tbsp chopped walnuts*

1 Melt the chocolate in the milk in a saucepan over a gentle heat, stirring from time to time. Pour into a bowl and leave to cool completely.

2 Whip the cream in a separate bowl until it just holds its shape. Beat in the chocolate mixture, a little at a time, until the mixture is smooth and creamy.

3 Tip the mixture into an ice-cream maker and, following the manufacturer's instructions, churn until almost frozen. Alternatively, pour into a container suitable for use in the freezer, freeze until ice crystals form around the edges, then whisk with a strong hand whisk or hand-held electric mixer until smooth.

4 Stir the marshmallows, glacé cherries, crushed biscuits and nuts into the iced mixture, then return to the freezer container and freeze until firm.

5 Allow the ice cream to soften at room temperature for 15–20 minutes before serving in scoops. Add a wafer and chocolate sauce to each portion, if desired.

ICED CHOCOLATE NUT GATEAU

SERVES 6–8

75g / 3oz / ¾ cup shelled hazelnuts
about 32 sponge fingers
150ml / ¼ pint / ⅔ cup cold strong black coffee
30ml / 2 tbsp brandy
475ml / 16fl oz / 2 cups double cream
75g / 3oz / generous ½ cup icing sugar, sifted
150g / 5oz plain chocolate, chopped into
small pieces
icing sugar and cocoa powder, for dusting

1 Preheat oven to 200°C/400°F/Gas 6. Spread out the hazelnuts on a baking sheet and toast them in the oven for 5 minutes until golden. Tip the nuts on to a clean dish towel and rub off the skins while still warm. Cool, then chop finely.

2 Line a 1.2 litre / 2 pint / 5 cup loaf tin with clear film and cut the sponge fingers to fit the base and sides. Reserve the remaining biscuits. Mix the coffee with the brandy in a shallow dish. Dip the sponge fingers briefly into the coffee mixture and return to the tin, sugary side down to fit neatly.

3 Whip the cream with the icing sugar until it holds soft peaks. Fold half the chopped chocolate into the cream with the hazelnuts. Use a gentle figure-of-eight action to distribute the chocolate and nuts evenly.

4 Melt the remaining chocolate in a bowl set over a pan of barely simmering water. Cool, then fold into the cream mixture. Spoon into the tin.

5 Moisten the remaining biscuits in the coffee mixture, be careful not to soak the biscuits, as they will collapse. Lay the coffee-moistened biscuits over the filling. Wrap and freeze until firm.

6 To serve, remove from the freezer 30 minutes before serving to allow the ice cream to soften slightly. Turn out on to a serving plate and dust with icing sugar and cocoa.

ICED CHOCOLATE AND MANDARIN GATEAU

Dip the sponge fingers in a mixture of strong black coffee and mandarin or orange liqueur. Omit the hazelnuts from the cream filling. About 30 minutes before serving, remove the frozen gâteau from the tin and place it on a serving plate. Cover with whipped cream flavoured with mandarin or orange liqueur. Pipe more whipped cream around the base of the gâteau. Decorate with plain or chocolate-dipped mandarin or orange segments.

ICE CREAM BOMBES

SERVES 6

*1 litre / 1¾ pints / 4 cups soft-scoop chocolate
ice cream
475ml / 16fl oz / 2 cups soft-scoop vanilla
ice cream
50g / 2oz / ⅓ cup plain chocolate chips
115g / 4oz toffees
75ml / 5 tbsp double cream*

<u>1</u> Divide the chocolate ice cream equally among six small cups. Push it roughly to the base and up the sides, leaving a small cup-shaped dip in the middle. Return to the freezer and leave for 45 minutes. Take the cups out again and smooth the ice cream in each into shape, keeping the centre hollow. Return to the freezer.

<u>2</u> Put the vanilla ice cream in a small bowl and break it up slightly with a spoon. Stir in the chocolate chips and use this mixture to fill the hollows in the cups of chocolate ice cream. Smooth the tops, then cover the cups with clear film, return to the freezer and leave overnight.

<u>3</u> Melt the toffees with the cream in a small pan over a very low heat, stirring constantly until smooth, warm and creamy.

<u>4</u> Turn out the bombes on to individual plates and pour the toffee sauce over the top. Serve immediately.

CHOCOLATE MINT ICE CREAM PIE

SERVES 8

75g / 3 oz plain chocolate chips
40g / 1½oz butter or margarine
50g / 2oz crisped rice cereal
1 litre / 1¾ pints / 4 cups mint-chocolate-chip ice cream
chocolate curls, to decorate

1 Line a 23 cm / 9 in pie tin with foil. Place a round of greaseproof paper over the foil in the bottom of the tin.
2 In a heatproof bowl set over a saucepan of simmering water melt the chocolate chips with the butter or margarine.
3 Remove the bowl from the heat and gently stir in the cereal, a little at a time.

4 Press the chocolate-cereal mixture evenly over the base and up the sides of the prepared tin, forming a 1 cm / ½ in rim. Chill until completely hard.
5 Carefully remove the cereal base from the tin and peel off the foil and paper. Return the base to the pie tin.

6 Remove the ice cream from the freezer and allow it to soften for 10 minutes.

7 Spread the ice cream evenly in the biscuit case crust. Freeze until firm.
8 Scatter the chocolate curls over the ice cream just before serving.

CHOCOLATE BISCUITS AND COOKIES

CHOC-CHIP NUT BISCUITS

MAKES 36
115g/4oz/1 cup plain flour
5ml/1 tsp baking powder
5ml/1 tsp salt
75g/3oz/6 tbsp butter or margarine
115g/4oz/1 cup caster sugar
50g/2oz/⅓ cup soft light brown sugar
1 egg
5ml/1 tsp vanilla essence
115g/4oz/⅔ cup plain chocolate chips
50g/2oz/½ cup hazelnuts, chopped

1 Preheat oven to 180°C/350°F/Gas 4. Grease 2–3 baking sheets. Sift the flour, baking powder and salt into a small bowl. Set the bowl aside.

2 With a hand-held electric mixer, cream the butter or margarine and sugars together. Beat in the egg and vanilla essence. Add the flour mixture and beat well on low speed.

3 Stir in the chocolate chips and half of the hazelnuts. Drop teaspoonfuls of the mixture on to the prepared baking sheets, to form 2 cm/¾ in mounds. Space the biscuits about 5 cm/2 in apart to allow room for spreading.

4 Flatten each biscuit lightly with a wet fork. Sprinkle the remaining hazelnuts on top of the biscuits and press lightly into the surface. Bake for 10–12 minutes, until golden brown. Transfer the biscuits to a wire rack and allow to cool.

CHOC-CHIP OAT BISCUITS

MAKES 60
115g/4oz/1 cup plain flour
2.5ml/½ tsp bicarbonate of soda
1.5ml/¼ tsp baking powder
1.5ml/¼ tsp salt
115g/4oz/1 cup butter or margarine, softened
115g/4oz/1 cup caster sugar
75g/3oz/½ cup light brown sugar
1 egg
1.5ml/¼ tsp vanilla essence
75g/3oz/scant 1 cup rolled oats
175g/6oz/1 cup plain chocolate chips

1 Preheat oven to 180°C/350°F/Gas 4. Grease 3–4 baking sheets. Sift the flour, bicarbonate of soda, baking powder and salt into a mixing bowl. Set the bowl aside.

2 With a hand-held electric mixer, cream the butter or margarine and sugars together in a bowl. Add the egg and vanilla essence and beat until light and fluffy.

3 Add the flour mixture and beat on low speed until thoroughly blended. Stir in the rolled oats and chocolate chips, mixing well with a wooden spoon. The dough should be crumbly.

4 Drop heaped teaspoonfuls on to the prepared baking sheets, spacing the dough about 2.5 cm/1 in apart. Bake for about 15 minutes until just firm around the edge but still soft to the touch in the centre. With a slotted spatula, transfer the biscuits to a wire rack and allow them to cool.

CHOCOLATE-DIPPED HAZELNUT CRESCENTS

MAKES ABOUT 35

275g / 10oz / 2 cups plain flour
pinch of salt
225g / 8oz / 1 cup unsalted butter, softened
75g / 3oz / 6 tbsp caster sugar
15ml / 1 tbsp hazelnut-flavoured liqueur
or water
5ml / 1 tsp vanilla essence
75g / 3oz plain chocolate, chopped into
small pieces
50g / 2oz / ½ cup hazelnuts, toasted and
finely chopped
icing sugar, for dusting
350g / 12oz plain chocolate, melted, for
dipping

1 Preheat oven to 160°C/325°F/Gas 3. Grease two large baking sheets. Sift the flour and salt into a bowl. In a separate bowl, beat the butter until creamy. Add the sugar and beat until fluffy, then beat in the hazelnut liqueur or water and the vanilla essence. Gently stir in the flour mixture, then the chocolate and hazelnuts.

2 With floured hands, shape the dough into 5 x 1 cm/2 x ½in crescent shapes. Place on the baking sheets, 5 cm/2 in apart. Bake for 20–25 minutes until the edges are set and the biscuits slightly golden. Remove the biscuits from the oven and cool on the baking sheets for 10 minutes, then transfer the biscuits to wire racks to cool completely.

3 Have the melted chocolate ready in a small bowl. Dust the biscuits lightly with icing sugar. Using a pair of kitchen tongs or your fingers, dip half of each crescent into the melted chocolate. Place the crescents on a non-stick baking sheet until the chocolate has set.

CHUNKY DOUBLE CHOCOLATE COOKIES

MAKES 18—20

115g/4oz/½ cup unsalted butter, softened
115g/4oz/⅔ cup light muscovado sugar
1 egg
5ml/1 tsp vanilla essence
150g/5oz/1¼ cups self-raising flour
75g/3oz/¾ cup porridge oats
115g/4oz plain chocolate, roughly chopped
115g/4oz white chocolate, roughly chopped

DOUBLE-CHOC ALMOND COOKIES:

Instead of the porridge oats, use 75g/3oz/¾ cup ground almonds. Omit the chopped chocolate and use 175g/6oz/1 cup chocolate chips instead. Top each heap of cake mixture with half a glacé cherry before baking.

1 Preheat oven to 190°C/375°F/Gas 5. Lightly grease two baking sheets. Cream the butter with the sugar in a bowl until pale and fluffy. Add the egg and vanilla essence and beat well.

2 Sift the flour over the mixture and fold in lightly with a metal spoon, then add the oats and chopped plain and white chocolate and stir until evenly mixed.

3 Place small spoonfuls of the mixture in 18—20 rocky heaps on the baking sheets, leaving space for spreading.

4 Bake for 12–15 minutes or until the biscuits are beginning to turn pale golden. Cool for 2–3 minutes on the baking sheets, then lift on to wire racks. The biscuits will be soft when freshly baked but will harden on cooling.

CHOCOLATE MARZIPAN COOKIES

MAKES ABOUT 36

*200g / 7oz / scant 1 cup unsalted butter,
softened*
*200g / 7oz / generous 1 cup light muscovado
sugar*
1 egg, beaten
300g / 11oz / 2¾ cups plain flour
60ml / 4 tbsp cocoa powder
200g / 7oz white almond paste
*115g / 4oz white chocolate, chopped into
small pieces*

1 Preheat oven to 190°C/375°F/Gas 5.
Lightly grease two large baking sheets.
Using a hand-held electric mixer, cream
the butter with the sugar in a mixing
bowl until pale and fluffy. Add the egg
and beat well.

2 Sift the flour and cocoa over the
mixture. Stir in with a wooden spoon
until all the flour mixture has been
smoothly incorporated, then use clean
hands to press the mixture together to
make a fairly soft dough.

3 Using a rolling pin and keeping your
touch light, roll out about half the dough
on a lightly floured surface to a thickness
of about 5 mm/¼ in. Using a 5 cm/2 in
plain or fluted biscuit cutter, cut out 36
rounds, re-rolling the dough as required.
Wrap the remaining dough in clear film
and set it aside.

4 Cut the almond paste into 36 equal
pieces. Roll into balls, flatten slightly and
place one on each round of dough. Roll
out the remaining dough, cut out more
rounds, then place on top of the almond
paste. Press the dough edges to seal.

5 Bake for 10–12 minutes, or until the
cookies have risen well and are beginning
to crack on the surface. Cool on the
baking sheet for about 2–3 minutes, then
finish cooling on a wire rack.

6 Melt the white chocolate, then either
drizzle it over the biscuits to decorate, or
spoon into a paper piping bag and quickly
pipe a design on to the biscuits.

VARIATION
Use glacé icing instead of melted
white chocolate to decorate the
cookies, if you prefer.

BLACK AND WHITE GINGER FLORENTINES

MAKES ABOUT 30

120ml/4fl oz/½ cup double cream
50g/2oz/¼ cup butter
50g/2oz/¼ cup granulated sugar
30ml/2 tbsp honey
150g/5oz/1¼ cups flaked almonds
40g/1½oz/6 tbsp plain flour
2.5ml/½ tsp ground ginger
50g/2oz/⅓ cup diced candied orange peel
75g/3oz/½ cup diced stem ginger
50g/2oz plain chocolate, chopped into small pieces
150g/5oz bittersweet chocolate, chopped into small pieces
150g/5oz fine quality white chocolate, chopped into small pieces

1 Preheat oven to 180°C/350°F/Gas 4. Lightly grease two large baking sheets. In a saucepan over a medium heat, stir the cream, butter, sugar and honey until the sugar dissolves. Bring the mixture to the boil, stirring constantly. Remove from the heat and stir in the almonds, flour and ground ginger. Stir in the candied peel, ginger and plain chocolate.

2 Drop teaspoons of the mixture on to the baking sheets at least 7.5 cm/3 in apart. Spread each round as thinly as possible with the back of the spoon.

3 Bake for 8–10 minutes or until the edges are golden brown and the biscuits are bubbling. Do not under-bake or they will be sticky, but be careful not to over-bake as they burn easily. Continue baking in batches. If you wish, use a 7.5 cm/3 in biscuit cutter to neaten the edges of the florentines while they are still on the baking sheet.

4 Allow the biscuits to cool on the baking sheets for 10 minutes, until they are firm enough to move. Using a metal palette knife, carefully lift the biscuits on to a wire rack to cool completely.

5 Melt the bittersweet chocolate in a heatproof bowl over barely simmering water. Cool slightly. Put the white chocolate in a separate bowl and melt in the same way, stirring frequently. Remove and cool for about 5 minutes, stirring occasionally.

6 Using a small metal palette knife, spread half the florentines with the bittersweet chocolate and half with the melted white chocolate. Place on a wire rack, chocolate side up. Chill for 10–15 minutes to set completely.

CHEWY CHOCOLATE BISCUITS
MAKES 18

4 egg whites
350g/12oz/2½ cups icing sugar
115g/4oz/1 cup cocoa powder
30ml/2 tbsp plain flour
5ml/1 tsp instant coffee
15ml/1 tbsp water
115g/4oz/1 cup walnuts, finely chopped

1 Preheat oven to 180°C/350°F/Gas 4. Line two baking sheets with non-stick baking paper.
2 With a hand-held electric mixer, beat the egg whites in a bowl until frothy.
3 Sift the icing sugar, cocoa powder, flour and coffee into the whites. Add the water and continue beating on low speed to blend, then on high speed for a few minutes until the mixture thickens. With a rubber spatula, fold in the walnuts.
4 Place generous spoonfuls of the mixture 2.5 cm/1 in apart on the prepared baking sheets. Bake for 12–15 minutes, or until firm and cracked on top but soft on the inside. With a metal spatula, transfer the biscuits to a wire rack to cool.

CHOCOLATE CRACKLE-TOPS

MAKES ABOUT 38

200g/7oz bittersweet or plain chocolate,
chopped into small pieces
90g/3½oz/7 tbsp unsalted butter
115g/4oz/½ cup caster sugar
3 eggs
5ml/1 tsp vanilla essence
200g/7oz/1¾ cups plain flour
25g/1oz/¼ cup cocoa powder
2.5ml/½ tsp baking powder
pinch of salt
175g/6oz/1½ cups icing sugar, for coating

1 Grease two or more large baking sheets. In a heavy-based saucepan over a low heat, melt the chocolate and butter until smooth, stirring frequently. Remove from the heat. Stir in the sugar until dissolved. Add the eggs, one at a time, beating well after each addition. Stir in the vanilla essence.

2 Sift the flour, cocoa, baking powder and salt into a bowl. Gradually stir into the chocolate mixture in batches to make a soft dough. Cover in clear film and chill for at least 1 hour until the dough is firm enough to hold its shape.

3 Preheat oven to 160°C/325°F/Gas 3. Place the icing sugar in a small, deep bowl. Using a small ice cream scoop or round teaspoon, scoop the dough into small balls and roll between your palms.

4 Drop the balls, one at a time, into the icing sugar and roll until heavily coated. Remove each ball with a slotted spoon and tap the spoon against the bowl to remove excess sugar. Place the balls on the baking sheets, about 4 cm/1½ in apart.

5 Bake the biscuits for 10–15 minutes or until the top of each feels slightly firm when touched with a fingertip. Leave for 2–3 minutes, until just set. Transfer to wire racks and leave to cool completely.

CHUNKY CHOCOLATE DROPS

MAKES ABOUT 18

*175g/6oz bittersweet or plain chocolate,
chopped into small pieces*
115g/4oz/½ cup unsalted butter, diced
2 eggs
115g/4oz/½ cup granulated sugar
50g/2oz/⅓ cup light brown sugar
40g/1½oz/6 tbsp plain flour
25g/1oz/¼ cup cocoa powder
5ml/1 tsp baking powder
10ml/2 tsp vanilla essence
pinch of salt
*115g/4oz/1 cup pecan nuts, toasted and
coarsely chopped*
175g/6oz/1 cup plain chocolate chips
*115g/4oz fine quality white chocolate,
chopped into small pieces*
*115g/4oz fine quality milk chocolate,
chopped into small pieces*

1 Preheat oven to 160°C/325°F/Gas 3. Grease two large baking sheets. In a medium saucepan over a low heat, melt the chocolate and butter until smooth, stirring frequently. Remove from the heat and leave to cool slightly.

2 In a large mixing bowl, beat the eggs and sugars until pale and creamy. Gradually pour in the melted chocolate mixture, beating well. Beat in the flour, cocoa, baking powder and vanilla essence. Stir in the remaining ingredients.

3 Drop heaped tablespoons of the mixture on to the baking sheets, 10 cm/4 in apart. Flatten each to a 7.5 cm/3 in round. (You will only get 4–6 biscuits on each sheet.) Bake for 8–10 minutes until the tops are shiny and cracked and the edges look crisp. Do not over-bake or the biscuits will break when they are removed from the baking sheets.

4 Remove the baking sheets to wire racks to cool for 2 minutes, until the biscuits are just set, then carefully transfer them to the wire racks to cool completely. Bake the biscuits in batches, if necessary. Store in airtight containers.

CHOCOLATE AMARETTI

MAKES ABOUT 24

115g / 4oz / 1 cup blanched whole almonds
115g / 4oz / ½ cup caster sugar
15ml / 1 tbsp cocoa powder
30ml / 2 tbsp icing sugar
2 egg whites
pinch of cream of tartar
5ml / 1 tsp almond essence
flaked almonds, to decorate

1 Preheat oven to 180°C / 350°F / Gas 4. Place the almonds on a small baking sheet and bake for 10–12 minutes, turning occasionally until golden brown. Cool to room temperature. Reduce the oven temperature to 160°C / 325°F / Gas 3.

2 Line a large baking sheet with non-stick baking paper. In a food processor, process the toasted almonds with half the caster sugar until the almonds are finely ground but not oily. Transfer the ground almonds to a bowl and stir in the cocoa powder and icing sugar. Set aside.

3 In a medium mixing bowl, beat the egg whites and cream of tartar with a hand-held mixer, until stiff peaks form. Sprinkle in the remaining caster sugar about 15ml / 1 tbsp at a time, beating well after each addition, and continue beating until the whites are glossy and stiff. Beat in the almond essence.

4 Sprinkle over the almond-sugar mixture and gently fold into the beaten egg whites until just blended. Spoon the mixture into a large piping bag fitted with a plain 1 cm / ½ in nozzle. Pipe 4 cm / 1½ in rounds about 2.5 cm / 1 in apart on the prepared baking sheet. Press a flaked almond into the centre of each biscuit.

5 Bake the biscuits for 12–15 minutes or until they are crisp. Cool on the baking sheet for 10 minutes. With a metal palette knife, transfer the biscuits to wire racks to cool completely. When cool, store in an airtight jar or biscuit tin. Serve after a dinner party with coffee, or use in trifles.

CHOCOLATE KISSES

MAKES 24

*75g/3oz dark plain chocolate, chopped into
small pieces*
*75g/3oz white chocolate, chopped into small
pieces*
115g/4oz/½ cup butter, softened
115g/4oz/½ cup caster sugar
2 eggs
225g/8oz/2 cups plain flour
icing sugar, to decorate

1 Melt the plain and white chocolates in separate bowls and set both aside to cool.
2 Beat the butter and caster sugar together until pale and fluffy. Beat in the eggs, one at a time. Then sift in the flour and mix well.

3 Halve the creamed mixture and divide it between the two bowls of chocolate. Mix each chocolate in thoroughly so that each forms a dough. Knead the doughs until smooth, wrap them separately in clear film and chill for 1 hour. Preheat oven to 190°C/375°F/Gas 5.

4 Shape slightly rounded teaspoonfuls of both doughs roughly into balls. Roll the balls between your palms to neaten them. Arrange the balls on greased baking sheets and bake for 10–12 minutes. Dust liberally with sifted icing sugar and cool on a wire rack.

MOCHA VIENNESE SWIRLS

MAKES ABOUT 20

*115g/4oz plain chocolate, chopped into
small pieces*

*200g/7oz/scant 1 cup unsalted butter,
softened*

90ml/6 tbsp icing sugar

30ml/2 tbsp strong black coffee

200g/7oz/1¾ cups plain flour

50g/2oz/½ cup cornflour

TO DECORATE

about 20 blanched almonds

*150g/5oz plain chocolate, chopped into
small pieces*

1 Preheat oven to 190°C/375°F/Gas 5. Melt the chocolate in a bowl over barely simmering water. Cream the butter with the icing sugar in a bowl until smooth and pale. Beat in the melted chocolate, then the strong black coffee.

2 Sift the plain flour and cornflour over the mixture. Fold in lightly and evenly to make a soft biscuit dough.

3 Lightly grease two large baking sheets. Spoon the dough into a piping bag fitted with a large star nozzle. Pipe about 20 swirls on the baking sheets, allowing room for spreading. Keep the nozzle close to the sheet so that the swirls are flat.

4 Press an almond into the centre of each swirl. Bake for about 15 minutes or until the biscuits are firm and starting to brown. Cool for about 10 minutes on the baking sheets, then lift carefully on to a wire rack to cool completely.

5 When cool, melt the chocolate and dip the base of each swirl to coat. Place on a sheet of non-stick baking paper and leave to set completely.

CHOCOLATE MACAROONS

MAKES 24

50g / 2oz plain chocolate, chopped into
small pieces
115g / 4oz / 1 cup blanched almonds
225g / 8oz / 1 cup granulated sugar
3 egg whites
2.5ml / ½ tsp vanilla essence
1.5ml / ¼ tsp almond essence
icing sugar, for dusting

<u>1</u> Preheat oven to 160°C/325°F/Gas 3.
Line two baking sheets with non-stick
baking paper.

VARIATION

For Chocolate Pine Nut Macaroons,
spread 50g/2oz/⅔ cup toasted pine
nuts in a shallow dish. Press the balls of
chocolate macaroon dough into the nuts
to cover one side and bake as described,
nut-side up.

<u>2</u> Melt the chocolate in the top of a
double boiler, or in a heatproof bowl
placed over a saucepan of barely
simmering water.
<u>3</u> Grind the almonds finely in a food
processor, blender or nut grinder.
Transfer to a mixing bowl.
<u>4</u> Add the sugar, egg whites, vanilla
essence and almond essence and stir to
blend. Stir in the chocolate. The mixture
should just hold its shape. If it is too soft,
chill it in the fridge for 15 minutes.

<u>5</u> Use a teaspoon and your hands to shape
the dough into walnut-size balls. Place on
the baking sheets and flatten slightly.
Brush each ball with a little water and sift
over a thin layer of icing sugar. Bake for
10–12 minutes, until just firm. With a
metal spatula, transfer to a wire rack to
cool completely.

CHOCOLATE CINNAMON TUILES

3 In a separate bowl, mix together the cocoa and cinnamon. Stir into the larger quantity of mixture until well combined. Leaving room for spreading, drop spoonfuls of the chocolate-flavoured mixture on to the prepared baking sheets, then spread each gently with a palette knife to make a neat round.

4 Using a small spoon, drizzle the reserved plain mixture over the rounds, swirling it lightly to give a marbled effect.

5 Bake for 4–6 minutes, until just set. Using a palette knife, lift each biscuit and drape it over a rolling pin, to give a curved shape as it hardens. Allow the tuiles to set, then remove them and finish cooling on a wire rack. Serve on the same day.

MAKES 12

1 egg white
50g/2oz/¼ cup caster sugar
30ml/2 tbsp plain flour
40g/1½oz/3 tbsp butter, melted
15ml/1 tbsp cocoa powder
2.5ml/½ tsp ground cinnamon

1 Preheat oven to 200°C/400°F/Gas 6. Lightly grease two large baking sheets. Whisk the egg white in a clean, grease-free bowl until it forms soft peaks. Gradually whisk in the sugar to make a smooth, glossy mixture.

2 Sift the flour over the meringue mixture and fold in evenly; try not to deflate the mixture. Stir in the butter. Transfer about 45ml/3 tbsp of the mixture to a small bowl and set it aside.

CHOCOLATE CUPS

Cream 150g/5oz/⅔ cup butter with 115g/4oz/½ cup caster sugar. Stir in 75g/3oz/1 cup porridge oats, 15ml/1 tbsp cocoa powder and 5ml/1 tsp vanilla essence. Roll to the size of golf balls and space well on greased baking sheets. Bake at 180°C/350°F/Gas 4 for 12–15 minutes. Cool slightly then drape over greased upturned glasses until cool and firm. Makes 8–10.

CHOCOLATE PRETZELS

MAKES 28

150g / 5oz / 1¼ cups plain flour
pinch of salt
25g / 1oz / ¼ cup cocoa powder
115g / 4oz / ½ cup butter, softened
115g / 4oz / ½ cup caster sugar
1 egg
1 egg white, lightly beaten, for glazing
sugar crystals, for sprinkling

1 Sift the plain flour, salt and cocoa powder into a bowl. Set aside. Grease two baking sheets.

2 With a hand-held electric mixer, cream the butter. Add the caster sugar and beat until fluffy. Beat in the egg. Stir in the dry ingredients. Gather the dough into a ball and chill for 1 hour.

3 Roll the dough into 28 small balls. Preheat the oven to 190°C/375°F/Gas 5. Roll each ball into a rope about 25 cm/10 in long. With each rope, form a loop with the two ends facing you. Twist the ends and fold back on to the circle, pressing in to make a pretzel shape. Place on the greased baking sheets.

4 Brush the pretzels with the egg white. Sprinkle sugar crystals over the tops and bake for 10–12 minutes until firm. Transfer to a wire rack to cool.

LITTLE CAKES, SLICES AND BARS

CHOCOLATE FAIRY CAKES

MAKES 24

*115g/4oz plain chocolate, chopped into
small pieces*
15ml/1 tbsp water
275g/10oz/2½ cups plain flour
5ml/1 tsp baking powder
2.5ml/½ tsp bicarbonate of soda
pinch of salt
300g/11oz/scant 1½ cups caster sugar
*175g/6oz/¾ cup butter or margarine, at
room temperature*
150ml/¼ pint/⅔ cup milk
5ml/1 tsp vanilla essence
3 eggs
FOR THE ICING
40g/1½ oz/3 tbsp butter or margarine
115g/4oz/1 cup icing sugar
2.5ml/½ tsp vanilla essence
15–30ml/1–2 tbsp milk

1 Preheat oven to 180°C/350°F/Gas 4.
Grease 24 bun tins, about 6.5 cm/2¾ in
in diameter and line with paper cases.
2 Make the icing. Soften the butter or
margarine. Place it in a bowl and stir in
the icing sugar, a little at a time. Add the
vanilla essence, then, a drop at a time,
beat in just enough milk to make a
creamy, spreadable mixture. Cover the
surface closely with clear film and set the
bowl aside.

3 Melt the chocolate with the water in a
heatproof bowl over simmering water.
Remove from the heat. Sift the flour,
baking powder, bicarbonate of soda, salt
and sugar into a large bowl. Add the
chocolate mixture, butter or margarine,
milk and vanilla essence.

4 With a hand-held electric mixer on
medium speed, beat the mixture until
smooth. Increase the speed to high and
beat for 2 minutes. Add the eggs, one at a
time, and beat for 1 minute after each
addition. Divide the mixture evenly
among the prepared bun tins.

5 Bake for 20–25 minutes or until a
skewer inserted into the centre of a cake
comes out clean. Cool in the tins for
10 minutes, then turn out to cool
completely on a wire rack. Spread the top
of each cake with the icing, swirling it
into a peak in the centre.

CHOCOLATE MINT-FILLED CUPCAKES

MAKES 12

225g/8oz/2 cups plain flour
5ml/1 tsp bicarbonate of soda
pinch of salt
50g/2oz/½ cup cocoa powder
150g/5oz/10 tbsp unsalted butter, softened
350g/12oz/1⅔ cups caster sugar
3 eggs
5ml/1 tsp peppermint essence
250ml/8 fl oz/1 cup milk

FOR THE MINT CREAM FILLING

300ml/½ pint/1¼ cups double cream or whipping cream
5ml/1 tsp peppermint essence

FOR THE CHOCOLATE MINT GLAZE

175g/6oz plain chocolate, chopped into small pieces
115g/4oz/½ cup unsalted butter
5ml/1 tsp peppermint essence

1 Preheat oven to 180°C/350°F/Gas 4. Line a 12-hole bun tin with paper cases, using the cases double if they are thin. Sift the flour, bicarbonate of soda, salt and cocoa powder into a bowl. Set aside.
2 In a large mixing bowl, beat the butter and sugar with a hand-held electric mixer for about 3–5 minutes until light and creamy. Add the eggs, one at a time, beating well after each addition and adding a small amount of the flour mixture if the egg mixture shows signs of curdling. Beat in the peppermint essence until thoroughly mixed.

3 With the hand-held electric mixer on a low speed, beat in the flour-cocoa mixture alternately with the milk, until just blended. Spoon into the paper cases, filling them about three-quarters full.
4 Bake for 12–15 minutes, until a cake tester inserted in the centre of one of the cupcakes comes out clean.

5 Lift the cupcakes on to a wire rack to cool completely. When cool, carefully remove the paper cases.
6 Prepare the mint cream filling. In a small bowl, whip the cream and peppermint essence until stiff. Fit a small, plain nozzle into a piping bag and spoon in the flavoured cream. Gently press the nozzle into the bottom of one of the cupcakes. Squeeze gently, releasing about 15ml/1 tbsp of the flavoured cream into the centre of the cake. Repeat with the remaining cupcakes, returning each one to the wire rack as it is filled.

7 Prepare the glaze. In a saucepan over a low heat, melt the chocolate and butter, stirring until smooth. Remove from heat and stir in the peppermint essence. Cool then spread on the top of each cake.

CHOCOLATE LEMON TARTLETS

MAKES 12 TARTLETS

1 quantity Chocolate Shortcrust Pastry
lemon twists and melted chocolate to decorate

FOR THE LEMON CUSTARD SAUCE
grated rind and juice of 1 lemon
350ml / 12fl oz / 1½ cups milk
6 egg yolks
50g / 2oz / ½ cup caster sugar

FOR THE LEMON CURD FILLING
grated rind and juice of 2 lemons
175g / 6oz / ¾ cup unsalted butter, diced
450g / 1lb / 2 cups granulated sugar
3 eggs, lightly beaten

FOR THE CHOCOLATE LAYER
175ml / 6fl oz / ¾ cup double cream
175g / 6oz bittersweet or plain chocolate,
chopped into small pieces
25g / 1oz / 2 tbsp unsalted butter, cut into
pieces

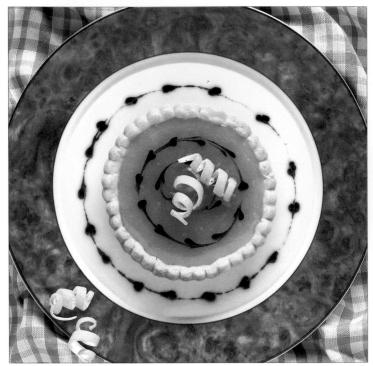

1 Prepare the custard sauce. Place the rind in a saucepan with the milk. Bring to the boil over a medium heat. Remove from the heat and allow to stand for 5 minutes to infuse. Strain the milk into a clean pan and reheat it gently.

2 In a bowl beat the yolks and sugar with a hand-held electric mixer for 2–3 minutes, until pale and thick. Pour over about 250ml / 8fl oz / 1 cup of the flavoured hot milk, beating vigorously.

3 Return the yolk mixture to the rest of the milk in the pan and cook gently, stirring constantly, over low heat until the mixture thickens and lightly coats the back of a spoon. (Do not allow sauce to boil or it will curdle.) Strain into a chilled bowl. Stir 30ml / 2 tbsp lemon juice into the sauce. Cool, stirring occasionally, then chill until ready to use.

4 Prepare the lemon curd filling. Combine the lemon rind, juice, butter and sugar in the top of a double boiler. Set over simmering water and heat gently until the butter has melted and the sugar has completely dissolved. Reduce the heat to low.

5 Stir the lightly beaten eggs into the butter mixture. Cook over a low heat, for 15 minutes, stirring constantly, until the mixture coats the back of a spoon.

6 Strain the lemon curd into a bowl and cover closely with clear film. Allow to cool, stirring occasionally, then chill to thicken, stirring occasionally.

7 Lightly butter twelve 7.5 cm / 3 in tartlet tins (if possible ones which have removable bases). On a lightly floured surface, roll out the pastry to a thickness of 3 mm / ⅛ in. Using a 10 cm / 4 in fluted cutter, cut out 12 rounds and press each one into a tartlet tin. Prick the bases with a fork. Place the tins on a baking sheet and chill for 30 minutes.

8 Preheat oven to 190°C / 375°F / Gas 5. Cut out rounds of foil and line each pastry case; fill with baking beans or rice. Bake blind for 5–8 minutes. Remove the foil with the beans and bake for 5 more minutes, until the cases are golden. Remove to rack to cool.

9 Prepare the chocolate layer. In a saucepan over a medium heat, bring the cream to the boil. Remove from the heat and add the chocolate all at once; stir until melted. Beat in the butter and cool slightly. Pour the filling into each tartlet to make a layer 5 mm / ¼ in thick. Chill for 10 minutes until set.

10 Remove the tartlets from the tins and spoon in a layer of lemon curd to come to the top of the pastry. Set aside, but do not chill. To serve, spoon a little lemon custard sauce on to a plate and place a tartlet in the centre. Decorate with a lemon twist. Dot the custard with melted chocolate. Draw a skewer through the chocolate to make heart motifs.

CHOCOLATE CREAM PUFFS

MAKES 12 LARGE CREAM PUFFS

115g / 4oz / 1 cup plain flour
30ml / 2 tbsp cocoa powder
250ml / 8fl oz / 1 cup water
2.5ml / ½ tsp salt
15ml / 1 tbsp granulated sugar
115g / 4oz / ½ cup unsalted butter, diced
4 eggs

FOR THE CHOCOLATE PASTRY CREAM

450ml / ¾ pint / 2 cups milk
6 egg yolks
115g / 4oz / ½ cup granulated sugar
50g / 2oz / ½ cup plain flour
*150g / 5oz plain chocolate, chopped into
small pieces*
115ml / 4fl oz / ½ cup whipping cream

FOR THE CHOCOLATE GLAZE

300ml / ½ pint / 1¼ cups whipping cream
50g / 2oz / ¼ cup unsalted butter, diced
*225g / 8oz bittersweet or plain chocolate,
chopped into small pieces*
15ml / 1 tbsp golden syrup
5ml / 1 tsp vanilla essence

1 Preheat oven to 220°C/425°F/Gas 7.
Lightly grease two large baking sheets.
Sift the flour and cocoa powder into a
bowl. In a saucepan over a medium heat,
bring to the boil the water, salt, sugar and
butter. Remove the pan from the heat and
add the flour and cocoa mixture all at
once, stirring vigorously until the
mixture is smooth and leaves the sides of
the pan clean.

2 Return the pan to the heat to cook the
choux pastry for 1 minute, beating
constantly. Remove from the heat.

3 With a hand-held electric mixer, beat in
4 of the eggs, one at a time, beating well
after each addition, until each is well
blended. The mixture should be thick and
shiny and just fall from a spoon. Spoon
the mixture into a large piping bag fitted
with a plain nozzle. Pipe 12 mounds
about 7.5 cm/3 in across at least 5 cm/
2 in apart on the baking sheet.

4 Bake for 35–40 minutes until puffed
and firm. Remove the puffs. Using a
serrated knife, slice off and reserve the
top third of each puff; return the opened
puffs to the oven for 5–10 minutes to dry
out. Remove to a wire rack to cool.

5 Prepare the pastry cream. Bring the
milk to the boil in a small pan. In a bowl,
heat the yolks and sugar until pale and
thick. Stir in the flour. Slowly pour about
250ml/8fl oz/1 cup of the hot milk into
the yolks, stirring constantly. Return the
yolk mixture to the remaining milk in the
pan and cook, stirring until the sauce
boils for 1 minute. Remove from the heat
and stir in the chocolate until smooth.

6 Strain into a bowl and cover closely
with clear film. Cool to room
temperature. In a bowl, whip the cream
until stiff. Fold into the pastry cream.

7 Using a large piping bag, fill each puff
bottom with pastry cream, then cover
each puff with its top. Arrange the cream
puffs on a large serving plate in a single
layer or as a pile.

8 Make the glaze by heating the cream,
butter, chocolate, syrup and vanilla
essence in a medium saucepan over low
heat until melted and smooth, stirring
frequently. Cool for 20–30 minutes until
slightly thickened. Pour a little glaze over
each of the cream puffs to serve.

CHOCOLATE RASPBERRY MACAROON BARS

2 In a medium bowl beat the butter, sugar, cocoa powder and salt with a hand-held electric mixer for about 1 minute, until well blended and creamy. Beat in the almond essence and the flour until the mixture forms a crumbly dough.

3 Turn the dough into the prepared tin and pat firmly over the base to make an even layer. Prick the dough with a fork. Bake for 20 minutes until the pastry has just set. Remove from the oven and increase the temperature to 190°C/375°F/Gas 5.

4 Make the topping. In a small bowl, combine the raspberry jam and the liqueur. Spread the mixture evenly over the chocolate crust, then sprinkle evenly with the chocolate chips.

5 In a food processor fitted with a metal blade, process the almonds, egg whites, salt, sugar and almond essence until well blended and foamy. Gently pour over the jam layer, spreading evenly to the edges of the tin. Sprinkle with the almonds.

6 Bake for 20–25 minutes more, until the top is golden and puffed. Cool in the tin on a wire rack for 20 minutes or until firm. Using the edges of the foil, carefully remove the bake from the tin and cool completely. Peel off the foil, and, using a sharp knife, cut into bars.

MAKES 16–18 BARS

115g/4oz/½ cup unsalted butter, softened
50g/2oz/⅓ cup icing sugar
25g/1oz/¼ cup cocoa powder
pinch of salt
5ml/1 tsp almond essence
115g/4oz/1 cup plain flour
FOR THE TOPPING
150g/5oz/½ cup seedless raspberry jam
15ml/1 tbsp raspberry-flavoured liqueur
175g/6oz/1 cup mini chocolate chips
175g/6oz/1½ cups ground almonds
4 egg whites
pinch of salt
225g/8oz/1¼ cups caster sugar
2.5ml/½ tsp almond essence
50g/2oz/¼ cup flaked almonds

1 Preheat oven to 160°C/325°F/Gas 3. Invert a 33 x 23 cm/13 x 9 in baking tin. Mould a sheet of foil over the tin and smooth the foil evenly around the corners. Lift off the foil and turn the tin right side up; line with the moulded foil. Grease the foil.

CHOCOLATE BUTTERSCOTCH BARS

MAKES 24

225g/8oz/2 cups plain flour
2.5ml/½ tsp baking powder
150g/5oz plain chocolate, chopped
115g/4oz/½ cup unsalted butter, diced
50g/2oz/⅓ cup light muscovado sugar
30ml/2 tbsp ground almonds

FOR THE TOPPING

175g/6oz/¾ cup unsalted butter, diced
115g/4oz/½ cup caster sugar
30ml/2 tbsp golden syrup
175ml/6fl oz/¾ cup condensed milk
150g/5oz/1¼ cups whole toasted hazelnuts
225g/8oz plain chocolate, chopped into small pieces

1 Preheat oven to 160°C/325°F/Gas 3. Grease a shallow 30 x 20 cm/12 x 8 in tin. Sift the flour and baking powder into a large bowl. Melt the chocolate in a bowl over a saucepan of simmering water.

2 Rub the butter into the flour until the mixture resembles coarse breadcrumbs, then stir in the sugar. Work in the melted chocolate and ground almonds to make a light biscuit dough.

3 Spread the dough roughly in the tin, then use a rubber spatula to press it down evenly into the sides and the corners. Prick the surface with a fork and bake for 25–30 minutes until firm. Leave to cool in the tin.

4 Make the topping. Heat the butter, sugar, golden syrup and condensed milk in a pan, stirring until the butter and sugar have melted. Simmer until golden, then stir in the hazelnuts.

5 Pour over the cooked base. Leave to set.

6 Melt the chocolate for the topping in a heatproof bowl over barely simmering water. Spread evenly over the butterscotch layer, then leave to set again before cutting into bars to serve.

CHOCOLATE WALNUT BARS

MAKES 24

50g/2oz/½ cup walnuts
50g/2oz/¼ cup caster sugar
115g/4oz/1 cup plain flour, sifted
75g/3oz unsalted butter, cut into pieces

FOR THE TOPPING

25g/1oz/2 tbsp unsalted butter
75ml/3fl oz/5 tbsp water
25g/1oz/¼ cup cocoa powder
115g/4oz/½ cup caster sugar
5ml/1 tsp vanilla essence
pinch of salt
2 eggs
icing sugar, for dusting

1 Preheat oven to 180°C/350°F/Gas 4. Grease the base and sides of a 20 cm/8 in square baking tin.

2 Grind the walnuts with 15–30ml/ 1–2 tbsp of the sugar in a food processor, blender or coffee grinder.

3 In a bowl, combine the ground walnuts, remaining sugar and flour. With your fingertips, rub in the butter until the mixture resembles coarse breadcrumbs. Alternatively, process all the ingredients in a food processor until the mixture resembles coarse breadcrumbs.

4 Pat the walnut mixture on to the base of the prepared tin in an even layer. Bake for 25 minutes.

5 Meanwhile make the topping. Heat the butter with the water in a saucepan over a medium heat. When all the butter has melted, gradually whisk in the cocoa powder and caster sugar. Remove from the heat, stir in the vanilla essence and salt and set the mixture aside to cool for 5 minutes. Whisk in the eggs until blended.

6 Pour the topping over the baked crust, return the baking tin to the oven and bake for about 20 minutes or until set. Transfer the tin to a wire rack to cool.

7 When the bake has cooled for 5 minutes, mark it into 6 x 2.5 cm/2½ x 1 in bars. Leave until completely cold, then separate the bars and transfer them to a wire rack. Dust lightly with icing sugar. Place the bars on a plate and serve.

COOK'S TIP

Look out for walnut pieces in the supermarket or health food store. They are cheaper than walnut halves and are perfect for this recipe. Ground almonds would also work well, but because they are so fine you need to take care not to over-process the mixture or they may become oily.

CHOCOLATE, DATE AND ORANGE BARS

Make the base as in the main recipe, but substitute hazelnuts for the walnuts. Roast the hazelnuts briefly in a hot oven or under the grill, rub off the skins using a clean, dry napkin or tea towel, then grind them with the sugar in a food processor. Complete the base and bake it as described, then set it aside.

Make the topping. Mix 225g/8oz/2 cups of sugar-rolled dates, 75g/3oz/6 tbsp butter and 120ml/4fl oz/½ cup water in a saucepan. Simmer, stirring occasionally, until the butter has dissolved and the dates have broken down to form a pulp. Stir in 50g/2oz/⅓ cup soft light brown sugar until dissolved. Remove the pan from the heat and beat in the grated rind of 1 orange, with 30ml/2 tbsp orange juice. Allow to cool.

Beat 175g/6oz/1½ cups self-raising flour and 1 egg into the date mixture, then spread the topping evenly over the hazelnut base. Bake in a preheated oven at 180°C/ 350°F/Gas 4 for 30 minutes. Cool in the tin, loosen around the edges with a knife then turn out so that the hazelnut base is now uppermost.

Glaze with 150g/5oz melted chocolate. Cut into bars when set.

CHOCOLATE AND TOFFEE BARS

MAKES 32

350g/12oz/2 cups soft light brown sugar
450g/1lb/2 cups butter or margarine, at room temperature
2 egg yolks
7.5ml/1½ tsp vanilla essence
450g/1lb/4 cups plain or wholemeal flour
2.5ml/½ tsp salt
175g/6oz plain chocolate, broken into squares
115g/4oz/1 cup walnuts or pecan nuts, chopped

1 Preheat oven to 180°C/350°F/Gas 4. Beat the sugar and butter or margarine in a mixing bowl until light and fluffy. Beat in the egg yolks and vanilla essence, then stir in the flour and salt to make a soft dough.
2 Spread the dough in a greased 33 x 23 x 5 cm/13 x 9 x 2 in baking tin. Level the surface. Bake for 25–30 minutes, until lightly browned. The texture will be soft.
3 Remove the bake from the oven and immediately place the chocolate on top. Set aside until the chocolate is soft, then spread it out with a spatula. Sprinkle with the chopped nuts.
4 While the bake is still warm, cut it into 5 x 4 cm/2 x 1½ in bars, remove from the tin and leave to cool on a wire rack.

CHOCOLATE PECAN SQUARES

MAKES 16

2 eggs
10ml/2 tsp vanilla essence
pinch of salt
175g/6oz/1½ cups pecan nuts, roughly chopped
50g/2oz/½ cup plain flour
50g/2oz/¼ cup granulated sugar
120ml/4fl oz/½ cup golden syrup
75g/3oz plain chocolate, chopped into small pieces
40g/1½oz/3 tbsp unsalted butter
16 pecan nut halves, to decorate

1 Preheat oven to 160°C/325°F/Gas 3. Line a 20 cm/8 in square baking tin with non-stick baking paper.
2 In a bowl, whisk the eggs with the vanilla essence and salt. In another bowl, mix together the pecan nuts and flour.
3 Put the sugar in a saucepan, add the golden syrup and bring to the boil. Remove from the heat and stir in the chocolate and butter with a wooden spoon until both have dissolved and the mixture is smooth. Stir in the beaten egg mixture, then fold in the pecan nuts and flour.
4 Pour the mixture into the prepared tin and bake for about 35 minutes or until firm to the touch. Cool in the tin for 10 minutes before turning out on a wire rack. Cut into 5 cm/2 in squares and press pecan halves into the tops while still warm. Cool completely before serving.

CHUNKY CHOCOLATE BARS

MAKES 12

*350g/12oz plain chocolate, chopped into
small pieces*
115g/4oz/½ cup unsalted butter
400g/14oz can condensed milk
225g/8oz digestive biscuits, broken
50g/2oz/⅓ cup raisins
*115g/4oz ready-to-eat dried peaches,
roughly chopped*
*50g/2oz/½ cup hazelnuts or pecan nuts,
roughly chopped*

1 Line a 28 x 18 cm/11 x 7 in cake tin
with clear film.
2 Melt the chocolate and butter in a large
heatproof bowl over a pan of simmering
water. Stir until well mixed.

3 Pour the condensed milk into the
chocolate and butter mixture. Beat with a
wooden spoon until creamy.
4 Add the broken biscuits, raisins,
chopped peaches and hazelnuts or pecans.
Mix well until all the ingredients are
coated in the rich chocolate sauce.

5 Tip the mixture into the prepared tin,
making sure it is pressed well into the
corners. Leave the top craggy. Cool, then
chill until set.
6 Lift the cake out of the tin using the
clear film and then peel off the film. Cut
into 12 bars and serve at once.

CHOCOLATE AND COCONUT SLICES

MAKES 24

175g/6oz digestive biscuits
115g/4oz/1 cup walnuts
50g/2oz/¼ cup caster sugar
pinch of salt
115g/4oz/½ cup butter or margarine, melted
75g/3oz/1 cup desiccated coconut
250g/9oz/1½ cups plain chocolate chips
250ml/8fl oz/1 cup sweetened condensed milk

1 Place the digestive biscuits in a paper bag, fold the top over so that the bag is sealed and use a rolling pin to crush the biscuits into coarse crumbs. Chop the walnuts into small pieces, and set aside.

2 Preheat oven to 180°C/350°F/Gas 4. Put a baking sheet inside to heat up.

3 In a bowl, combine the crushed biscuits, sugar, salt and melted butter or margarine. Press the mixture evenly over the base of an ungreased 33 x 23 cm/ 13 x 9 in baking dish.

4 Sprinkle the coconut over the biscuit base, then scatter over the chocolate chips. Pour the condensed milk evenly over the chocolate. Sprinkle the walnuts on top. Place on the hot baking sheet and bake for 30 minutes. Turn out on a wire rack and allow to cool. When cold, cut into slices.

WHITE CHOCOLATE MACADAMIA SLICES

MAKES 16

150g/5oz/1¼ cups macadamia nuts,
blanched almonds or hazelnuts
400g/14oz white chocolate, broken into
squares
115g/4oz/½ cup ready-to-eat dried apricots
75g/3oz/6 tbsp unsalted butter
5ml/1 tsp vanilla essence
3 eggs
150g/5oz/scant 1 cup light muscovado sugar
115g/4oz/1 cup self-raising flour

1 Preheat oven to 190°C/375°F/Gas 5. Lightly grease two 20 cm/8 in round sandwich cake tins and line the base of each with greaseproof paper or non-stick baking paper.

2 Roughly chop the nuts and half the white chocolate, making sure that the pieces are more or less the same size, then use scissors to cut the apricots to similar size pieces.

3 In a heatproof bowl over a saucepan of barely simmering water, melt the remaining white chocolate with the butter. Remove from the heat and stir in the vanilla essence.

4 Whisk the eggs and sugar together in a mixing bowl until thick and pale, then pour in the melted chocolate mixture, whisking constantly.

5 Sift the flour over the mixture and fold it in evenly. Finally, stir in the nuts, chopped white chocolate and chopped dried apricots.

6 Spoon into the tins and level the tops. Bake for 30–35 minutes or until the top is firm and crusty. Cool in the tins before cutting each cake into 8 slices.

CRANBERRY AND CHOCOLATE SQUARES

MAKES 12

150g/5oz/1¼ cups self-raising flour, plus
extra for dusting
115g/4oz/½ cup unsalted butter
60ml/4 tbsp cocoa powder
215g/7½oz/1¼ cups light muscovado sugar
2 eggs, beaten
115g/4oz/1⅓ cups fresh or thawed frozen
cranberries
75ml/5 tbsp coarsely grated plain chocolate,
for sprinkling

FOR THE TOPPING

150ml/¼ pint/⅔ cup soured cream
75g/3oz/6 tbsp caster sugar
30ml/2 tbsp self-raising flour
50g/2oz/4 tbsp soft margarine
1 egg, beaten
2.5ml/½ tsp vanilla essence

1 Preheat oven to 180°C/350°F/Gas 4. Grease a 27 x 18 cm/10½ x 7 in cake tin and dust lightly with flour. Combine the butter, cocoa powder and sugar in a saucepan and stir over a low heat until melted and smooth.

2 Remove the melted mixture from the heat and stir in the flour and eggs, beating until thoroughly mixed.

3 Stir in the cranberries, then spread the mixture in the tin. Make the topping by mixing all the ingredients in a bowl. Beat until smooth, then spread over the base.

4 Sprinkle with the grated chocolate and bake for 40–45 minutes, or until risen and firm. Cool in the tin for 10 minutes. Then cut neatly into 12 squares. Remove from the tin and cool on a wire rack.

NUT AND CHOCOLATE CHIP BROWNIES

MAKES 16

150g / 5oz plain chocolate, chopped into small pieces
120ml / 4fl oz / ½ cup sunflower oil
215g / 7½oz / 1¼ cups light muscovado sugar
2 eggs
5ml / 1 tsp vanilla essence
65g / 2½oz / generous ½ cup self-raising flour
60ml / 4 tbsp cocoa powder
75g / 3oz / ¾ cup walnuts or pecan nuts, chopped
60ml / 4 tbsp milk chocolate chips

1 Preheat oven to 180°C/350°F/Gas 4. Lightly grease a shallow 19 cm/7½ in square cake tin. Melt the plain chocolate in a heatproof bowl over a saucepan of barely simmering water.

2 Beat the oil, sugar, eggs and vanilla essence together in a large bowl. Stir in the melted chocolate, then beat well until evenly mixed and smooth.

3 Sift the flour and cocoa powder into the bowl and fold in thoroughly. Stir in the chopped nuts and chocolate chips, tip into the prepared tin and spread evenly to the edges.

4 Bake for 30–35 minutes, or until the top is firm and crusty. Cool in the tin before cutting into squares.

LOW-FAT BROWNIES

MAKES 9

75ml / 5 tbsp fat-reduced cocoa powder
15ml / 1 tbsp caster sugar
75ml / 5 tbsp skimmed milk
3 large bananas, mashed
175g / 6oz / 1 cup soft light brown sugar
5ml / 1 tsp vanilla essence
5 egg whites
75g / 3oz / ¾ cup self-raising flour
75g / 3oz / ¾ cup oat bran
15ml / 1 tbsp icing sugar, for dusting

1 Preheat oven to 180°C/350°F/Gas 4. Line a 20 cm/8 in square cake tin with non-stick baking paper. Blend the cocoa powder and caster sugar with the milk in a bowl. Add the bananas, soft brown sugar and vanilla essence.

2 In a mixing bowl, lightly beat the egg whites with a fork. Add the chocolate mixture and continue to beat well. Sift the flour over the mixture and fold in with the oat bran. Pour the mixture into the prepared cake tin.

3 Bake for 40 minutes or until the top is firm and crusty. Cool in the tin before cutting into squares. Lightly dust the brownies with icing sugar before serving.

MARBLED BROWNIES

MAKES 24

*225g / 8oz plain chocolate, chopped into
small pieces*
75g / 3oz / 6 tbsp butter, diced
4 eggs
300g / 11oz / scant 1½ cups granulated sugar
150g / 5oz / 1¼ cups plain flour
2.5ml / ½ tsp salt
5ml / 1 tsp baking powder
10ml / 2 tsp vanilla essence
115g / 4oz / 1 cup walnuts, chopped
FOR THE PLAIN MIXTURE
50g / 2oz / ¼ cup butter, at room temperature
175g / 6oz / ¾ cup cream cheese
75g / 3oz / 6 tbsp granulated sugar
2 eggs
25g / 1oz / ¼ cup plain flour
5ml / 1 tsp vanilla essence

1 Preheat oven to 180°C / 350°F / Gas 4.
Line a 33 x 23 cm / 13 x 9 in baking tin
with greaseproof paper or non-stick
baking paper. Grease the paper lightly.

2 Melt the chocolate with the butter in a
heatproof bowl over barely simmering
water, stirring constantly until smooth.
Set the mixture aside to cool.
3 Meanwhile, beat the eggs in a bowl
until light and fluffy. Gradually add the
sugar and continue beating until blended.
Sift over the flour, salt and baking powder
and fold in gently but thoroughly.

4 Stir in the cooled chocolate mixture.
Add the vanilla essence and walnuts.
Measure and set aside 475ml / 16fl oz /
2 cups of the chocolate mixture.

5 For the plain mixture, cream the butter
and cream cheese in a bowl. Add the
sugar and beat well. Beat in the eggs,
flour and vanilla essence.
6 Spread the unmeasured chocolate
mixture in the tin. Pour over the plain
mixture. Drop spoonfuls of the reserved
chocolate mixture on top.

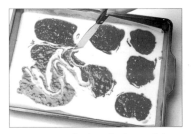

7 With a metal palette knife, swirl the
mixtures to marble them. Do not blend
completely. Bake for 35–45 minutes,
until just set. Turn out when cool and cut
into squares for serving.

WHITE CHOCOLATE BROWNIES WITH MILK CHOCOLATE MACADAMIA TOPPING

SERVES 12

115g/4oz/1 cup plain flour
2.5ml/½ tsp baking powder
pinch of salt
175g/6oz fine quality white chocolate,
chopped into small pieces
115g/4oz/½ cup caster sugar
115g/4oz/½ cup unsalted butter, cut into
small pieces
2 eggs, lightly beaten
5ml/1 tsp vanilla essence
175g/6oz plain chocolate chips or plain
chocolate, chopped into small pieces

FOR THE TOPPING

200g/7oz milk chocolate, chopped into
small pieces
175g/6oz/1½ cups unsalted macadamia
nuts, chopped

<u>1</u> Preheat oven to 180°C/350°F/Gas 4. Grease a 23 cm/9 in springform tin. Sift together the flour, baking powder and salt, set aside.

<u>2</u> In a medium saucepan over a low heat, melt the white chocolate, sugar and butter until smooth, stirring frequently. Cool slightly, then beat in the eggs and vanilla essence. Stir in the flour mixture until well blended. Stir in the chocolate chips or chopped chocolate. Spread evenly in the prepared tin.

<u>3</u> Bake for 20–25 minutes, until a cake tester inserted in the cake tin comes out clean; do not over-bake. Remove the cake from the oven and place the tin on a heatproof surface.

<u>4</u> Sprinkle the chopped milk chocolate evenly over the cake and return it to the oven for 1 minute.

<u>5</u> Remove the cake from the oven again and gently spread the softened chocolate evenly over the top. Sprinkle with the macadamia nuts and gently press them into the chocolate. Cool on a wire rack for 30 minutes, then chill, for about 1 hour, until set. Run a sharp knife around the side of the tin to loosen, then unclip the side of the springform tin and remove it carefully. Cut into thin wedges.

DOUBLE CHOCOLATE CHIP MUFFINS

MAKES 16

400g/14oz/3½ cups plain flour
15ml/1 tbsp baking powder
30ml/2 tbsp cocoa powder
115g/4oz/⅔ cup dark muscovado sugar
2 eggs
150ml/¼ pint/⅔ cup soured cream
150ml/¼ pint/⅔ cup milk
60ml/4 tbsp sunflower oil
175g/6oz white chocolate, chopped into
small pieces
175g/6oz plain chocolate, chopped into
small pieces
cocoa powder, for dusting

1 Preheat oven to 180°C/350°F/Gas 4.
Place 16 paper muffin cases in muffin tins
or deep patty tins. Sift the flour, baking
powder and cocoa into a bowl and stir in
the sugar. Make a well in the centre.

2 In a separate bowl, beat the eggs with
the soured cream, milk and oil, then stir
into the well in the dry ingredients. Beat
well, gradually incorporating all the
surrounding flour mixture to make a
thick and creamy batter.

3 Stir the white and plain chocolate
pieces into the batter mixture.

4 Spoon the chocolate mixture into the
muffin cases, filling them almost to the
top. Bake for 25–30 minutes, until well
risen and firm to the touch. Cool on a
wire rack, then dust the muffins lightly
with cocoa powder.

CHOCOLATE WALNUT MUFFINS

MAKES 12

175g / 6oz / ¾ cup unsalted butter
150g / 5oz plain chocolate, chopped into
small pieces
200g / 7oz / scant 1 cup caster sugar
50g / 2oz / ⅓ cup soft dark brown sugar
4 eggs
5ml / 1 tsp vanilla essence
1.5ml / ¼ tsp almond essence
110g / 3¾oz / scant 1 cup plain flour
15ml / 1 tbsp cocoa powder
115g / 4oz / 1 cup walnuts or pecan
nuts, chopped

1 Preheat oven to 180°C / 350°F / Gas 4.
Grease a 12-cup muffin tin, or use paper
cases supported in a bun tin.

2 Melt the butter with the chocolate in
the top of a double boiler or in a
heatproof bowl set over a saucepan of
simmering water. Transfer to a large
mixing bowl.
3 Stir both the sugars into the chocolate
mixture. Mix in the eggs, one at a time,
then add the vanilla and almond essences.

4 Sift over the flour and cocoa, fold in,
then stir in the walnuts or pecan nuts.
5 Fill the muffin cups or cases almost to
the top and bake for 30–35 minutes, until
a skewer inserted in a muffin comes out
clean but slightly sticky. Leave to stand
for 5 minutes before cooling the muffins
on a rack.

CHOCOLATE CINNAMON DOUGHNUTS

MAKES 16

500g / 1¼lb / 5 cups strong plain flour
30ml / 2 tbsp cocoa powder
2.5ml / ½ tsp salt
1 sachet easy-blend dried yeast
300ml / ½ pint / 1¼ cups hand-hot milk
40g / 1½oz / 3 tbsp butter, melted
1 egg, beaten
115g / 4oz plain chocolate, broken into 16 pieces
sunflower oil, for deep frying

FOR THE COATING

45ml / 3 tbsp caster sugar
15ml / 1 tbsp cocoa powder
5ml / 1 tsp ground cinnamon

1 Sift the flour, cocoa and salt into a large bowl. Stir in the yeast. Make a well in the centre and add the milk, melted butter and egg. Stir, gradually incorporating the surrounding dry ingredients, to make a soft and pliable dough.

2 Knead the dough on a lightly floured surface for about 5 minutes, until smooth and elastic. Return to the clean bowl, cover with clear film or a clean dry dish towel and leave in a warm place until the dough has doubled in bulk.

3 Knead the dough lightly again, then divide into 16 pieces. Shape each into a round, press a piece of plain chocolate into the centre, then fold the dough over to enclose the filling, pressing firmly to make sure the edges are sealed. Re-shape the doughnuts when sealed, if necessary.

4 Heat the oil for frying to 180°C / 350°F or until a cube of dried bread browns in 30–45 seconds. Deep fry the doughnuts in batches. As each doughnut rises and turns golden brown, turn it over to cook the other side. Drain the cooked doughnuts well on kitchen paper.

5 Mix the sugar, cocoa and cinnamon in a shallow bowl. Toss the doughnuts in the mixture to coat them evenly. Pile on a plate and serve warm.

VARIATION

Instead of using a square of plain chocolate to fill each doughnut, try chocolate spread instead. Use about 5ml / 1 tsp of the spread for each doughnut. Seal well before frying.

CHOCOLATE ORANGE SPONGE DROPS

MAKES ABOUT 14
2 eggs
50g / 2 oz / ¼ cup caster sugar
2.5ml / ½ tsp grated orange rind
50g / 2oz / ½ cup plain flour
60ml / 4 tbsp finely shredded orange marmalade
40g / 1½oz plain chocolate, chopped into small pieces

1 Preheat oven to 200°C/400°F/Gas 6. Line three baking sheets with baking parchment. Put the eggs and sugar in a large heatproof bowl and whisk over a pan of simmering water until the mixture is thick and pale.

2 Remove the bowl from the pan of water and continue whisking until the mixture is cool. Whisk in the grated orange rind. Sift the flour over the whisked mixture and fold it in gently.

3 Put spoonfuls of the mixture on the baking sheets, spacing them well apart to allow for spreading. The mixture will make 28–30 drops. Bake for about 8 minutes or until the biscuits are golden. Allow them to cool on the baking sheets for a few minutes, then use a spatula to transfer them to a wire rack to cool completely. Sandwich the biscuits together in pairs with the marmalade.

4 Melt the chocolate in a heatproof bowl set over a pan of barely simmering water. Drizzle or pipe the chocolate over the tops of the sponge drops. Leave to set before serving.

BRIOCHES AU CHOCOLAT

MAKES 12

250g/9oz/2¼ cups strong white flour
pinch of salt
30ml/2 tbsp caster sugar
1 sachet easy-blend dried yeast
3 eggs, beaten, plus extra beaten egg,
for glazing
45ml/3 tbsp hand-hot milk
115g/4oz/½ cup unsalted butter, diced
175g/6oz plain chocolate, broken into
squares

1 Sift the flour and salt into a large mixing bowl and stir in the sugar and yeast. Make a well in the centre of the mixture and add the eggs and milk.

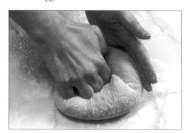

2 Beat the egg and milk mixture well, gradually incorporating the surrounding dry ingredients to make a fairly soft dough. Turn the dough on to a lightly floured surface and knead well for about 5 minutes, until smooth and elastic, adding a little more flour if necessary.
3 Add the butter to the dough, a few pieces at a time, kneading until each addition is absorbed before adding the next. When all the butter has been incorporated and small bubbles appear in the dough, wrap it in clear film and chill for at least 1 hour. If you intend serving the brioches for breakfast, the dough can be left overnight.

4 Lightly grease 12 individual brioche tins set on a baking sheet or a 12-hole brioche or patty tin. Divide the brioche dough into 12 pieces and shape each into a smooth round. Place a chocolate square in the centre of each round. Bring up the sides of the dough and press the edges firmly together to seal, use a little beaten egg if necessary.
5 Place the brioches, join side down, in the prepared tins. Cover and leave them in a warm place for about 30 minutes or until doubled in size. Preheat oven to 200°C/400°F/Gas 6.

6 Brush the brioches with beaten egg. Bake for 12–15 minutes, until well risen and golden brown. Place on wire racks and leave until they have cooled slightly. They should be served warm and can be made in advance and reheated if necessary. Do not serve straight from the oven, as the chocolate will be very hot.

COOK'S TIP

Brioches freeze well for up to
1 month. Thaw at room temperature,
then reheat on baking sheets in a low
oven and serve warm, but not hot.
For a richer variation serve with
melted chocolate drizzled over the
top of the brioches.

SWEETS, TRUFFLES AND DRINKS

CHOCOLATE AND CHERRY COLETTES

MAKES 18–20

115g/4oz plain dark chocolate, chopped into
small pieces
75g/3oz white or milk chocolate, chopped
into small pieces
25g/1oz/2 tbsp unsalted butter, melted
15ml/1 tbsp Kirsch or brandy
60ml/4 tbsp double cream
18–20 maraschino cherries or liqueur-soaked
cherries
milk chocolate curls, to decorate

1 Melt the dark chocolate, then remove it from the heat. Spoon into 18–20 foil sweet cases, spread evenly up the sides with a small brush, then leave the cases in a cool place until the chocolate has set.

2 Melt the white or milk chocolate with the butter. Remove from the heat and stir in the Kirsch or brandy, then the cream. Cool until the mixture is thick enough to hold its shape.

3 Carefully peel away the paper from the chocolate cases. Place one cherry in each chocolate case. Spoon the white or milk chocolate cream mixture into a piping bag fitted with a small star nozzle and pipe over the cherries until the cases are full. Top each colette with a generous swirl, and decorate with milk chocolate curls. Leave to set before serving.

COGNAC AND GINGER CREAMS

MAKES 18–20
*300g/11oz plain dark chocolate, chopped
into small pieces
45ml/3 tbsp double cream
30ml/2 tbsp cognac
4 pieces of stem ginger, finely chopped, plus
15ml/1 tbsp syrup from the jar
crystallized ginger, to decorate*

1 Polish the insides of 18–20 chocolate moulds carefully with cotton wool. Melt about two-thirds of the chocolate in a heatproof bowl over a saucepan of barely simmering water, then spoon a little into each mould. Reserve a little of the melted chocolate, for sealing the creams.

2 Using a small brush, sweep the chocolate up the sides of the moulds to coat them evenly, then invert them on to a sheet of greaseproof paper and set aside until the chocolate has set.

CHOCOLATE MARSHMALLOW DIPS
Have ready a large baking sheet lined with non-stick baking paper. Melt 175g/6oz plain or bittersweet chocolate in a heatproof bowl over barely simmering water. Stir until smooth. Remove the pan from the heat, but leave the bowl in place, so that the chocolate does not solidify too soon. You will need 15–20 large or 30–35 small marshmallows. Using cocktail sticks, spear each marshmallow and coat in the chocolate. Roll in ground hazelnuts. Place on the lined baking sheet and chill until set before removing the skewers. Place each marshmallow dip in a foil sweet case.

3 Melt the remaining chopped chocolate over simmering water, then stir in the cream, cognac, stem ginger and ginger syrup, mixing well. Spoon into the chocolate-lined moulds. If the reserved chocolate has solidified, melt, then spoon a little into each mould to seal.

4 Leave the chocolates in a cool place (not the fridge) until set. To remove them from the moulds, gently press them out on to a cool surface, such as a marble slab. Decorate with small pieces of crystallized ginger. Keep the chocolates cool if not serving them immediately.

CHOCOLATE TRUFFLES

MAKES 20 LARGE OR 30 MEDIUM TRUFFLES

250ml/8fl oz/1 cup double cream
275g/10oz fine quality bittersweet or plain chocolate, chopped into small pieces
40g/1½oz/3 tbsp unsalted butter, cut into small pieces
45ml/3 tbsp brandy, whisky or liqueur of own choice
cocoa powder, for dusting (optional)
finely chopped pistachio nuts, to decorate (optional)
400g/14oz bittersweet chocolate, to decorate (optional)

<u>1</u> Pour the cream into a saucepan. Bring to the boil over a medium heat. Remove from the heat and add the chocolate, all at once. Stir gently until melted. Stir in the butter until melted, then stir in the brandy, whisky or liqueur. Strain into a bowl and cool to room temperature. Cover the mixture with clear film and chill for 4 hours or overnight.

<u>2</u> Line a large baking sheet with non-stick baking paper. Using a small ice cream scoop, melon baller or tablespoon, scrape up the mixture into 20 large balls or 30 medium balls and place on the lined baking sheet. Dip the scoop or spoon in cold water from time to time, to prevent the mixture from sticking.

<u>3</u> If dusting with cocoa powder, sift a thick layer of cocoa on to a dish or pie plate. Roll the truffles in the cocoa, rounding them between the palms of your hands. (Dust your hands with cocoa to prevent the truffles from sticking.) Do not worry if the truffles are not perfectly round as an irregular shape looks more authentic. Alternatively, roll the truffles in very finely chopped pistachios. Chill on the paper-lined baking sheet until firm. Keep in the fridge for up to 10 days or freeze for up to 2 months.

<u>4</u> If coating with chocolate, do not roll the truffles in cocoa, but freeze them for 1 hour. For perfect results, temper the chocolate. Alternatively, simply melt it in a heatproof bowl over a saucepan of barely simmering water. Using a fork, dip the truffles, one at a time, into the melted chocolate, tapping the fork on the edge of the bowl to shake off excess. Place on a baking sheet, lined with non-stick baking paper. If the chocolate begins to thicken, reheat it gently until smooth. Chill the truffles until set.

MALT WHISKY TRUFFLES

MAKES 25–30

*200g/7oz plain dark chocolate, chopped into
small pieces
150ml/¼ pint/⅔ cup double cream
45ml/3 tbsp malt whisky
115g/4oz/¾ cup icing sugar
cocoa powder, for coating*

<u>1</u> Melt the chocolate in a heatproof bowl
over a saucepan of simmering water, stir
until smooth, then cool slightly.

<u>2</u> Using a wire whisk, whip the cream
with the whisky in a bowl until thick
enough to hold its shape.

<u>3</u> Stir in the melted chocolate and icing
sugar, mixing evenly, then leave until firm
enough to handle.

<u>4</u> Dust your hands with cocoa powder
and shape the mixture into bite-size balls.
Coat in cocoa powder and pack into
pretty cases or boxes. Store in the fridge
for up to 3–4 days if necessary.

TRUFFLE-FILLED EASTER EGG

MAKES 1 LARGE, HOLLOW EASTER EGG

*350g/12oz plain couverture chocolate,
tempered, or plain, milk or white chocolate,
melted*
Chocolate Truffles

1 Line a small baking sheet with non-stick baking paper. Using a small ladle or spoon, pour in enough melted chocolate to coat both halves of an Easter egg mould. Tilt the half-moulds slowly to coat the sides completely; pour any excess chocolate back into the bowl. Set the half-moulds, open side down, on the prepared baking sheet and leave for 1–2 minutes until just set.

2 Apply a second coat of chocolate and chill for 1–3 minutes more, until set. Repeat a third time, then replace the moulds on the baking sheet and chill for at least 1 hour or until the chocolate has set completely. (Work quickly to avoid having to temper the chocolate again; untempered chocolate can be reheated if it hardens.)

3 To remove the set chocolate, place a half-mould, open side up, on a board. Carefully trim any drops of chocolate from the edge of the mould. Gently insert the point of a small knife between the chocolate and the mould to break the air lock. Repeat with the second mould.

4 Holding the mould open side down, squeeze firmly to release the egg half. Repeat with the other half and chill, loosely covered. (Do not touch the chocolate surface with your fingers, as they will leave prints.) Reserve any melted chocolate to reheat for "glue".

5 To assemble the egg, hold one half of the egg with a piece of folded kitchen paper or foil and fill with small truffles. If necessary, use the remaining melted chocolate as "glue". Spread a small amount on to the rim of the egg half and, holding the empty egg half with a piece of kitchen paper or foil, press it on to the filled half, making sure the rims are aligned and carefully joined.

6 Hold for several seconds, then prop up the egg with the folded paper or foil and chill to set. If you like, decorate the egg with ribbons or Easter decorations.

CHOCOLATE CHRISTMAS CUPS

MAKES ABOUT 35 CUPS

275g/10oz plain chocolate, chopped into
small pieces
175g/6oz cold cooked Christmas pudding
75ml/2½fl oz/5 tbsp brandy or whisky
chocolate leaves and crystallized cranberries
to decorate

1 Melt the chocolate and use to coat the
bottom and sides of about 35 sweet cases.
Allow to set, then repeat, reheating the
melted chocolate if necessary. Leave the
chocolate cups to cool and set. Reserve
the remaining chocolate. Crumble the
Christmas pudding into a small bowl,
sprinkle with brandy or whisky and allow
to stand for 30–40 minutes, until the
liquor is absorbed.
2 Spoon a little of the pudding mixture
into each cup, smoothing the top. Reheat
the remaining chocolate and spoon over
the top of each cup to cover the surface.
Leave to set, then peel off the cases and
place in clean foil cases. Decorate with
chocolate leaves and crystallized berries.

MARZIPAN LOGS

MAKES ABOUT 12

225g/8oz marzipan, at room temperature
115g/4oz/⅔ cup candied orange peel,
chopped
30ml/2 tbsp orange-flavoured liqueur
15ml/1 tbsp soft light brown sugar
edible gold powder
75g/3oz plain chocolate, melted
gold-coated sweets

1 Knead the marzipan well, then mix in
the chopped peel and liqueur. Set aside
for about 1 hour, to dry.
2 Break off small pieces of the mixture
and roll them into log shapes.
3 Dip the tops of half of the marzipan logs
in the sugar and brush them lightly with
edible gold powder.
4 Dip the remaining logs in the melted
chocolate. Place on non-stick baking
paper and press a gold-coated sweet in
the centre of each. When set, arrange all
the logs on a plate.

PEPPERMINT CHOCOLATE STICKS

MAKES ABOUT 80

115g/4oz/½ cup granulated sugar
150ml/¼ pint/⅔ cup water
2.5ml/½ tsp peppermint essence
200g/7oz plain dark chocolate, chopped into
small pieces
60ml/4 tbsp toasted desiccated coconut

1 Lightly oil a large baking sheet. Place the sugar and water in a small, heavy-based saucepan and heat gently, stirring until the sugar has dissolved.
2 Bring to the boil and boil rapidly without stirring until the syrup registers 138°C/280°F on a sugar thermometer. Remove the pan from the heat and stir in the peppermint essence.

3 Pour the mixture on to the greased baking sheet and leave until set.

4 Break up the peppermint mixture into a small bowl and use the end of a rolling pin to crush it into small pieces.
5 Melt the chocolate. Remove from the heat and stir in the mint pieces and desiccated coconut.

6 Lay a 30 x 25cm/12 x 10in sheet of non-stick baking paper on a flat surface. Spread the chocolate mixture over the paper, leaving a narrow border all around, to make a rectangle measuring about 25 x 20cm/10 x 8in. Leave to set. When firm, use a sharp knife to cut into thin sticks, each about 6cm/2½in long.

CHOCOLATE ALMOND TORRONNE

MAKES ABOUT 20 SLICES

115g/4oz plain dark chocolate, chopped into
small pieces
50g/2oz/¼ cup unsalted butter
1 egg white
115g/4oz/½ cup caster sugar
75g/3oz/¾ cup chopped toasted almonds
50g/2oz/½ cup ground almonds
75ml/5 tbsp chopped candied peel

FOR THE COATING

175g/6oz white chocolate, chopped into small
pieces
25g/1oz/2 tbsp unsalted butter
115g/4oz/1 cup flaked almonds, toasted

1 Melt the chocolate with the butter in a heatproof bowl over a saucepan of barely simmering water until smooth.

2 In a clean, grease-free bowl, whisk the egg white with the sugar until stiff. Gradually beat in the melted chocolate mixture, then stir in the toasted almonds, ground almonds and peel.

3 Tip the mixture on to a large sheet of non-stick baking paper and shape into a thick roll.

4 As the mixture cools, use the paper to press the roll firmly into a triangular shape. When you are satisfied with the shape, twist the paper over the triangular roll and chill until completely set.

5 Make the coating. Melt the white chocolate with the butter in a heatproof bowl over a saucepan of simmering water. Unwrap the chocolate roll and with a clean knife spread the white chocolate quickly over the surface. Press the flaked almonds in a thin even coating over the chocolate, working quickly before the chocolate sets.

6 Chill the coated chocolate roll again until firm, then cut the torronne into fairly thin slices to serve. Torronne is ideal to finish a dinner party.

DOUBLE CHOCOLATE-DIPPED FRUIT

MAKES 24 COATED PIECES

fruits – about 24 pieces (strawberries, cherries, orange segments, large seedless grapes, physalis (Cape gooseberries), kumquats, stoned prunes, stoned dates, dried apricots, dried peaches or dried pears)
115g/4oz white chocolate, chopped into small pieces
115g/4oz bittersweet or plain chocolate, chopped into small pieces

1 Clean and prepare fruits; wipe strawberries with a soft cloth or brush gently with pastry brush. Wash firm-skinned fruits such as cherries and grapes and dry well. Peel and leave whole or cut up any fruits being used.

CHOCOLATE PEPPERMINT CREAMS

1 egg white
90ml/6 tbsp double cream
5ml/1 tsp peppermint essence
675g/1½lb/5½ cups icing sugar, plus extra for dusting
few drops of green food colouring
175g/6oz plain chocolate, chopped into small pieces

1 Beat the egg white lightly in a bowl. Mix in the cream and peppermint essence, then gradually add the icing sugar to make a firm, pliable dough. Work in 1–2 drops of green food colouring (apply it from a cocktail stick if you are anxious about adding too much colour) until the dough is an even, pale green.
2 On a surface dusted with icing sugar, roll out the dough to a thickness of about 1cm/½in. Stamp out 4cm/1½in rounds of squares and place on a baking sheet lined with non-stick baking paper. Leave to dry for at least 8 hours, turning once.
3 Melt the chocolate in a bowl over barely simmering water. Allow to cool slightly. Spread chocolate over the top of each peppermint cream, and place them on fresh sheets of non-stick paper. Chill until set.

2 Melt the white chocolate. Remove from the heat and cool to tepid (about 29°C/84°F), stirring frequently. Line a baking sheet with non-stick baking paper. Holding each fruit by the stem or end and at an angle, dip about two-thirds of the fruit into the chocolate. Allow the excess to drip off and place on the baking sheet. Chill the fruits for about 20 minutes until the chocolate sets.

3 Melt the bittersweet or plain chocolate, stirring frequently until smooth.

4 Remove the chocolate from the heat and cool to just below body temperature, about 30°C/86°F. Take each white chocolate-coated fruit in turn from the baking sheet and, holding by the stem or end and at the opposite angle, dip the bottom third of each piece into the dark chocolate, creating a chevron effect. Set on the baking sheet. Chill for 15 minutes or until set. Before serving, allow the fruit to stand at room temperature 10–15 minutes before serving.

CHOCOLATE-COATED NUT BRITTLE

MAKES 20–24 PIECES

115g/4oz/1 cup mixed pecan nuts and whole almonds
115g/4oz/½ cup caster sugar
60ml/4 tbsp water
200g/7oz plain dark chocolate, chopped into small pieces

1 Lightly grease a baking sheet with butter or oil. Mix the nuts, sugar and water in a heavy-based saucepan. Place the pan over a gentle heat, stirring until all the sugar has dissolved.
2 Bring to the boil, then lower the heat to moderate and cook until the mixture turns a rich golden brown and registers 155°C/310°F on a sugar thermometer. If you do not have a sugar thermometer, test the syrup by adding a few drops to a cup of iced water. The mixture should solidify to a very brittle mass.

CHOCOLATE-COATED HAZELNUTS

Roast about 225g/8oz/2 cups hazelnuts in the oven or under the grill. Allow to cool. Melt the chocolate in a heatproof bowl over a pan of barely simmering water. Remove from the heat, but leave the bowl over the water so that the chocolate remains liquid. Have ready about 30 paper sweet cases, arranged on baking sheets. Add the roasted hazelnuts to the melted chocolate and stir to coat. Using two spoons, carefully scoop up a cluster of two or three chocolate-coated nuts. Carefully transfer the cluster to a paper sweet case. Leave the nut clusters in a cool place until set.

3 Quickly remove the pan from the heat and tip the mixture on to the prepared baking sheet, spreading it evenly. Leave until completely cold and hard.

4 Break the nut brittle into bite-size pieces. Melt the chocolate and dip the pieces to half-coat them. Leave on a sheet of non-stick baking paper to set.

Chocolate Nut Clusters

Makes about 30

525ml / 21fl oz / 2½ cups double cream
25g / 1oz / 2 tbsp unsalted butter, cut into small pieces
350ml / 12fl oz / 1½ cups golden syrup
200g / 7oz / scant 1 cup granulated sugar
75g / 3oz / ½ cup light brown sugar
pinch of salt
15ml / 1 tbsp vanilla essence
350g / 12oz / 3 cups combination of hazelnuts, pecans, walnuts, brazil nuts and unsalted peanuts
400g / 14oz plain chocolate, chopped into small pieces
15g / ½oz / 1 tbsp white vegetable fat

1 Lightly brush two baking sheets with vegetable oil. In a large heavy-based saucepan over a medium heat, cook the cream, butter, golden syrup, sugars and salt, stirring occasionally for about 3 minutes, until the sugars dissolve and the butter melts.

2 Bring to the boil and continue cooking, stirring frequently for about 1 hour, until the caramel reaches 119°C / 238°F on a sugar thermometer, or until a small amount of caramel dropped into a cup of iced water forms a hard ball.
3 Plunge the bottom of the pan into cold water to stop cooking. Cool slightly, then stir in the vanilla essence.

4 Stir the nuts into the caramel until well coated. Using an oiled tablespoon, drop spoonfuls of nut mixture on to the prepared sheets, about 2.5cm / 1in apart. If the mixture hardens, return to the heat to soften. Chill the clusters for 30 minutes until firm and cold, or leave in a cool place until hardened.
5 Using a metal palette knife, transfer the clusters to a wire rack placed over a baking sheet to catch drips. In a medium saucepan, over a low heat, melt the chocolate with the white vegetable fat, stirring until smooth. Set aside to cool slightly.

6 Spoon chocolate over each cluster, being sure to cover completely.

7 Place on a wire rack over a baking sheet. Allow to set for 2 hours until hardened. Store in an airtight container.

CHOCOLATE FUDGE TRIANGLES

MAKES ABOUT 48 TRIANGLES

600g/1lb 5oz fine quality white chocolate, chopped into small pieces
375g/13oz can sweetened condensed milk
15ml/1 tbsp vanilla essence
7.5ml/1½ tsp lemon juice
pinch of salt
175g/6oz/1½ cups hazelnuts or pecan nuts, chopped (optional)
175g/6oz plain chocolate, chopped into small pieces
40g/1½oz/3 tbsp unsalted butter, cut into small pieces
50g/2oz bittersweet chocolate, for drizzling

1 Line a 20cm/8in square baking tin with foil. Brush the foil lightly with oil. In a saucepan over low heat, melt the white chocolate and condensed milk until smooth, stirring frequently. Remove from the heat and stir in the vanilla essence, lemon juice and salt. Stir in the nuts if using. Spread half the mixture in the tin. Chill for 15 minutes.

2 In a saucepan over low heat, melt the plain chocolate and butter until smooth, stirring frequently. Remove from the heat, cool slightly, then pour over the chilled white layer and chill for 15 minutes until set.

3 Gently re-heat the remaining white chocolate mixture and pour over the set chocolate layer. Smooth the top, then chill for 2–4 hours until set.

4 Using the foil as a guide, remove the fudge from the pan and turn it on to a cutting board. Lift off the foil and use a sharp knife to cut the fudge into 24 squares. Cut each square into a triangle. Melt the bittersweet chocolate in a heatproof bowl over a pan of barely simmering water. Cool slightly, then drizzle over the triangles.

EASY CHOCOLATE HAZELNUT FUDGE

MAKES 16 SQUARES

150ml / ¼ pint / ⅔ cup evaporated milk
350g / 12oz / 1½ cups sugar
large pinch of salt
50g / 2oz / ½ cup hazelnuts, halved
350g / 12oz / 2 cups plain chocolate chips

<u>1</u> Generously grease a 20cm/8in square cake tin.

<u>2</u> Place the evaporated milk, sugar and salt in a heavy-based saucepan. Bring to the boil over a medium heat, stirring constantly. Lower the heat and simmer gently, stirring, for about 5 minutes.

<u>3</u> Remove the pan from the heat and add the hazelnuts and chocolate chips. Stir gently with a metal spoon until the chocolate has completely melted.

<u>4</u> Quickly pour the fudge mixture into the prepared tin and spread evenly. Leave to cool and set.

<u>5</u> When the chocolate hazelnut fudge has set, cut it into 2.5cm/1in squares. Store in an airtight container, separating the layers with greaseproof paper or non-stick baking paper.

TWO-TONE FUDGE

Make the Easy Chocolate Hazelnut Fudge and spread it in a 23cm/9in square cake tin, to make a slightly thinner layer than for the main recipe. While it is cooling, make a batch of plain fudge, substituting white chocolate drops for the plain chocolate chips and leaving out the hazelnuts. Let the plain fudge cool slightly before pouring it carefully over the dark chocolate layer. Use a palette knife or slim metal spatula to spread the plain layer to the corners, then set aside to set as before. Cut into squares.

RICH CHOCOLATE PISTACHIO FUDGE

MAKES 36

250g/9oz/generous 1 cup granulated sugar
375g/13oz can sweetened condensed milk
50g/2oz/¼ cup unsalted butter
5ml/1 tsp vanilla essence
115g/4oz plain dark chocolate, grated
75g/3oz/¾ cup pistachio nuts, almonds
or hazelnuts

CHOCOLATE AND MARSHMALLOW FUDGE

25g/1oz/2 tbsp butter
350g/12oz/1½ cups granulated sugar
175ml/6fl oz/¾ cup evaporated milk
pinch of salt
115g/4oz/2 cups white mini
marshmallows
225g/8oz /1¼ cups chocolate chips
5ml/1 tsp vanilla essence
115g/4oz/½ cup chopped walnuts
(optional)

1 Generously grease an 18cm/7 in cake tin. Mix the butter, sugar, evaporated milk and salt in a heavy-based saucepan. Stir over a medium heat until the sugar has dissolved, then bring to the boil and cook for 3–5 minutes or until thickened, stirring all the time.

2 Remove the pan from the heat and beat in the marshmallows and chocolate chips until dissolved. Beat in the vanilla essence. Scrape the mixture into the prepared cake tin and press it evenly into the corners, using a metal palette knife. Level the surface.

3 If using the walnuts, sprinkle them over the fudge and press them in to the surface. Set the fudge aside to cool. Before it has set completely, mark it into squares with a sharp knife. Chill until firm before cutting the fudge up and serving it.

1 Grease a 19cm/7½in square cake tin and line with non-stick baking paper. Mix the sugar, condensed milk and butter in a heavy-based pan. Heat gently, stirring occasionally, until the sugar has dissolved completely and the mixture is smooth.

2 Bring the mixture to the boil, stirring occasionally, and boil until it registers 116°C/240°F on a sugar thermometer or until a small amount of the mixture dropped into a cup of iced water forms a soft ball.

3 Remove the pan from the heat and beat in the vanilla essence, chocolate and nuts. Beat vigorously until the mixture is smooth and creamy.

4 Pour the mixture into the prepared cake tin and spread evenly. Leave until just set, then mark into squares. Leave to set completely before cutting into squares and removing from the tin. Store in an airtight container in a cool place.

TRUFFLE-FILLED FILO CUPS

MAKES ABOUT 24 CUPS

*3–6 sheets fresh or thawed frozen filo pastry,
depending on size
40g/1½ oz/3 tbsp unsalted butter, melted
sugar, for sprinkling
pared strips of lemon zest, to decorate*

**FOR THE CHOCOLATE TRUFFLE
MIXTURE**

*250ml/8fl oz/1 cup double cream
225g/8oz bittersweet or plain chocolate,
chopped into small pieces
50g/2oz/¼ cup unsalted butter, cut into
small pieces
30ml/2 tbsp brandy or liqueur*

1 Prepare the truffle mixture. In a
saucepan over a medium heat, bring the
cream to a boil. Remove from the heat
and add the pieces of chocolate, stirring
until melted. Beat in the butter and add
the brandy or liqueur. Strain into a bowl
and chill for 1 hour until thick.

2 Preheat oven to 200°C/400°F/Gas 6.
Grease a 12-hole bun tray. Cut the filo
sheets into 6cm/2½ in squares. Cover
with a damp dish towel. Place one square
on a work surface. Brush lightly with
melted butter, turn over and brush the
other side. Sprinkle with a pinch of sugar.
Butter another square and place it over
the first at an angle; sprinkle with sugar.
Butter a third square and place over the
first two, unevenly, so the corners form
an uneven edge. Press the layered square
into one of the holes in the bun tray.

3 Continue to fill the tray, working
quickly so that the filo does not have time
to dry out. Bake the filo cups for 4–6
minutes, until golden. Cool for 10
minutes on the bun tray then carefully
transfer to a wire rack and cool
completely.

4 Stir the chocolate mixture; it should be
just thick enough to pipe. Spoon the
mixture into a piping bag fitted with a
medium star nozzle and pipe a swirl into
each filo cup. Decorate each with tiny
strips of lemon zest.

MEXICAN HOT CHOCOLATE

SERVES 4

1 litre / 1¾ pints / 4 cups milk
1 cinnamon stick
2 whole cloves
115g / 4oz plain dark chocolate, chopped into
small pieces
2–3 drops of almond essence

1 Heat the milk gently with the spices in a saucepan until almost boiling, then stir in the plain chocolate over a moderate heat until melted.

2 Strain into a blender, add the almond essence and whizz on high speed for about 30 seconds until frothy. Alternatively, whisk the mixture with a hand-held electric mixer or wire whisk.

3 Pour into warmed heatproof glasses and serve immediately.

WHITE HOT CHOCOLATE

SERVES 4

1.75 litres / 3 pints / 7½ cups milk
175g / 6oz white chocolate, chopped into
small pieces
10ml / 2 tsp coffee powder
10ml / 2 tsp orange-flavoured liqueur
(optional)
whipped cream and ground cinnamon, to serve

1 Pour the milk into a large heavy-based saucepan and heat until almost boiling. As soon as bubbles form around the edge of the pan remove the milk from the heat.

2 Add the white chocolate, coffee powder and orange-flavoured liqueur, if using. Stir until all the chocolate has melted and the mixture is smooth.

3 Pour the hot chocolate into four mugs. Top each with a swirl or spoonful of whipped cream and a sprinkling of ground cinnamon. Serve immediately.

ICED MINT AND CHOCOLATE COOLER

SERVES 4

60ml/4 tbsp drinking chocolate
400ml/14fl oz/1⅔ cups chilled milk
150ml/¼ pint/⅔ cup natural yogurt
2.5ml/½ tsp peppermint essence
4 scoops of chocolate ice cream
mint leaves and chocolate shapes, to decorate

1 Place the drinking chocolate in a small pan and stir in about 120ml/4fl oz/½ cup of the milk. Heat gently, stirring, until almost boiling, then remove the pan from the heat.

2 Pour the hot chocolate milk into a heatproof bowl or large jug and whisk in the remaining milk. Add the natural yogurt and peppermint essence and whisk again.

3 Pour the mixture into four tall glasses, filling them no more than three-quarters full. Top each drink with a scoop of ice cream. Decorate with mint leaves and chocolate shapes. Serve immediately.

CHOCOLATE VANILLA COOLER

Make the drink as in the main recipe, but use single cream instead of the natural yogurt and 5ml/1 tsp natural vanilla essence instead of the peppermint essence.

MOCHA COOLER

Make the drink as in the main recipe, but dissolve the chocolate in 120ml/4fl oz/½ cup strong black coffee, and reduce the milk to 300ml/½ pint/1¼ cups. Use cream instead of yogurt and leave the essence out.

IRISH CHOCOLATE VELVET

SERVES 4

250ml/8fl oz/1 cup double cream
400ml/14fl oz/1⅔ cups milk
115g/4oz milk chocolate, chopped into small pieces
30ml/2 tbsp cocoa powder
60ml/4 tbsp Irish whiskey
whipped cream, for topping
chocolate curls, to decorate

1 Using a hand-held electric mixer, whip half the cream in a bowl until it is thick enough to hold its shape.

2 Place the milk and chocolate in a saucepan and heat gently, stirring, until the chocolate has melted.

3 Whisk in the cocoa, then bring to the boil. Remove from the heat and stir in the remaining cream and the Irish whiskey.

4 Pour quickly into four warmed heatproof mugs or glasses and top each serving with a generous spoonful of the whipped cream, then the chocolate curls. Serve with Peppermint Sticks for extra indulgence.

HOT CHOCOLATE AND CHOC-TIPPED BISCUITS

SERVES 2

FOR THE CHOC-TIPPED BISCUITS

115g/4oz/½ cup soft margarine
15ml/3 tbsp icing sugar, sifted
150g/5oz/1¼ cups plain flour
few drops of vanilla essence
75g/3oz plain chocolate, chopped into small pieces.

FOR THE HOT CHOCOLATE

90ml/6 tbsp drinking chocolate powder, plus a little extra for sprinkling
30ml/2 tbsp caster sugar, or more according to taste
600ml/1 pint/2½ cups milk
2 large squirts of cream (optional)

1 Preheat oven to 180°C/350°F/Gas 4 and lightly grease two baking sheets. Make the choc-tipped biscuits. Put the margarine and icing sugar in a bowl and beat them together until very soft. Mix in the flour and vanilla essence.

2 Put the mixture in a large piping bag fitted with a large star nozzle. Pipe ten neat lines, each 13cm/5in long, on the baking sheets. Leave a little room between each biscuit. They will not spread much on cooking, but you need to be able to remove them easily. Cook for 15–20 minutes until the biscuits are pale golden brown. Allow to cool slightly before lifting on to a wire rack.

3 Put the chocolate in a heatproof bowl over a saucepan of barely simmering water and leave to melt. Stir until creamy, then remove the bowl of melted chocolate from the heat. Dip both ends of each biscuit in the chocolate, put back on the rack and leave to cool and set.

4 To make the drinking chocolate, put the drinking chocolate powder and the sugar in a saucepan. Add the milk and bring it to the boil, whisking all the time. Divide between two tall mugs. Add more sugar if needed. Top each drink with a squirt of cream, if you like.

SAUCES, FROSTINGS AND ICINGS

SIMPLE BUTTERCREAM

MAKES ABOUT 350G/12OZ

75g/3oz butter or soft margarine
225g/8oz/1½ cups icing sugar
5ml/1 tsp vanilla essence
10–15ml/2–3 tsp milk

1 If using butter, allow it to come to room temperature so that it can easily be creamed. Sift the icing sugar. Put the butter or margarine in a bowl. Add about a quarter of the icing sugar and beat with a hand-held electric mixer until fluffy.

2 Using a metal spoon, add the remaining sifted icing sugar, a little at a time, beating well with the electric mixer after each addition. Icing sugar is so fine that if you add too much of it at one time, it tends to fly out of the bowl.

3 Beat in 5ml/1 tsp of the milk. The mixture should be light and creamy, with a spreadable consistency. Add the vanilla essence, then more milk if necessary, but not too much, or it will be too sloppy to draw into peaks. Use as a filling and/or topping on layer cakes and cupcakes.

CHOCOLATE BUTTERCREAM

ENOUGH TO FILL A 20CM/8IN ROUND LAYER CAKE

75g/3oz/6 tbsp unsalted butter or margarine, softened
175g/6oz/1 cup icing sugar
15ml/1 tbsp cocoa powder
2.5ml/½ tsp vanilla essence

1 Place all the ingredients in a large bowl.

2 Beat well to a smooth spreadable consistency.

VARIATIONS

Coffee Buttercream: Stir 10ml/2 tsp instant coffee into 15ml/1 tbsp boiling water. Beat into the icing instead of the milk.
Mocha Buttercream: Stir 5ml/1 tsp cocoa powder into 10ml/2 tsp boiling water. Beat into the icing. Add a little coffee essence.
Orange Buttercream: Use orange juice instead of the milk and vanilla essence, and add 10ml/2 tsp finely grated orange rind. Omit the rind if using the icing for piping.

WHITE CHOCOLATE FROSTING

ENOUGH TO COVER A 20CM/8IN ROUND CAKE

175g/6oz white chocolate, chopped into small pieces
75g/3oz/6 tbsp unsalted butter
115g/4oz/¾ cup icing sugar
90ml/6 tbsp double cream

1 Melt the chocolate with the butter in a heatproof bowl over a saucepan of barely simmering water. Remove the bowl from the heat and beat in the icing sugar, a little at a time, using a wire whisk.

2 Whip the cream in a separate bowl until it just holds its shape, then beat into the chocolate mixture. Allow the mixture to cool, stirring occasionally, until it begins to hold its shape. Use immediately.

COOK'S TIP

White chocolate frosting is a rich frosting suitable for a dark chocolate sponge without a filling. Use a palette knife to form peaks for an attractive finish.

FUDGE FROSTING

MAKES 350G/12OZ

50g/2oz plain chocolate, chopped into
small pieces
225g/8oz/2 cups icing sugar, sifted
50g/2oz/¼ cup butter or margarine
45ml/3 tbsp milk or single cream
15ml/1 tbsp vanilla essence

COOK'S TIP

When you have covered the cake
with the frosting, use the back of a
spoon or the tines of a fork to swirl
the fudge frosting and create an
attractive pattern on the cake, but do
this quickly, as it sets very fast.

1 Put the chocolate, icing sugar, butter or
margarine, milk or cream and vanilla
essence in a heavy-based saucepan.
2 Stir over a very low heat until the
chocolate and butter or margarine melt.
Turn off the heat, stir until smooth.

3 Beat the icing frequently as it cools until
it thickens sufficiently to use for
spreading or piping. Use immediately and
work quickly once it has reached the right
consistency. This is a popular frosting and
can be used for many kinds of cakes.

SATIN CHOCOLATE ICING

MAKES 225G/8OZ
*175g/6oz plain or bittersweet
chocolate, chopped into small pieces
150ml/¼ pint/⅔ cup double cream
2.5ml/½ tsp instant coffee powder*

COOK'S TIP
Do not touch the icing once it has
hardened or the attractive satin finish
will be spoilt. Cakes covered with
this icing need little by way of
decoration, but half-dipped cherries
look very effective.

1 Put the chocolate, cream and coffee in a
small heavy-based saucepan. Place the
cake to be iced on a wire rack over a
baking sheet or tray.

2 Place the saucepan over a very low heat
and stir the mixture with a wooden spoon
until all the pieces of plain or bittersweet
chocolate have melted and the mixture is
smooth and evenly blended.

3 Remove from the heat and immediately
pour the icing over the cake, letting it run
down the sides slowly to coat it
completely. Spread the icing with a
palette knife or slim spatula as necessary,
working quickly before the icing has time
to thicken.

CHOCOLATE FONDANT
**ENOUGH TO COVER AND DECORATE
A 23CM/9IN ROUND CAKE**
*350g/12oz plain chocolate, chopped into
small pieces
60ml/4 tbsp liquid glucose
2 egg whites
900g/2lb/7 cups icing sugar*

1 Put the chocolate and glucose in a
heatproof bowl. Place over a
saucepan of barely simmering water
and leave to melt, stirring the
mixture occasionally. When it is
smooth, remove the bowl from the
heat and cool slightly.
2 In a clean, grease-free bowl, whisk the
egg whites with a hand-held electric
mixer until soft peaks form, then stir
into the chocolate mixture with about
45ml/3 tbsp of the icing sugar.
3 Continue to beat the icing,
gradually adding enough of the
remaining icing sugar to make a stiff
paste. Wrap the fondant in clear film
if not using immediately.

BITTERSWEET CHOCOLATE SAUCE

QUICK CHOCOLATE SAUCE
MAKES 225ML/8FL OZ/1 CUP
150ml/¼ pint/⅔ cup double cream
15ml/1 tbsp caster sugar
*150g/5oz plain chocolate, chopped into
small pieces*
*30ml/2 tbsp dark rum or whisky
(optional)*

1 Bring the cream and sugar to the
boil. Remove from the heat, add the
chocolate and stir until melted. Stir
in the rum or whisky.
2 Pour the chocolate sauce into a jar.
When cool, cover and store for up to
10 days. Reheat by standing the jar in
a saucepan of simmering water, or
remove the lid and microwave on
High power for 2 minutes. Stir
before serving.

MAKES ABOUT 350ML/12FL OZ
45ml/3 tbsp granulated sugar
120ml/4fl oz/½ cup water
*175g/6oz bittersweet chocolate, chopped into
small pieces*
25g/1oz/2 tbsp unsalted butter, diced
60–90ml/4–6 tbsp single cream
2.5ml/½ tsp vanilla essence

1 Combine the sugar and water in a
heavy-based saucepan. Bring to the boil
over a medium heat, stirring constantly
until all the sugar has dissolved.

2 Add the chocolate and butter to the
syrup, stir with a wooden spoon, then
remove the pan from the heat and
continue to stir until smooth.

3 Stir in the single cream and vanilla
essence. Serve the sauce warm, over
vanilla ice cream, profiteroles, poached
pears or crêpes.

GLOSSY CHOCOLATE SAUCE

SERVES 6
115g/4oz/½ cup caster sugar
60ml/4 tbsp water
*175g/6oz plain chocolate, chopped into
small pieces*
25g/1oz/2 tbsp unsalted butter
30ml/2 tbsp brandy or orange juice

COOK'S TIP
Any of these sauces would make a
chocolate fondue, with fruit and
dessert biscuits as dippers.

1 Place the caster sugar and water in a
heavy-based saucepan and heat gently,
stirring occasionally with a wooden spoon
until all the sugar has dissolved.

2 Stir in the chocolate until melted, then
add the butter in the same way. Do not
allow the sauce to boil. Stir in the brandy
or orange juice and serve warm.

CHOCOLATE FUDGE SAUCE

SERVES 6

150ml / ¼ pint / ⅔ cup double cream
50g / 2oz / ¼ cup butter
50g / 2oz / ¼ cup vanilla sugar
175g / 6oz plain chocolate, chopped into
small pieces
30ml / 2 tbsp brandy

1 Heat the cream with the butter and sugar in a bowl over a saucepan of barely simmering water. Stir until smooth, then leave to cool.

2 Add the chocolate to the cream mixture. Stir over simmering water until it is melted and thoroughly combined.

3 Stir in the brandy a little at a time, then cool to room temperature.

CHOCOLATE-GANACHE
ENOUGH TO COVER A 23CM / 9IN
ROUND CAKE

225g / 8oz plain chocolate, chopped into
small pieces
250ml / 8fl oz / 1 cup double cream

Melt the chocolate with the cream in a saucepan over a low heat. Pour into a bowl, leave to cool, then whisk until the mixture begins to hold its shape.

WHITE CHOCOLATE AND ORANGE SAUCE

SERVES 6

150ml / ¼ pint / ⅔ cup double cream
50g / 2oz / ¼ cup butter
45ml / 3 tbsp caster sugar
175g / 6oz white chocolate, chopped into
small pieces
30ml / 2 tbsp orange-flavoured liqueur
finely grated rind of 1 orange

COOK'S TIP

Serve with ice cream, or with hot waffles or fresh crêpes.

1 Pour the cream into a heavy-based saucepan. Cut the butter into cubes and add it to the pan, with the sugar. Heat gently, stirring the mixture occasionally until the butter has melted.

2 Add the chocolate to the cream. Stir over a very low heat until it is melted and thoroughly combined.
3 Stir in the orange rind, then add the liqueur a little at a time. Leave to cool.

CHOCOLATE SUPPLIERS AROUND THE WORLD

AUSTRALIA
Chocolatier Australia
224 Waterdale Road, Ivanhoe,
Victoria 3079 Tel: (3) 94 99 70 22

The Chocolate Box
761 Burke Road, Camberwell,
Victoria 3124 Tel: (3) 98 13 13 77

Darren Taylor's Handmade Chocolates
Seet Art, 96 Oxford Street, Paddington,
New South Wales 2021
Tel: (2) 93 61 66 17

Sweet William Chocolates
4 William Street, Paddington, New
South Wales 2021 Tel: (2) 93 31 54 68

Simon Johnson
181 Harris Street, Pyrmont, New South
Wales 2009 Tel: (2) 95 52 25 22

Haigh's Chocolates
Beehive Corner, 2 Rundle Mall,
Adelaide, South Australia
Tel: (8) 23 12 844

AUSTRIA
Altmann & Kühne
Graben 30, 1010 Wien
Tel: (1) 53 30 927

Demels
14 Kohlmarkt, 1010 Wien
Tel: (1) 53 51 717

Hotel Imperial
Kärtner Ring 16, A-1051 Wien
Tel: (1) 50 11 03 13
Fax: (1) 50 10 355

Mirabell Salzburger Confiserie
Hauptstrasse 14-16, A-5082 Grödig
Tel: (62) 46 20 110

BELGIUM
Charlemagne
Place Jacques Brel 8, 4040 Herstal
Tel: (41) 64 66 44

Godiva
Wapenstilstandstraat 5, 1081 Brussels
Tel: (2) 42 21 711

Kim's Chocolates
Nieuwlandlaan 12, Industriezone B-615,
B-3200 Aarschot
Tel: (16) 55 15 80

Neuhaus
Postbox 2, B - 1602 Vlenzenbeek
Tel: (2) 56 82 211

Pierre Colas
2 Rue Campagne, 4577 Modave
Tel: (2) 64 80 893

Wittamer
12 Place du Grand Sablon, Grote Zavel
12, 1000 Brussels Tel: (2) 51 28 451

FRANCE
Bonnat
8 Cours Senozan, 38500 Voiron
Tel: (76) 05 28 09

Christian Constant
26 Rue du Bac, 75007 Paris
Tel: (47) 03 30 00

Cluizel
La Fontaine au Chocolat
101 & 210 Rue Saint Honoré,
75001, Paris Tel: (1) 42 44 11 66

Fauchon
26-30 Place de la Madeleine,
75008 Paris Tel: (1) 47 42 60 11

Lalonde
59 Rue St Dizier, 54400 Nancy
Tel: 83 53 31 57

La Maison du Chocolat
225 Rue Faubourg St Honoré,
75008 Paris Tel: (1) 42 27 39 44

Le Roux
18 Rue du Port-Maria, 56170 Quiberon
Tel: 97 50 06 83

Richart Design et Chocolat
258 Bd. Saint-Germain, 75007 Paris
Tel: (1) 45 55 66 00

Chocolaterie Valrhona
BP 40, 26600 Tain L'Hermitage
Tel: 75 07 90 90

Weiss
18 Avenue Denfert-Rochereau,
42000 St Etienne
Tel: 77 49 41 41

GERMANY
Confiserie Heinemann
Krefelder Strasse 645
41066 München-Gladbach
Tel: (2161) 6930

Dreimeister
Weststrasse 47 - 49, Werl,
Westönnen Tel: 29 22 8 20 45

Feodora
Vertriebszentrale Bremen,
Postfach 105803, D28058 Bremen
Tel: (421) 59 90 61

Bremer Chocolade-Fabrik Hachez
Westerstrasse 32, D-28199 Bremen
Tel: (421) 59 50 64 62

Leysieffer
Benzstrasse 9, 49076 Osnabrück
Tel: (541) 91 420

Stollwerck
Stollwerckstrasse 27-31, 51149 Köln
Tel: (22) 03 430

Van Houten
Am Stamgleis, 22844 Norderstedt
Tel: (5) 26 020

GREAT BRITAIN
Ackermans
9 Goldhurst Terrace, Finchley Road,
London, NW6 3HX
Tel: (0171) 624 2742

Charbonnel et Walker
1 The Royal Arcade, 28 Old Bond
Street, London, W1X 4BT
Tel: (0171) 491 0939

Gerard Ronay
3 Warple Way, London, W3 0RF
Tel: (0181) 730 818

Godiva
247 Regent Street, London, W1
Tel: (0171) 409 0963

Grania & Sarnia
6 Sterne Street, London, W12 8AD
Tel: (0181) 749 8274

Green & Black
Whole Earth Food, 269 Portobello
Road, London, W1 1LR
Tel: (0171) 229 7545

JB Confectionery
Unit 3, The Palmerston Centre,
Oxford Road, Harrow, Middlesex
HA3 7RG Tel: (0181) 863 0011

Mortimer & Bennett
33 Turnham Green Terrace, London,
W4 1RG Tel: (0181) 995 4145

Rococo Chocolates
321 Kings Road, London, SW3 5EP
Tel: (0171) 352 5857
Fax: (0171) 352 7360

Sara Jayne
517 Old York Road, London, SW18 1TF
Tel: (0181) 874 8500

The Chocolate Society
Clay Pit Lane, Roecliffe, Near
Boroughbridge, N. Yorks, YO5 9LS
Tel: (01423) 322 230

The Cool Chile Company
P.O. Box 5702, London, W11 2GS
Tel: (0171) 229 9360

Town & Country Chocolates
52 Oxford Road, Denham, Uxbridge,
Middlesex, UB9 4DH
Tel: (01895) 256 166

ITALY
Caffarel/Peyrano
Via Gianevello 41 - 10062 Luserna,
S. Giovanni (TO), Piedmont
Tel: (121) 90 10 86

Maglio Arte Dolciaria
73024 Maglio, La Via Gioacchino
Toma 4 Tel: (836) 25 723

Majani
Via Lunga 19/C, Crespellano (BO)
Tel: 51 96 91 57

Perugina
Nestlé Italiana
Via Pievaiola, San Sisto, PGIT
Tel: (75) 52 761

MEXICO
Chocolatera de Jalisco
Av Narianotero 1420, Apartado Postal
33121, 44510 Guadalajara, Halisco

SPAIN
Blanxart
Tambor del Bruc, 13-08970 Sant Joan
Despi, Barcelona Tel: (3) 373 3761

Ludomar
Ciudad de la Asunción 58, 08030
Barcelona Tel: (72) 203 662

Ramón Roca
Mercaders, 6 17004, Gerona
Tel: (72) 203 662

Chocolates Valor
Pianista Gonzalo Soriano, 13 Villajoyosa
Tel: (6) 589 050

SWITZERLAND
Lindt & Sprüngli
Seestrasse 204, CH-8802 Kilchberg
Tel: (1) 71 62 233

Sprüngli
Bahnhofstrasse 21, 8022 Zurich
Tel: (1) 21 15 777

THE NETHERLANDS
Bensdorp
Heerenstraat 51, Postbus 4, 1400 AA
Bussum Tel: (35) 69 74 911

Gerkens Cacao
Veerdijk 82, Postbus 82, 1530 AB
Wormer Tel: (35) 69 74 911

Cacao De Zaan
Stationsstraat 76, Postbus 2, 1540 AA
Koog aan de Zaan
Tel: (75) 62 83 601

Droste
PO Box 5, 8170AA Vaassen
Tel: (578) 57 82 00

USA
Dilettante Chocolates
416 Broadway, Seattle, WA 98102
Tel: (206) 328 1530

Fran's
2805 East Madison, Seattle, Washington,
WA 98122-4020
Tel: (206) 322 0233

Ghirardelli
900 North Point Street, San Francisco,
CA 94109 Tel: (415) 474 1414

Joseph Schmidt Confections
3489 16th Street, San Francisco,
CA 9411 Tel: (415) 861 8682

Richard Donnelly Fine Chocolates
1509 Mission Street, Santa Cruz,
CA 95060 Tel: (408) 458 4214

Moonstruck Chocolatier
6663 SW BVTN Hillsdale Highway,
STE194, Portland, Oregon, OR9 7225
Tel: (503) 283 8843

ACKNOWLEDGEMENTS
Thanks to the following companies for
supplying chocolates for photography:

Ackermans, Alfred Ritter, Bendicks
(Mayfair) Ltd, Charbonnel et Walker,
The Cool Chile Company, The
Chocolate Society, Richard Donnelly,
Feodora Chocolate, Ghirardelli
Chocolate Company, Grania & Sarni,
Green and Black, The Jenks Group, JB
Confectionery, Leonidas, Lessiters,
Nestlé Rowntree Ltd, Parsons Trading
Ltd, Perugina, Richart Design et
Chocolat, Rococo, Ryne Quality
Confectionery, Joseph Schmidt, Town &
Country Chocolates, Trustin.

Thanks also to Stefano Raimondi of the
Italian Trade Centre, Patrizia De Vito of
the Associazione Industrie Dolciarie in
Rome, Elaine Ashton of Grania and
Sarnia, Dan Mortimer of Mortimer and
Bennet, David Lyle of Town and Country
Chocolates and John Bacon of JB
Confectionery.
    Christine McFadden is particularly
indebted to the late Sophie Coe, and her
husband Michael Coe, for their book The
True History of Chocolate, and to Chantal
Coady for the information in The
Chocolate Companion.

INDEX

PICTURE ACKNOWLEDGEMENTS

Thanks to the following picture libraries for supplying additional images in the book.
AKG, London: pp9(br) *Columbus discovers the New World*, Bernhard Rode; 10(br) *First landing on Guanaja*, wood engraving; 19(b) *Goethe in the Countryside*, Johann Tischbein; 24(b) *Healing plants, cacao*, from FE Bilz; 6 (bl) & 61(tr) Poster for chocolate, *Mother's Cocoa in Danger*.

Bridgeman Art Library: 6(r) *Cacao Van Houten*, Privit Livemont, Victoria and Albert, London; 18(r) *The chocolate girl*, Jean-Etienne Liotard, Dresden Gemäldegalerie; 19 *Still life*, Philippe Rousseau, Musée des Beaux Arts, Reims, Peter Willi; 20(t) *Cardinal Mazarin*, French School, Musée Condé, Chantilly; 20(bl) *Tapestry of Louis XIV's marriage*, Gobelins, Mobilier National, Paris; 22(br) *A cup of chocolate*, Sir John Lavery, Whitford and Hughes, London; 23(r) American poster for chocolate; 26(b) *Cocoa plantation in the Isle of Grenada*, O'Shea Gallery, London; 60(bl) *Cacao Van Houten*, Privet Livemont, Victoria and Albert, London; 60(br) Box of Cadbury's assorted chocolates, c1913.

Mansell Collection: pp25(b).
Public Records Office : pp6(l);

11(t); 27(t); 28(t); 30(br); p57(br).

Visual Arts Library: pp8(l); 9(l); 10 *Montezuma offering chocolate to Herman Cortés*, PG Miguel, Artephot/Oronoz; 15(t) *Mexican making chocolate*, Codex Tuleda, Artephot/Oronoz; 20(r) *A horseman and a lady drinking chocolate*, Bonnart, Vision; 25(l) *Still Life: Chocolate set*, Luis Melendez, Museo del Prado, Madrid, Artephot/Oronoz; 26(b) *The morning cocoa*, Longhi; 25(tr) *The breakfast*, François Boucher, Musée du Louvre, Artephot/Oronoz; 25(tl) *Physiologie du Goût ou Méditations de Gastronomie Transcendante*, E Baneste; 29(br) *Advertisement, Chocolat Menier*, F Bouisset, Artephot/Perrin; 16(tl) *Cacao Van Houten*, Artephot/Perrin; 16(tr) Poster for Chocolate, H Gerbault; 48(tl) Poster for French Chocolate and Tea Company, Steilen, Artephot/Perrin; 49(l) Chocolat Capentier poster; 58(br) Chocolat Mondia, Artephot/Vision; 59(l) *Portrait of Madame Du Barry*, Greuze, Artephot/Varga; 61(br) *Chocolat Masson*, Grasset, Artephot/Perrin.

Other pictures supplied courtesy of Bendick's (Mayfair) Ltd: 16(bl), Cadburys Ltd: 28(bl); 42(b); 43(bl); 60(tr). Fran's: 62. Godiva: 37(bl) 58(t). Nestlé Rowntree Ltd: 1; 27(b); 34(br) 36(tr&l), Rococo: 17(bl).

SELECTED BIBLIOGRAPHY

NATHALIE BAILLEUX, HERVÉ BIZEUL, JOHN FELTWELL, RÉGINE KOPP, CORBY KUMMER, PIERRE LABANNE, CRISTINA PAULY, ODILE PERRARD, MARIAROSA SCHIAFFINO, PREFACE JEANNE BOURIN 1995 *The Book of Chocolate*. Paris, New York: Flammarion.
BLYTHMAN, JOANNA 1996 *The Food We Eat*. London: Michael Joseph.
COADY, CHANTAL 1993 *Chocolate: The Food of the Gods*. London: Pavilion Books.
COADY, CHANTAL 1995 *The Chocolate Companion*. London: Quintet Publishing.
COE, SOPHIE D. AND MICHAEL D. 1996 *The True History of Chocolate*. London: Thames and Hudson.
COX, CAT 1993 *Chocolate Unwrapped: The Politics of Pleasure*. London: The Women's Environmental Network.
GAGE, THOMAS 1648 *The English-American His Travail by Land and Sea, or a New Survey of the West Indies*. London.
HEAD, BRANDON 1905 *The Food of the Gods*. London: George Routledge & Sons.

McGEE, HAROLD 1984 *On Food and Cooking: The Science and Lore of the Kitchen*. London, Australia: George Allen & Unwin.
MONTIGNAC, MICHEL 1991 *Dine Out and Lose Weight*. London: Artulen UK.
RICHART DESIGN ET CHOCOLAT *Le Petit Livre Blanc du Chocolat*.
SHERR, JEREMY *The Homoeopathic Proving of Chocolate*. Dynamis School.
Spicing up the Palate: Studies of Flavourings – Ancient and Modern. Proceedings of the Oxford Symposium on Food and Cookery 1992. Totnes, Devon: Prospect Books.
STOBART, TOM 1977 *Herbs, Spices and Flavourings*. Penguin Books.
TRAGER, JAMES 1995 *The Food Chronology*. Ontario: Fitzhenry & Whiteside.
WATERHOUSE, DEBRA 1995 *Why Women Need Chocolate*. London: Vermilion.
WHYMPER, R. 1921 *Cocoa and Chocolate: Their Chemistry and Manufacture*. London: J. & A. Churchill.
WILLIAMS, C. TREVOR 1953 *Chocolate and Confectionery*. London.

NOTES

NOTES

NOTES

NOTES

NOTES

NOTES